MW00777299

ADMIRAL DAN GALLERY

ADMIRAL DAN GALLERY

The Life and Wit of a Navy Original

C. HERBERT GILLILAND
and ROBERT SHENK

NAVAL INSTITUTE PRESS   ANNAPOLIS, MARYLAND

Naval Institute Press
291 Wood Road
Annapolis, MD 21402

Library of Congress Cataloging-in-Publication Data
Gilliland, C. Herbert.
    Admiral Dan Gallery : the life and wit of a Navy original / C. Herbert Gilliland & Robert Shenk.
        p.   cm.
    Includes index.
    ISBN 1-55750-337-0 (alk. paper)
    1. Gallery, Daniel V.   2. Admirals—United States Biography.   3. United States. Navy Biography.   4. United States—History, Naval—20th century.   I. Shenk, Robert, 1943–   .
II. Gallery, Daniel V.   III. Title.
E746.G35G55   1999
359'.0092—dc21
    [B]   99-23174

Printed in the United States of America on acid-free paper ∞

06 05 04 03 02 01 00 99   9 8 7 6 5 4 3 2
First printing

Frontispiece: Daniel V. Gallery, USN, during World War II. *U.S. Navy*

Numerous excerpts from the following works, copyright by Daniel V. Gallery, were used by permission of W. W. Norton & Company: *Eight Bells, and All's Well,* 1965 (including excerpts about the USS *Idaho,* about Gallery's hanging by his toe, and about Little League in San Juan); *Clear the Decks!* 1951 (including the excerpt on the attack on Panama); *Twenty Million Tons Under the Sea,* 1956 (including the excerpt on the suicide of Cszhech); *Now, Hear This!* 1965 (including "Water Shortage"); and *The* Pueblo *Incident,* 1970 (including the excerpt on "What Price Human Life"). The article, "St. Brendan's Day Eve," printed in *Shipmate,* March 1971, pp. 11–14, is used by permission. Other Gallery quotations (including but not limited to excerpts from diaries, personal letters and correspondence, and other works in the Gallery Collection in Special Collections at the United States Naval Academy and quotations from other works for which Mrs. Gallery holds copyright) are used by permission of Vera D. Gallery.

To Marion S. Gilliland and Captain C. H. Gilliland Sr., MC, USNR

and

Juanita Strait

Contents

"Admiral Dan": A Reminiscence by Herman Wouk

THIS BOOK IS ABOUT a man I knew well and deeply admired, one of the most fortunate encounters in my life, Admiral Daniel V. Gallery. It includes copious excerpts from his lively, often controversial writings, and revealing glimpses into his personal correspondence down the decades. "Admiral Dan" had a way with words, and this very readable, well-researched biography emerges almost as a vivid self-portrait of a true navy original, and a memorable fighting admiral.

The operative word here is "fighting." Dan Gallery seldom backed off from a fight in peace or war, and more often than not went looking for one. That may be how we came to meet. In March 1951 *The Caine Mutiny* was published in the shadow of a gigantically successful war novel, James Jones's *From Here to Eternity,* attracting at first scant attention from critics or public. In the United States Navy, however, it caused a stir, because of the figure of Captain Philip Francis Queeg. The navy at the time had a perfectionist image of itself, inculcated at Annapolis, which Captain Queeg hardly exemplified. There was much hostility to my picture of the hooligan navy in which I had served, and little recognition of my regard for the service and the way it had transformed my own life. In July, while I was still digesting my disappointment at what looked like a literary misfire, I received a wonderful letter about the novel (quoted in this book in full) on the two-star stationery of one Admiral Daniel Gallery.

Remember, I had finished my war only six years earlier as a lieutenant, senior grade. Admirals were as remote and awesome to me as senators or movie stars, and here was one of those luminaries, telling me that—contrary to all the navy harrumphing—I had done in my novel exactly what I had set out to do, and had done it well! Dan Gallery may have heard so much abuse of my *Mutiny* that he decided to read it for himself to see what the fuss was about. It was in his nature to make up his own mind about matters in dispute, and if he was taking a lone stand, so much the better. Anyway, that letter was the start of a lifelong friendship.

Aristotle (I once was a philosophy major) defines friendships as of three varieties: *pleasure, use,* or *virtue.* In great friendships, these three elements tend to fuse. Certainly such was the case of my bond with Daniel Gallery. The pleasure was that of getting to know well a taciturn warrior of strong character, intellectual depth, and sharp wit. The use was simple and decisive. I could not have written *The Winds of War* and *War and Remembrance* with the military accuracy I can claim for those works had I not known Admiral Gallery. He was my chief naval consultant throughout, he opened all doors to me, and his creative suggestions were important; it was his idea, for instance, that Victor Henry go to Berlin as the naval attaché. As for virtue in the Aristotelian sense, neither of us may have been exemplars of lofty moral character, but we were both religious, he a practicing Catholic and I an observant Jew. We had our abrasive differences, but we got along from the outset.

The extended hand of friendship came from him. He wrote again, suggesting that we meet in a fancy New York rendezvous, the Oak Room bar at the Plaza. I came there on the watch for a formidable presence. A short lean man in a brown jacket and a bow tie, with large ears and a quizzical face, approached me. "Herman Wouk? I'm Dan Gallery." No resplendent blue-and-gold uniform, no majestic bearing, just a small man in brown.

Over drinks he came to the point quickly, after some pleasant words about my novel. Dan Gallery wanted a literary agent. He had placed some articles and a story or two in the *Saturday Evening Post,* and though still on active duty, he was bent on pursuing a writing career as well. I did refer him to my own able agent, who in time took him on, much to their mutual profit. It was a piquant reversal of roles, there in the Oak

Room bar, for a reserve lieutenant to be doing an admiral a favor, and to be on equal terms with him, because he was aspiring to my turf. Moreover, I liked his straight-talking style, utterly without side. He became more formidable and also more likable as our conversation went on. His views on the navy were decidedly his own, and not reverential.

It ended with his inviting me to sail with him on his next sortie as a carrier division commander. My wife agreed, after making me promise not to be catapulted off the flight deck, and it was a reserve lieutenant's pipe dream cruise. The admiral put me up in his own flag suite, displacing the ship's captain from his quarters, and ordered his steward to serve me the salads and vegetable dishes I could eat. Our conversations were far-ranging, I watched day and night flight operations from the flag bridge, and I observed something of Gallery's buzz-saw aspect when performance was not up to his standard. The day the ship was returning to port, Dan casually mentioned that the air group would fly off the ship to its base, he was going to fly a plane himself, and how would I like to come with him? I sort of gulped, "Why, sure. " How could I reply, "No thanks, my wife won't let me"? So I got catapulted, but not in Dan's plane, after all. I guess he decided to let someone less rusty fly me back to terra firma.

At this point I yield to the authors of this fine and thorough naval biography to take up the story of Admiral Dan, including details of how we helped each other in our literary work. There are dark shadows in his story, as well as brilliant episodes of ingenuity and heroism. He was a hard drinker, and an opinionated maverick on matters of high public policy, which almost cost him his career. This book is the unadorned truth about Daniel V. Gallery. Take him for all in all, he was a credit to the United States Navy, to his country, and to his faith; a decidedly human gentleman with human failings, more than balanced by rare willpower, brainpower, and humor. I am honored to write these brief scattered words about my remarkable departed friend, Admiral Dan.

Introduction

IN 1995, WHILE WORKING in a local library, one of us happened upon an intriguing article written years ago by a naval officer, describing his wartime experience as a commander of an airbase in Iceland. Iceland seemed a quite desolate location in which to set a few Quonset huts and an airstrip for conducting antisubmarine patrols—but this site obviously had been made quite livable by the humor, practical jokes, and otherwise engaging personality of its skipper—an officer named Dan Gallery.

Later at the Naval Academy we overheard a librarian say, "Of course the midshipmen are always reading up on the *U-505*." The *U-505* (as it turns out) was a German submarine that an American task group had boarded on the high seas and captured in 1944. That seemed a highly unlikely, rather swashbuckling episode for the twentieth century, but it not only had happened, but had been conceived long in advance of the occasion, was meticulously planned, and was creatively carried out, all at the direction of this same officer.

About the same time, we learned that the "Gallery Papers" were held by the Nimitz Library of the Naval Academy.

Gradually it dawned on us that here was a flamboyant figure—a splendid wartime leader with great daring and principle and an unusual imagination—who had not been much studied despite the wealth of literature about World War II. Admittedly, Gallery did not shake the world or shape strategic events to the extent that other famous figures have. But his personality was simply magnetic. Later we learned that Gallery had attained substantial public success after the war as a writer of essays, short stories, even some novels. As this writing career had originated in the midst of his naval career, it had been highly controversial, not only because of Gallery's characteristic outspokenness, but because many naval officers believed then (as some believe now) that when you're in the navy, every bit of your spare time is *navy* time—or at least, it's certainly not for writing for publication.

All these subjects drew our interest, and suggested that here was an ideal subject for a biography. However, it would have to be a biography of an unusual kind. The story of Dan Gallery was not only the story of a naval officer, but was also (we increasingly began to understand) the story of an "ideas man," someone who could think creatively and express himself in highly original terms. That is, Gallery's notorious wit didn't just appear after he became an admiral and began to publish articles in the national press; it was a prime element in his naval leadership. Overall, Gallery's vocations as naval officer and as thinker/writer were so intertwined that it is impossible to get across the personality of the man without also presenting his voice.

So, rather than write a traditional biography, which would tell the Gallery navy story in straight narrative, we showcase some of Gallery's own writing as a part of our presentation. Primarily, we do this by appending a Gallery letter or article or story at the end of each chapter, an item in one way or another representative of that particular stage of his career. To illustrate his midshipman period, for example, we present his letter to his dad about the famous episode of his knocking out the secretary of the navy's son. To exemplify Gallery in wartime we present the article which made him nationally known: his report of the capture of the *U-505* itself. Beyond these selections, even in our own narrative we also listen a good deal to Dan, partly because in some cases he is our only source for information (few of his contemporaries are around to fill in details), but also because of the general interest of his anecdotes. We do our best to present Dan's voice at every stage of his life. It is an unfortunate tendency to remember a famous person only as he left the public arena, in his last expressions, which may not be his best. As we hope to suggest, Dan's ingenuity, his love of a colorful anecdote, and his general joy of life were ever-present, lifelong features of his remarkable personality.

This, then, from several viewpoints (including his own), is the life of Dan Gallery—a lively, inventive, religious, fun-loving, patriotic, inspiring, provocative, quick-tempered, hard-headed, and often exasperating naval officer. We were intrigued to make his acquaintance. We hope you find his story interesting and rewarding, too.

C. Herbert Gilliland and Robert Shenk

ADMIRAL DAN GALLERY

An Irish Childhood in Chicago

MORE SO THAN MOST, much about Dan Gallery can be traced
directly to his childhood, and specifically to his parents—including his
strength of will, his religious character, his literary gift, even his very
naval career itself.

Dan was born in Chicago, Illinois, on July 10, 1901, at 49 McCallister
Place, in an Irish neighborhood about a mile west of the Loop.[1] His
ancestry was wholly Irish, all his grandparents except one immigrating
to the United States from Ireland around 1845 during the potato famine
that ravaged that small country.[2] The family was Roman Catholic and
very proud of the fact. Besides going to Catholic schools, at various
times Dan attended mass in all the four Catholic churches—Irish, Italian, French, and Jesuit—that were located within a mile of his house.
To this one should add that John Ireland, the "fighting archbishop" of
St. Paul,[3] was a close family friend, two of Dan's great-aunts were nuns,
Grandpa William J. Onahan was one of the first papal knights of the
Midwest (he spoke at the founding of Marquette University), and Dan's
next oldest brother, "John Ireland Gallery," destined by Dan's father and
mother for the priesthood, would in fact become a priest.

But Dan wasn't excessively respectful of all this religious presence.
When he was about six his mother took him to visit one of his great-
aunts at the Sacred Heart convent at Grosse Ile. There Dan committed
some offense (later he couldn't remember what) that condemned him to

sit in the visitor's parlor for an hour of contrition and meditation. He thought he was being unfairly treated.

> I remember sitting there in the little parlor for about fifteen minutes getting madder and madder by the minute. Finally the injustice of it all was just too much and I blew my stack. I hauled down all the pictures from the wall, busted the glass in them, and heaved them into the fireplace. I tipped over all the tables and chairs, rolled the rug into a heap, and sat back to see what would happen next.
>
> Since Pop wasn't there, and since you can't haul a young man's pants down [to whip him] in a convent, the pay-off was not too bad. I was only sent to bed without my supper.[4]

Still, often the moral examples and stern admonitions Dan received did have an effect on him. Dan greatly respected the kindness his grandfather showed the poor, and was later to regard the moral training he had received at St. Ignatius High School as superbly preparatory for naval discipline. Indeed, "In some ways the Navy discipline was easier because it was more impersonal. No Navy duty officer ever put the fear of God into me the way that Father Leahy could."[5]

But the fear of God was only one of many influences at work. Not only did he have the "gangster" influence of a bunch of kids who lived down the block—they swore, stole things, told dirty stories, and had some pretty tough scraps[6]—but he had ill habits of his own. Dan and his brothers had regular fist fights, he consistently ignored the local cops, and once (with a friend) he set fire to a neighbor's front porch. For most of these offenses he was punished (usually by being "beaten on the after end"), but not always. After all, he was usually a good citizen.

> I never stole anything much when I was a kid, and I was obedient to Mama, Papa, and my teachers except when I was pretty sure the odds were about a hundred to one that I could get away with something really worthwhile. But I didn't mind heaving rocks through the neighbors' windows on Halloween and other appropriate occasions.
>
> One time I got shagged by a cop. I had hit him with a small rock when his back was turned. He was about a hundred feet away,

so it was a good peg. He chased me right to our front door, which
I slammed in his face just in time.

Luckily my dad was home. He didn't like cops.[7]

Dan's father's experience as a lawyer was that the cops often beat up
good citizens to try to get them to own up to crimes they couldn't solve.
So in this case his husky dad outfaced the cop, who soon turned away.

Dan may have gotten some of his high spirits—as well as some of his
literary talent—from his mother. Mary Onahan Gallery ("Molly" in her
younger days) had once aspired to be a journalist, and in her youth she
published short pieces in several newspapers. But she suffered a bit from
censorship. For instance, still smarting from her convent education, in
one of her early literary efforts Mary shed doubt on the wisdom of having cloistered nuns teach young women. The article was already in proof
and the paper's editor was impatiently wiring Mary to return it, but her
father angrily ordered her to destroy the piece. When she ignored that
directive, her father mentioned the situation to his friend Archbishop
Ireland, who happened to be passing through the city. The archbishop
sent for Mary. As she later recalled,

> He held out his hand to me and said, his grey eyes twinkling with
> laughter: "Well, well, well, Molly so you're in hot water as usual."
>
> "Yes, Archbishop," said I meekly.

He went over the article with her, and acknowledged that it was well-
written and contained some truth. But he argued it would do harm,
that it would discredit all she was to write later, and that "You of all
people should not say it." Molly was obliged to go home and tear up the
essay.[8]

A bit later, Molly got her revenge. She published a long, unauthorized
article in one of the Chicago papers entitled "Adventures of an Archbishop" and signed herself "Henri de Savigny," a pen name which temporarily hid her identity. The article was reprinted in the *New York Sun*,
among other papers, and (worth noting) elicited an offer of employment
for its author on the part of the *Sun*'s editor, the great journalist Charles
Anderson Dana. In the article, Mary told some of the archbishop's own
stories, stories which she apparently had heard him recount in the family home.

Most of the longer stories had to do with the intrigues within the Vatican. One of the shorter anecdotes, however, was a story the archbishop had narrated about his Civil War experience.

> When Archbishop Ireland was a chaplain in the Union Army, some of the soldiers were on the point of desertion. They sought several pretexts to remain behind, saying they were needed to take care of the wounded. Finally they declared that they had no cartridges anyhow, and so there "was no use goin' and settin' themselves up as targets to be shot at."
>
> Father Ireland turned on them sharply and said: "Come with me. I'll show you where the cartridges are." And he actually did. The soldiers were perforce obliged to go to the front.[9]

This story was printed in several American newspapers. When asked about it, the archbishop acknowledged the incident. So far, so good.

But then a Frenchman did some "creative writing." As Mary later recounted:

> One day in Paris as [Archbishop Ireland] was stepping into a cab he glanced carelessly at a newspaper he had just bought (*Figaro*), when his eye was arrested by the words "Monseigneur Ireland— Bon Evêque et Bon Soldat" (Good Bishop and Good Soldier). It was the story of the cartridges but with this addition: Father Ireland, according to *Figaro,* not only distributed the cartridges, but at a critical point in the battle, when the soldiers were about to turn and flee in sudden panic, the brave chaplain rushed to the front and, waving the American flag, sang the *Marseillaise,* rallying the soldiers and winning the battle.
>
> The Archbishop naively added as he told this story: "I couldn't sing the *Marseillaise;* couldn't sing anything to save my life," an admission with which many of his friends will sadly agree.[10]

Because of her unauthorized storytelling, Molly was for a while in disgrace with the archbishop.

Many aspects of Dan's character were no doubt formed by his mother, who grew up a very devout Catholic even as she retained a flair with the pen. While raising her six children and long afterwards, Mary continued to delight readers with occasional letters to the "Voice of the People" section of the *Chicago Tribune* and elsewhere, and in 1929 she published a book about her father and his friends with Loyola University Press.[11] About this time, she reportedly began a long (although unsuccessful) fight with the United States Congress for the fortification of the island of Guam, no doubt influenced in this by the insights of her naval sons.[12] Still, to hear Dan tell it, despite the considerable talent of his mother, by far the chief and most formative authority in his life was the old man.

Daniel V. Gallery, Senior, was a person for whom young Dan had the greatest respect. In Dan's schooling, for instance, the elder Gallery's influence proved far more important than any of the boy's own teachers.

> Every night after dinner Pop and the four boys would adjourn to the study room and do the homework. When we finished he would look it over and if it was correct, that was that. If it wasn't, he would hand it back and just say, "Number so and so answer is wrong."
>
> He never told us just what was wrong or how to correct it. We had to dope that our ourselves, although sometimes on difficult problems he would ask leading questions that might give us a clue. Some of the problems in arithmetic *were* difficult. . . .
>
> But Pop could do them and he never had to look in the back of the book for the answer. He had a keen, logical mind, and when our feeble brains were baffled by some outrageous conundrum which he could solve easily, it made him mad. When Pop got mad he got mad all over and no matter how tough the problem was, it wasn't as tough as Pop. So you just got busy and worked the goddam thing right.[13]

Dan would come to regard both his father and his Jesuit instructors at high school as much better teachers than the instructors at the Naval Academy, for they went beyond memorization, helping him to understand the roots of each subject. As a result of their good teaching, he led his high school class at St. Ignatius for two years. However, with his father's early help, Dan always claimed he hadn't needed the Jesuits much, either.[14]

For Daniel V. Gallery, Senior, his children—perhaps especially his sons—were his greatest interest. Dan Senior would follow their endeavors intensely throughout his life, keeping detailed logs of their achieve-

This family photograph was taken in October 1912. Dan (then age eleven) stands between John and Dan, Senior, who holds son Philip. William Onahan stands to the right of his mother, Mary. Margaret is on her mother's left, while Marcia or "Babe" is seated in the front. *Courtesy of Mrs. Daniel V. Gallery*

ments, maintaining large scrapbooks, and regularly adding snapshots to the collections. Many of these photos were taken during family vacations, either at a cabin on Fox Lake (sixty miles northwest of Chicago), or at Twin Lake at Pottawatamie Park (on the eastern shore of Lake Michigan).[15] In these summer spots, Dan "took to the water like a fish. I learned to swim, to row, to paddle a canoe, and to sail a boat. I loved the water and felt at home on it right from the start."[16] The elder Gallery encouraged all these activities, and clearly the children put their hearts into them.

But they did so as a closely knit group. As a result of their father's exhortation, there was even some formal "naval" organization among the young people. At a very young age the children were grouped into two family "watches," with the eldest three children—Dan, John, and "Onie" (William Onahan)—in "The Starboard Watch," and the youngest three—Margaret, Philip, and "Babe" (Marcia)—in the "Port."[17] These watches seem originally to have been designed for Christmas activities, but in Dan's later letters they are referred to in other contexts, too. Clearly they infected the children's imaginations.

Such naval organization was both a result of the father's interests and prophetic of the part he would play in his sons' careers. Having been thwarted in his own military ambition by the loss of his sight in one eye, the elder Gallery so focused on vicarious fulfillment that he successfully encouraged three of his sons (Dan, Onie, and Philip) to attend the Naval Academy. Even John (the priest) was to join the navy as a chaplain during World War II. However, although his father certainly was the prime

The three members of the Gallery family "Starboard Watch," Dan, Onie (William Onahan), and John, in the summer of 1906. Dan was just turning five. *Courtesy of Mrs. Daniel V. Gallery*

mover in the sons' joining the navy as Dan always claimed,[18] and while the family greatly respected all things naval in other ways too (going aboard the Great Lakes sidewheeler USS *Wolverine* once a year, buying surplus navy equipment, and so on[19]), the Naval Academy wasn't either Dan Senior or Dan Junior's original college of choice. *Contra* Dan's autobiography, when the elder Gallery first wrote Congressman Thomas Gallagher about Dan on March 30, 1917, he said his son was interested in going to *West Point*. Only on news that there was no nomination free for the Military Academy did the senior Gallery mention the Naval Academy (neither the first nor the last father to instantly shift his sights for his son). When Congressman Gallagher answered Dan Senior's second letter,[20] saying that a nomination to Annapolis was indeed open, all talk of West Point ceased.

In the spring of 1917, Dan was withdrawn from St. Ignatius, and with the help of tutors began prepping for the Naval Academy academic examination, which he took and passed in late June (one of some five hundred of fourteen hundred nominees nationwide to do so).[21] Though Dan fainted during the subsequent physical exam, he nevertheless passed it, too, and he was sworn into service as a midshipman on August 1.[22] There was one small difficulty, however. Evidencing just a bit of teenage rebellion even against this very strong-willed parent, Dan was determined to run away (or at least so he would later claim) rather than enter the academy wearing the short pants of boyhood, as his father desired. Since his father had consistently refused to buy him any long jeans, in early 1917 Dan had entered an essay contest run by a local department store—and won first prize among forty entries. The topic was "clothing" and the prize was a suit of clothes.[23] As a result, Dan was able to dress as an adult when he entered the gates of the Naval Academy—prepared now to deal manfully with a powerful authority of a somewhat different kind.

With his father's strong encouragement, Dan would exemplify at Annapolis both the high spirits and the temper that had marked his childhood in Chicago, and that would characterize his entire professional life. At the same time, the religious orientation Dan received in his childhood became deeply rooted in his character. Finally, wherever he served or settled, Dan always retained great love for the city of

Not long before beginning his naval career, young Dan won a new suit by writing an essay. Here he poses with his mother in his prize. Mrs. Gallery is rather well-dressed, too. *Courtesy of Mrs. Daniel V. Gallery*

Chicago itself. Eventually he was able to honor his debt to that city in full measure.

ALL THE OTHER selections that end chapters in this book were written by Dan Junior, and are included to illustrate both his wit and his voice—important aspects both of his naval leadership and of his writing career. However, it is appropriate that we first hear from Dan's father.

When the elder Gallery found that Dan would not be able to come home for Christmas his first year at the Naval Academy, he wrote the following letter to his son.[24] Besides manifesting Dan Senior's own talent with words, the letter reveals the nature of the fatherly support that had inspired Dan from the very start.

One of the Great Names of the Navy

December 22, 1917

My dear Dan:

I am thinking now of my boy and his other Christmas days. Because of imperfect equipment he could not do justice to his first Christmas dinner; he has striven at each dinner since to atone for it. He did not speak English at that first Christmas dinner, but chatted gaily in his native tongue, adding much to the vivacity of the table talk. His method of locomotion at that time was crude, and his radius of action limited. He could however disappear with astonishing celerity under chair or sofa when question was made about trouble or uproar in his vicinity, being certain that unjust blame therefor would be his. When extracted from his seclusion, the cherubic smile of conscious innocence that beamed from his dust veiled countenance prevailed over the clearest proof of guilt.

My waking hours at home were spent with him. Not content, he frequently while a baby demanded my sleeping hours, and at the unseemly time of 2 a.m. ordered me to turn out, tote him and sing Hear Dem Bells, and The Night Before Christmas and many other of the old familiar melodies. When he learned to toddle, where I went he went, taking with us his brothers and sisters as they too learned to toddle. His mind was active. After he began to acquire the language his persistent "Why, Papa," often embarrassed me for a sufficient answer. We talked of everything and he understood. The passing Christmas days saw him grow from baby to child and from child to boy. The promise of worth and capacity, evident in his earliest actions, was confirmed as the years went by. He was a pleasure to us at home, though far from an angel. At school he led whether in work or play.

He delighted in mechanics, in contriving, in planning and in construction. West Point and its fine engineering course he and I looked forward to from the time he was a tot. Though the Navy, its deeds, its ships and its heroes fascinated him we were forgetful or not conscious that in Annapolis he would find the precise satisfaction of his bent, and a more thorough training in the subjects that enlisted his interest.

Unexpectedly there came an appointment to the Naval Academy. The change from West Point and the sudden coming of something that was long wished, but always seemed vague and distant upset him somewhat and ended many plans for the time just ahead. He was startled by the abrupt ending of his school days. At dinner, after studying his lessons for next day, he was informed he had studied his last lesson at St. Ignatius. He might well be startled.

Day and night and Sunday for seven weeks thereafter he worked to exhaustion in covering the subjects of examination. That he stood up under the strain and finished his work in much less than the usual time, proved he had grit and bottom and habit of study. As eager as himself that he should succeed, I was sometimes not considerate, and drove him hard.

The examination over, there followed a period of uncertainty, waiting for the result. He knew of no reason to be uneasy. I was in doubt about algebra and unnerved him by saying he probably had not passed. I preferred the joy of unanticipated success to the bitter disappointment of unanticipated failure. When the news came over the wire that he had won, he was lifted into the clouds. That evening he could not sit still. There was no need to wish him pleasant dreams. My gratification was as great and no better concealed.

The last week of his life as a boy and as a civilian was his most crowded week. His friends showered him with congratulations and feasted him with lunches and dinners. Theatres, ball games and amusement parks filled day and evening. Perhaps his engagements with his dentist should not be reckoned among the high times. To him came the popularity that always comes to the winner. He had become a person of consequence.

Happy as I was over the splendid prospects his new life opened to him, I cherished the boyhood he was leaving behind. Among the photographs taken that week, are three I like best. They are the figure of a boy clad in knickers that I had so often seen starting on his way to school. My last glimpse of that boy was as he was going down the steps in the Administration Building with a number of others, at the Naval Academy, to put on the uniform of his life profession.

You are very dear to me, my boy, and I am proud of you. I believe in you. You have brains, good sense, a pleasant manner and a genial disposition. You know how to work and to concentrate. The story of your success in the past will be the story of your future. You will make your name one of the great names of the Navy.

A Merry Christmas to you, Dan, and a Happy New Year. Get that star!

Yours,
D.V.G.

Three Years at Annapolis

WITH HIS FATHER, Daniel V. Gallery, Junior, walked through the main gates of the United States Naval Academy on August 1, 1917. Soon he passed by the officer of the day, Lt. Comdr. (later Fleet Admiral) William F. Halsey, whose white uniform, sword, and campaign ribbons made a great impression on the young man.[1] In 1930 Gallery was to give this soon-to-be-famous naval leader his first hop in an aircraft right here in Annapolis, and shortly afterwards would ask the commander for a recommendation to postgraduate school.[2] At the same time, Gallery would ask a recommendation from another naval figure he knew— Capt. (later Fleet Admiral) Ernest J. King.[3] Both of these officers would not only impress Dan, but be impressed *by* Dan, and become his good friends. But on the day that he entered the academy and for a long time after, his father remained the most important figure in Dan Gallery's life.

For as he had guided the studies of his four sons each evening in their Chicago home, so the father continued to offer Dan regular guidance and exhortation, now by letter. Although for the most part only Dan's side of the correspondence remains, it is clear from Dan's continual reference to and defense of his academic record that the elder Gallery was consistently expressing concern about Dan's failure to top the academic ladder.

Actually, Dan was doing pretty well academically at the academy.

Dan as a midshipman. *Courtesy of Mrs. Daniel V. Gallery*

According to Gallery, there wasn't much actual teaching going on there at the time. You taught yourself.

> Subjects were math, English, French and Spanish, physics, electrical and steam engineering, chemistry, ordnance, mechanical drawing, seamanship, and navigation. You spent half the day studying in your room and half in the classrooms. Most of the "teachers" were naval officers doing a hitch of shore duty. They hardly ever tried to teach and probably wouldn't have been much help if they had.

Periods in the classrooms were mainly quiz sessions upon what the mids had memorized. Dan's letters are full of his reports on these quiz marks, which seem to range around what we might call a "B" or "B-plus." Gallery later said, "I got through plebe year without much difficulty in studies,"[4] and apparently he never had much problem. He ended up graduating forty-seventh in a class of 546[5] (an additional 148 did not graduate). But that kind of performance was not good enough for his old man.

Indeed, at one point in the middle of Dan's plebe year the elder Gallery could not contain himself. Troubled by what he regarded as his son's mediocre average in English, the father wrote the academy superintendent, Rear Adm. E. W. Eberle, a letter that is remarkable both for its obsequiousness and for its offer of assistance to the academy in motivating his son.

January 4, 1918

My dear Admiral Eberle:

Permit me to congratulate the country and you on your promotion. The Government has no more important work than the education of its young naval officers. Under your direction the affairs of the Academy have been splendidly managed. The administrative problems caused by the vast increase in the number of Midshipmen were solved without loss to its highest standard. Your promotion is not a sufficient recognition of your services.

If the rules of the Academy allow, may the enclosed note be delivered to Mr. Washburn, Professor of English? The average of my boy Midshipman Daniel V. Gallery, Jr. for three months in English is 3.04. His previous training and records warrant 3.40. My guess is that he is resting. As Mr. Washburn is in charge of his section this month, he may suggest to me where the fault lies. Knowing his capacity, I feel Dan will yet be among the highest and that I can stimulate his efforts to that end.

I wish you a Happy New Year.

Yours Truly,
Daniel V. Gallery

Given the crammed schedule Dan described to his folks, the notion that one's child was likely to be "resting" four months into the academy's plebe year seems pretty unlikely. And while it might seem curious that someone with the "gift of the gab" that Dan Gallery would later manifest wouldn't show much of it in English classes, probably the assignments didn't offer his imagination much play. In any case, certainly this academy professor was not "resting," or didn't want to appear to do so. Professor H. C. Washburn took four pages of type to explain to Dan's father that Dan had a mild problem in spelling, and then sent two additional pages in reply to another letter from the elder Gallery.[6] But, after all, Dan Senior had sent his request in the first place via the academy superintendent.

Dan Junior's opinion of his English grades (frequently expressed) was the perennial complaint of students in first-year college English: that the grades merely reflected the professor's whims. In any case, the senior Gallery shared with his son the gist of his exchange of letters with academy officials, and offered Dan some additional "exhortation." He seems to have continued to press the issue. As Dan later remarked with apparent understatement, "Any time he felt I needed parental guidance he was never backward about giving it."[7] At least once in these academy years Dan did get his back up in response to his father's badgering. Below is part of a letter Dan wrote in his last year at the academy:

Dear Papa:

I think you put things a little too strong in that last letter. I'll admit I rated being bawled out but you said several things I don't agree with. You said I had violated my word of honor and cannot be trusted. . . . When I said last Sep that I intended to star I was merely stating my honest intentions and did not intend to make any promises. . . . That I have not starred is my own fault but it does not mean I lied when I said I intended to. You also said I am a bum and that a bum is a person completely lacking in all principles of manhood. If I were such a character I would have not lasted $2\frac{1}{2}$ years here. I have been lazy as far as studies are concerned but no one can say I have been a bum in other respects. I may be a damned fool for letting my opportunities slide by but a damned fool can have a lot of manhood in him.[8]

Apparently the father got the point. After this, Dan's midshipman letters don't express any anger toward his dad.

Besides reflecting on his weekly marks, Dan comments most regularly (not only in almost every letter from the academy, but even on summer cruises) on another special subject: his attendance at mass or holy communion. Given the strong religious background of the family, his parents would naturally have been interested in his continuing to go to mass regularly on his leaving home. But the frequency with which Dan mentions his mass attendance or occasionally his reason for *not* attending—"I did not go to Holy Communion today. On account of the Masqueraders [the academy drama group] last night we did not get to bed until 12.30 and I was too tired to get up at 5.00"[9]—suggests that the father may have been expressing his concerns about this subject, too.

On the other hand, after he became an officer Dan would record his attendance at Mass in his personal diary, and no doubt similar comments could be found in many midshipman letters home. Certainly most of the other subjects in Dan's letters—pay, leave, academy rules, occasional demerits, the latest "hop" (and who Dan was "dragging"), requests for foodstuffs from home, hopes for summer cruises, interest in navy billets—were pretty typical of contemporary midshipman concerns. Also, like academy-trained adolescents before and since, Dan very quickly expressed jealousy as to his prerogatives as a midshipman. Many years later, *Admiral* Gallery would lament the replacement of the very tough "rocks and shoals" system of military justice by the Uniform Code (UCMJ), and would become so worked up over the subject that he had to be counselled in a letter from the judge advocate general that his publishing these beliefs would be "inflammatory."[10] But even as an academy "youngster" (sophomore) Dan was most upset when, as a result of some new plebes' complaints to their parents (complaints somehow forwarded to the secretary of the navy and academy superintendent, who came down hard) he was suddenly unable to dish out to the plebes the hazing he personally had been forced to endure a very short time before.

> Now a youngster cannot even tell a plebe to brace up without exposing himself to the danger of going down for hazing. Now if a plebe feels like it he can carry on at the table all the time. . . . I would consider it a great misfortune if I had gone through here without rating plebe and being run and hazed.

Gallery no doubt means it when he says he believes hazing helps to make a plebe into a responsible officer, but his opinion that it also "develops a deference for rank" and helps to "reduce [a plebe's] idea of his own importance" suggests that the relative prerogatives of youngsters and plebes were in the forefront of his mind.[11]

One other subject greatly occupied Gallery's attention in these letters home: academy sports. Initially Gallery tried out for the basketball team, and he talked in his letters of swimming and playing intramural baseball. He admired those who went out for crew, and zealously followed navy football (like everyone else). At one point, every letter for weeks expressed anxiety about whether there would be an Army-Navy game that year or not. (Until 1919, there wasn't. The 1917 and 1918 games were cancelled because of the war.) But in his youngster year Gallery was to find his own athletic niche—as a wrestler.

Gallery had trained as a wrestler in the Hebrew Institute program in Chicago,[12] so he wasn't a beginner. Although he only weighed some 127 pounds, he was wiry and fast. Moreover, he had invented an unusual hold.

> [I] had one hold that was peculiarly adapted to my lanky frame, although I never saw anyone else use it. It was a scissors on the near arm and a far-side half nelson. . . . It was such an unusual hold that when you first applied it your opponent's reaction seemed to be, "What the hell is this crazy guy doing now?"
>
> If you did it right, you wound up a few seconds later flat on your gut with your opponent's body stretched across yours at right angles, belly up. His arms were pinned under your body, and nothing but his heels and shoulders touched the mat. The shoulders touching gave you a pin fall.
>
> I used that hold time and time again.[13]

In his second year at Annapolis, Gallery wrestled intercollegiately, first in the bantamweight and later in the "special weight" class, and except for one draw (later awarded on appeal to a wrestler from Columbia[14]), Gallery won every match. Although the academy was outlawed from wrestling at the intercollegiate championships while Gallery was a mid (academy competitors were regarded as "professionals" because all mids had to take a few hours of instruction in self-defense, including wrestling[15]), the academy team was probably the best college program in the country. Navy regularly beat the best other college teams in head-to-

Dan in wrestling gear in front of an arcade of Bancroft Hall on academy grounds. *Courtesy of Mrs. Daniel V. Gallery*

head contests, which drew thousands of spectators (after football and crew, wrestling was the most popular spectator sport).

The next year (1919–20), although a fellow academy wrestler beat him once or twice, Gallery won every one of his intercollegiate bouts, telegramming home to his parents on successive occasions, "THREW PRINCETON MAN IN 8 MINUTES THIRTY SECONDS," "THREW WILLIAMS IN

TWO MINUTES TWENTY SECONDS NAVY EIGHTEEN PENN FOURTEEN," and "THREW ACKERLY CORNELLS CAPTAIN AND INTERCOLLEGIATE CHAMPION THREE MINUTES."[16] A subtitle of a *Naval Academy Log* story about the victory over Yale read "FIVE STRAIGHT FALLS FOR HANDSOME DAN."[17] After the season, Dan was selected to try out for the Olympic wrestling team.

In the meantime, naval authorities had decided not to extend the whole 1921 academy class for a fourth year. In 1916 the academic program had been cut from four to three years on account of World War I, and the traditional four-year program was now being reinstated. But the navy allowed the top half of the Class of 1921 to go on and finish in 1921, after just three years. Standing in the top ten percent of his full class, Gallery graduated on June 3, 1921, about a month shy of nineteen years of age. In early July he went to New York for Olympic elimination contests. While he lost one of his matches and was formally eliminated from "freestyle" wrestling, he was chosen as an extra to compete in the "Greco-Roman" part of the Olympics. On July 27 the navy Olympic athletes boarded the cruiser USS *Frederick* for Antwerp.[18]

There were two slight problems with Dan's Olympic quest. First, "Greco-Roman" wrestling, took some getting accustomed to on the part of U.S. athletes. For them it was in many respects a completely new sport. Second, and more important, Gallery had been growing from the 120-pound, sixty-seven-inch dark-haired and blue-eyed lad who had entered the academy at age sixteen, and for the Olympics he was required to move up in weight. Hence he had to compete with heavier, stronger opponents in the lightweight (135-pound) class.[19] Gallery won his first Olympic match against the Netherlands champion, but later lost to the powerful Finnish wrestler who would go on to win the Olympic championship. He lost in the lower medal rounds, too. The move to the 135-pound class was unfortunate. The eventual 125-pound Olympic champion was Ackerly, from Cornell.[20] As we've seen, Gallery had pinned him only a few months before.

Gallery regarded this Olympic adventure as a rare experience, as indeed it was. Besides wrestling, while in Antwerp he got his first flight in an airplane, a fifteen-minute excursion which cost fifty francs. After the games he went on to visit Belgian battlefields and the cities of Brussels, Cologne, Coblenz, and Wiesbaden.[21] Then he visited the small city of Maurs in southern France to see the daughter of the mayor, whom he knew through academy-arranged correspondence—Dan had been practicing his French in letters to her; Marie had practiced her English writing back. Ensign Gallery and Ens. Eddie Willkie found that no one in that town of twenty-five hundred had ever seen an American naval uniform, and the pair were lionized in their short visit as "Olympic champions."

> Eddie was an All-American football player as well as a wrestler. He weighed 230 pounds in his stockinged feet, was 6 foot 6, and hard as a rock. Marie spread word around town before we arrived that Eddie had won the world's heavyweight championship at Antwerp and that I had won the lightweight title. We meant to correct this error but never got around to it.

As Gallery put it, "it was a matter of the Republic of France entertaining the United States Navy."[22]

After this, the athletes were stranded in Europe for another three weeks, as the *Frederick* had to go to aid the *Pittsburgh,* which had gone aground in the Baltic. Dan and classmate Ens. Larry Litchfield had a great time visiting Berlin, Prague, and Vienna—until they ran out of money. In order to get back to Antwerp, they had to borrow railroad fare from two strangers, one an American civilian, the other a West Point cadet! Finally, the navy team steamed back to the States aboard the civilian transport *Pocahontas.*[23] This cruise added to the adventure, for Dan got to know several young women en route, including the twin daughters of the U.S. consul general at Brussels, Thelma and Gloria Morgan, later to become known as society figures Lady Furness and Gloria Vanderbilt.[24] Socially as well as professionally, then, Dan had begun stepping out.

Overall, Dan (also known at the academy as "Diz," "Dizzy Dan," "Dizzums," or "Irish,"[25]) seems to have taken his academy beginnings in stride. Plebe year seems not to have especially fazed him, and he very quickly adopted a pro-academy ethos. After that, academics never took too much of an effort; wrestling engaged his ambition and aggressiveness; and his many friendships would last his entire naval life. (Indeed, as he almost never held grudges and seldom cast disparagements at others, friendship became something of a Gallery art.) Finally, despite Dan's

Wrestling team letterman Dan and friends with their drags, on the water.
Courtesy of Mrs. Daniel V. Gallery

youth (he was fourth or fifth from the class "baby"[26]), the shortened academy term of three years seems to have been quite lengthy enough to inform his intelligence and shape a strong naval sense. As for his post-academy Olympic experience, that whole exciting trip was an auspicious and fitting beginning to a very colorful naval career. Symbolically it was a step forward on the very high road that Dan's father had set out for him.

DESPITE GALLERY'S great success as a collegiate wrestler, his most notorious athletic performance was in an informal "boxing match." Gallery's knowledge of the sport was limited to a dozen or more boyhood scraps. One of his fighting experiences subsequent to his midshipman career occurred at a bar in an officer's club in 1926. Dan was then a lieutenant junior grade, and a young woman asked him to cut in on the lieutenant commander with whom she would be dancing. When he did so the lieutenant commander objected—and Dan blacked his eye.[27] Dan's entire career as a boxer was like this—informal and spontaneous. Still, this was the early part of the century, and young men were supposed to know how to handle themselves. Moreover, masculine figures didn't mind throwing out a few taunts to assert their manhood, and settling quarrels by fighting was encouraged in the military, as elsewhere.

At the same time, the world was at war when Gallery entered the academy, and then as since some young men joined this or that military program to avoid front-line service. As it happened, the secretary of the navy at the time was Josephus Daniels, and Josephus's son Worth Bagley Daniels was a plebe. When this son chose to resign some five weeks after the signing of the armistice, several upperclassmen including Dan objected, calling young Daniels a draft dodger. In a couple of letters home, Dan described the subsequent events.

Fighting the Secretary's Son

December 22, 1918

Dear Papa,

Merry Christmas! The enclosed marks are not much of a Christmas present so I am send[ing], "The Fighting Fleets," by Paine too. Paine has actually been on destroyers during arguments with the subs so it ought to give a pretty good story of the life over there.

I was agreeably surprised with my math and steam marks. If I can hold the pace in those and get back to normal in English again I ought to break some of my records this month.

I had a scrap last week. Young Daniels put in his resignation and I called him a draft dodger. That was a week ago. He wanted to go out behind the gunshed then and there and settle it with our fists. That is a bouncing offense if you are ragged so I told him I would settle it in the gym with gloves. That is the usual way to settle scraps around here but that did not suit him. He said that the day his resignation was accepted and he shoved off that he would come up to my room and knock the stuffing out of me. He is 20 yrs. old and has about 15 pounds on me. His resignation was accepted Friday and he came around that afternoon. Carl [Koops] and I cleared the room for action and then Carl stood watch outside while Daniels and I had it out. I knocked him out in five minutes and when he came back to earth he said he was satisfied and had enough. He did not want to shake at first but he did before he left. I have no visible signs of the battle while he will have a beautiful shiner to explain to the Secretary.

There is no danger of any trouble over the affair as Daniels said it was closed as far as he was concerned and I think he is man enough to stand by it. He was a cit [civilian] when the battle took place so I don't see how anything can happen.

I wish I could be home and have a real Christmas and see the tree again. Carl and I are going to decorate the room but it won't come anywhere near being a real Christmas. I hope everyone at home enjoys the Day.

     Dan.

DAN WAS SURPRISED to find that the episode had not reached its conclusion. A week later, he wrote the following letter to his dad.

December 29, 1918

Dear Papa,

I got a nice scare last week. I was called down to see the Com [the commandant, Capt. W. H. Standley, later chief of Naval Operations— eds.] and of course knew right away what it was about. I had to wait for half an hour and while waiting I had imagined every kind of a fate from hanging to life in the brig. When I was called in he asked me for the straight dope on the scrap, confidentially, and after I told him enough about it to bilge a regiment he told me that my conduct was entirely blameless. This coming from the Commandant personally means that I have nothing to worry about.

I don't believe the Secretary would try to make things uncomfortable. He could not bounce me without walking right into the accusation that he did it for personal reasons.

All the big papers here had stories about half a column on the affair. They all had the same wrong dope the Trib had. The New York Herald was the only paper giving the straight story. It had half a column on the fourth page and said a youngster cleaned up Daniels. A Boston and an Indiana paper had hot editorials on the wrong side. The class president is having the straight dope written up for the Associated Press now that the Com has said it was O.K.

Toward the beginning of the year I gave Daniels a workout which would have been nothing but a matter of course to a *real* plebe. He however was highly indignant at my impudence in hazing the Secretary of the Navy's son. On that account he has had it in for me all along. The fact that he had 20 pounds weight on me and a rep. as a boxer which I have not also made him anxious for the fight. Two other fellows who called him a draft dodger almost got down on their knees to him when he looked cross about it.

There were no eye witnesses to the scrap. Koops helped us clear for action and then stood guard at the end of the corridor while the battle was in progress. There were no interruptions, as roughhouses are not uncommon and no one pays any attention to a little racket.

I got myself in solid with the class by the affair. Quite a number of fellows that I never knew before say howdy when we meet now. It was also the scandal of Crabtown for several days and I got acquainted with several femmes on account of it. . . .

    Dan

Gallery as a Blackshoe

AFTER THE OLYMPICS, Gallery reported to the first of a series of surface ("blackshoe") assignments, shipboard duty which would last over five years. Although in his later recollection he would tend to play down the importance of these early sea tours, it is clear that they were vital to his development, not only enhancing his technical knowledge but also grounding this future naval aviator in a kind of leadership of ordinary sailors hard to come by in officer-dominated aviation squadrons. As we'll see, Gallery learned the navy literally from the steam pipes and cargo holds up. At the same time, he kept up his sports interests, and learned what it was like to "go on the beach" with his buddies in ports throughout the world. Overall, in these tours of duty, in which he was formally assigned to five different ships and temporarily rode three or four more, Gallery went through an extensive naval learning experience.

Gallery first reported to the old battleship *Delaware* in late November 1920. On his midshipman cruise aboard the battleship *Maine,* he had spent ten days in the boiler room. As he wrote his father, "I fired, sliced, pulled fires, tended water, and railroaded coal from the bunkers. I will not mind the heat much when I get home. . . ."[1] So, when the *Delaware* began coaling ship a couple of days after he reported aboard as an ensign, he thought he could set an example for the sailors. However, he so wore himself out shovelling coal that he failed to get up at reveille the next morning, and got three days' restriction to his room for it.[2]

When Gallery got out of hack, he got back on the right foot, beginning with some signals and gunnery duty at sea, and standard junior officer assignments while in port, such as boat officer, beach guard, and safety observer during target practice. A couple of months later, while the fleet transited the Panama Canal to tour down the west coast of South America, Dan got himself temporarily stationed aboard the battleship *Arizona* to help train the Atlantic fleet wrestling team. (In the fleet championships back in Panama, his team beat the Pacific Fleet, winning three of five bouts.[3]) On rejoining the *Delaware* he was set to learn the engineering plant. He began literally at the bottom of the ship. "My mornings are taken up with tracing out water and steam lines and getting acquainted with the machinery," he pointed out in March of 1921.[4] A couple of months later, he played a part in overhauling the evaporator, the ice machines, distillers, and several boat engines while in temporary charge of the Auxiliary Division, and he learned a good deal about engines by making parts in the machine shop.[5]

Ever the competitor, Dan originally had hopes of being in a crack engineering department: "Besides winning the speed run we are leading the coal burners in economy in fuel consumption and prevention of smoke. We are steaming fourth in the whole navy at present in the competition for the engineering trophy."[6] But he was frustrated. On a full power trial of battlewagons steaming line abreast north from Guantánamo, a bad load of coal picked up just before sailing doomed the ship to come in last, five miles astern the other battleships: "It was, you might say, a bit embarrassing. If we had been a submarine, we would have pulled the plug and submerged." Apparently angry over some sarcastic personal remarks from the captain, the chief engineer blistered both officers and men for their general incompetence, blaming them all for the ship's bad showing. In Gallery's reflections on the leadership of the chief engineer, we see that he was learning more than engineering from his experiences:

> That tirade from the chief, who should have stood up for his own people, almost caused mutiny. It taught me . . .—if you are

the victim of a bum rap from above, take it and shut up. Don't pass it on down.[7]

In June Dan was detached from the *Delaware* and sent to several weeks of engineering school at Newport, assigned to the destroyer *Herndon*. There, among other things, he and three others tore down a steering engine and repaired it; he had done nothing like it before. While on the same ship he stood watch "with firemen and lowly enginemen,"[8] and in the same training stint he was umpire during full power trials on the destroyer *Ford*. By August 31 Gallery had received orders as chief engineer of the USS *Stevens*, a twelve-hundred ton four-stack destroyer in very bad shape that, because of personnel drawdowns after World War I, was manned with only half a crew. Because he regarded battleships as the prime duty, Gallery was a bit disappointed, but he resolved to make the most of this assignment.[9] Here again Gallery began to learn the ropes quickly. He greatly improved oil consumption (working up to third of seventeen ships in the division in the two-thirds of a year he was aboard[10]), and he came to appreciate the responsibility of his position as department head:

> I am the boss now and get the blame if the wheels don't go round properly or the credit if they do. . . . If I were still on a battlewagon I would probably still be a snotty ensign and junior officer of a division.[11]

Gallery was proud of the spirit among his men,[12] and noted with satisfaction at one point that he had been acting commanding officer for three weeks while the CO and XO were on leave.[13]

Still, his tour on the *Stevens* was not without complications. Immediately after reporting, Gallery was in the engine room when the *Stevens* was shifting berths from one buoy to another, some three hundred yards from the steep, rocky shore. The oil pumps began losing suction and so Dan left the engine room for the fireroom to help fix the pumps, leaving a first class machinist's mate with an excellent record on watch on the forward throttles. By mistake the machinist's mate answered a forward one-third bell with a one-third astern throttle (while the other engineer properly set his throttle one-third ahead). The commanding officer found his ship unaccountably pulling toward the shore, so he asked for two-thirds ahead speed on both engines, which the machin-ist's mate again acknowledged properly while further opening the wrong throttle. The same mistake occurred when the CO called for standard, and then for full, speed. Effectively out of control, the *Stevens* hit the rocks with both propellers going full speed—one ahead, one astern.

Dan was greatly chagrined about it:

> The whole fleet saw it happen and from another ship it just looked like we were a gang of dumbells and simply backed up on the beach till we couldn't go any farther. They probably thought we were trying to cut across the island and take the overland route.[14]

Naturally the propellers were both badly mangled, though luckily the rest of the ship escaped damage. Although the machinist's mate was Gallery's man and Dan was quite worried about the incident, he person-ally escaped the court-martial inquiries standard to grounding incidents because he had been going about his own duty in the fireroom while the wrong throttle was opened. (Gallery attributed the problem to the machinist mate's rough liberty the night before.)

Similarly a month later, when, due to an engineering casualty, the ship lost way in a storm and rolled desperately in the trough ("forty degrees each way," according to the telegram Dan sent his father[15]), Gallery was not blamed, for he had reported the poor state of the equip-ment before. It was a frightening experience, nevertheless:

> For two hours we had a merry time of it. It was blowing blue blazes and our little bucket would first stand on one beams end and then snap over and stand on the other. . . . I was down in the fireroom trying to get the water out of the oil. Every time the ship rolled we would all slide across the floor plates and pile up against the low side of the ship. When she rolled back we would go flying across to the other side. All this time we were without lights and most of my green firemen were scared stiff and thought we were bound for Davy Jones.[16]

Several months after that the ships suffered a collision due to shiphan-dling error, and Gallery was again not blameworthy, having been on

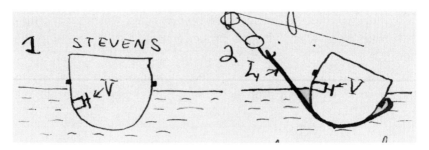

Gallery drew this diagram of his scheme to tip the destroyer USS *Stevens,* and sent it in a letter to his dad. The problem was to get at and close a valve "V" some four feet below the water line (Figure 1). Gallery proposed to pass a heavy line "L" from the port side under the keel of the vessel, then pass it up to a heavy tackle secured to the dock, then lead the fall back to the starboard side of the ship (Figure 2). At that point the whole ship's company would heave around on the fall, and tip the ship. The captain bought Gallery's idea, and the procedure worked. *Gallery Papers, U.S. Naval Academy Special Collections, Nimitz Library*

duty in the engine room as required. However, the commanding officer was relieved on account of the collision.[17]

With a new commander, the *Stevens* was ordered to decommission at the Navy Yard in Philadelphia along with 156 other destroyers. In this decommissioning work—a very important job, as it turns out, for many of these same four-stackers were sent to Britain in 1940 under Roosevelt's famous "destroyers for bases" deal—Gallery first illustrated something of the technical ingenuity that was to mark his naval career, and which was partly responsible for setting him on a fast track promotionally. In a letter to his father, he sketched a technical procedure he had invented:

> There was a big valve below the water line which we had not been able to close. Everyone said we would have to go into dry dock and let the navy yard fix it. We had a scheme however for getting the valve above the water so we could work on it by which we would avoid going into dry dock and thereby save the navy several hundred dollars. . . .

. . . To do this we had to roll about 4 feet of the starboard side
out of the water. All the wise ones and the old timers said it couldn't
be done, but we tried it anyway. We hooked a heavy line to the port
side of the ship, led it under the keel and up on the starboard side.
Then we hooked a heavy tackle to the line, secured the tackle on
the dock, and led the fall back on the ship. Then the whole ship's
company heaved in on the fall, pulling the port side under the
water, and rolling the starboard side out. The idea worked fine, we
got the valve above the water line and fixed it. . . .[18]

Again, Gallery had come up with this scheme; upon his suggesting it,
he and his CO worked the details out together. The commander then
included a very brief description of the episode in an article he wrote
for the U.S. Naval Institute *Proceedings,*[19] an event which may have first
stimulated Gallery to think about professional publication, though it
would be some ten years before he would try it.

Having decommissioned the *Stevens* in the summer of 1922, Gallery
was ordered to the destroyer *Case,* but in that same yard the armored
cruiser *Pittsburgh* was fitting out for a two-year cruise as flagship of
Naval Forces Europe. An officer ordered to the *Pittsburgh* did not want
the European cruise, so Gallery traded with him.[20]

Gallery was first assigned as material officer on this ship, but within
a few weeks he was also given the Boiler Division to head up. He quickly
qualified to stand engineering watches underway, finding that because
of his small ship experience, he was more confident and generally more
competent than the other ensigns. He credited his *Stevens* assignment:
"There is nothing like running a destroyer with half a crew to knock out
the sort of timid feeling that most people have for handling powerful
machinery."[21] Apparently he did his work well aboard the *Pittsburgh.* In
September 1923 he was appointed senior assistant engineer, and later
in the year he was relieved of engineering duties and made turret officer
of the after turret and senior watch officer on deck,[22] a position with
substantial protocol responsibilities in port (such as greeting visitors,
ordering signals, and making the ship smart in appearance).

But Gallery in retrospect didn't have much to say about these professional duties. Instead he remembered most vividly the extracurricular
activities ashore, as the *Pittsburgh* "showed the flag" from Philadelphia

W.S.S. Pittsburgh going through Kiel Canal
Summer 1923

On its grand European tour, the armored cruiser *Pittsburgh* (CA 4) visited ten different ports in the Baltic alone. Here, *Pittsburgh* transits the Kiel Canal in the summer of 1923. *Gallery Papers, U.S. Naval Academy Special Collections, Nimitz Library*

to Gibraltar, to Constantinople and throughout the Mediterranean, out into the Atlantic and up to ports in England, northern France, into the Baltic, and back, "stopp[ing] practically everywhere where the port had deep enough water for us."[23]

While aboard his first two ships, Gallery had been very involved in activities beyond his own primary duties. He had coached wrestling, played baseball and tennis, led a ship's platoon in a parade, and taken part in various off-hours activities. As he wrote his father shortly after reporting aboard the *Stevens,* "I have seen a couple of shows, thrown a couple of dinner parties on the ship, and taken in a couple of shindigs. I also looked up a femme the other day who I used to drag youngster year at the Academy."[24] But in the ports of Europe (especially Constantinople, where the *Pittsburgh* spent many months[25]), he could expand his accustomed social life. In his autobiography Gallery doesn't recount his sprees in any detail, only reporting that "in a complement of eighty

Dan captained ball teams from the USS *Pittsburgh* when they played during the ship's visit to Cairo in the spring of 1923. *Courtesy of Mrs. Daniel V. Gallery*

officers only two had to be sent home with black marks on their records (liquor, of course). . . . The J.O.'s got into many minor jams, but were able to worm their way out."[26] Actually, besides daylight battlefield tours, city visits, and baseball games, Europe seems to have been one long round of dinner parties and (especially) associated night life. It is noteworthy that the only episode Gallery recounts at any length in his autobiography includes its share of "fighting spirit." The incident took place the ship's last night in Constantinople after a long stay:

> Just before the last liberty boat left the Dolma Bagtche landing to take the boys back to the ship at midnight, the liberty party observed an old naval custom and beat up the squad of Turkish soldiers who were guarding the landing. So far, so good. Nothing unusual about that.
>
> But an hour or so later [Ens. Ash Pleasants] and I drove down to the landing, paid off the *arabache* driver and started dickering with a Turk boatman to row us out to the ship. We were both clean, sober, and ready to stand "eight-to-eight" (it says here). We didn't want no trouble with nobody.
>
> The Turk guards were still licking the wounds inflicted by our liberty party an hour before and were just aching for someone from the *Pittsburgh* to appear so they could wreak vengeance.

As soon as they heard us say "Pittsbourg" to the caïque pilot they let us have it. . . . After sweeping up the dock with us they tossed us into the boat and told the caïque coxswain to shove off.

As we were pulling away from the landing I thought I saw a chance to get in the parting shot in this battle. The sergeant commanding the squad was standing on the edge of the dock making derogatory comments in Arabic about me and Ash and there was a long boat hook with a bronze end lying in the bottom of the caïque.

Forgetting that the boatman was a Turk, I grabbed the boat hook and was about to clout the sergeant in the ear with it. The boatman dropped his oars, whipped out a long curved scimitar and flung me back in the stern sheets with the point of his knife poised an inch from my jugular vein.

He made some ill-tempered remarks in Turkish and then pulled back to the dock, where I was hauled out of the boat and beat up some more. Finally the soldiers let him take us back to the ship.[27]

Gallery said he and Pleasants made no report of the incident, lest the investigators misinterpret the events.

All in all, Gallery regarded this eighteen-month European cruise as "prime duty for a young ensign."[28] Professionally, to be sure, it seems to have been less significant duty than his other shipboard assignments, for he spent much of his time on the beach, and although the *Pittsburgh* certainly engaged in a great deal of coastal navigation, deck seamanship and sea detail, the ship took part in relatively few fleet operations while he was aboard her. But Gallery certainly honed his world awareness and social skills by visiting so many foreign countries and historical sites— from Gallipoli to the Pyramids to the Holy Land to Rome to Pompeii— and the multitude of watering holes that went along with them.

Gallery left the *Pittsburgh* in January 1924 and embarked on the armored cruiser *Colorado* for home in order to train for the 1924 Olympics. However, the Olympic wrestling rules had meantime changed so as to outlaw scissors holds, and as Gallery's unique hold was ruled a scissors (and he was also a bit out of shape), this time he didn't make the team. In early June he was assigned to the navy supply ship *Rappahannock*, which was steaming for the West Coast.[29] On this vessel he would stand underway officer of the deck watches (running the ship from the bridge) and again head up First Division (the boatswain's mates). His service aboard was pretty brief, as on reaching Seattle the ship was given orders to report to Mare Island for decommissioning, and shortly after that Gallery was given orders to leave her.

But it was not uneventful duty. One Monday morning while the ship was at a berth in the Mare Island shipyard, a sailor was reported missing at muster. Later that morning Gallery was inspecting his spaces and had occasion to enter Number One hold. There he found a body, which he believed was the sailor's. He immediately returned topside to inform the commanding officer, a Lt. Comdr. Butler Rhodes, and to fetch a stretcher, a stretcher bearer, and a hospital apprentice. With the commanding officer directly behind him and the others tagging after, Gallery hurried back down the hold, leading the way by flashlight. Then he heard a crash. Perhaps disoriented, the captain had fallen down through the flap hatch at the top of the ladder, the same hatch through which the seamen apparently had fallen sometime over the past weekend. The captain also was killed.[30] Although the board of inquest at which Gallery testified was perfunctory—it ruled the incident accidental—according to a note Dan's father wrote in his log, Dan was "very much shaken by [the] tragedy."[31]

But whatever ship he went aboard (even in wartime) Gallery was more typically cheerful. During the *Rappahannock*'s transit from Norfolk south toward the Panama Canal many months before, the crew had seen some lighter moments. Or at least it had, if we can believe the incident narrated below, taken from a 1952 Gallery letter to an old friend.

> Your letter really reached way back. Do you remember that time on the *Rappahannock* when I had the morning watch and you were fishing off the stern? We were off the coast of Florida bound for Panama on course 175, (or 176 I forget which—sure sign of old age), making 150 turns or 12.5 knots. Cape Canaveral light was bearing 230 degrees (229 MAG, 234 PSC), dist 14.5 miles and I was supposed to call Warrick to relieve me at 0700.
>
> All of a sudden a sailor comes running up to the bridge and yells, "Mr. Butler says stop the ship—he's got a big fish on his line." So I

sent the guy back to ask, "Which end of the line?", and you were sore for a week because a 20 foot marlin got away.[32]

Could it have happened? Well, sailors have at other times fished off fantails while cruising near Florida, and marlins that get away do average about twenty feet in length. . . .

In any case, upon his transfer from the *Rappahannock* Gallery has served in navy ships of several different kinds and sizes, and has held billets in engineering, deck, and gunnery departments. He's handled enlisted men in firerooms, in enginerooms, in cargo holds, on gun turrets and on the main deck, and in wrestling and baseball games, too. The small ship assignment, especially, has taught him confidence and self-reliance, while his enthusiasm for sports has afforded him the opportunity to interact with enlisted men in an unofficial, off-duty atmosphere, and learn to be "part of the crew."

Finally, he has been steaming throughout the world. With his next ship's cruise to Australia and back he will have walked on six continents, sailed many of the world's seas and oceans, and personally visited more ports than most navy people ever see. He has also had to handle himself in tense situations: while he has not been in combat, he's been in a collision, a grounding, and a near-foundering, and he has seen what disaster accidents can work, too. Most important, perhaps, Dan has kept his sense of humor through it all. For leadership purposes, it would be hard to over-emphasize the importance of this prominent feature of his personality.

GALLERY WAS TO serve as a blackshoe aboard one other vessel—by far, the pick of the lot. After spending Christmas 1924 on leave at home, in January 1925, he reported to the USS *Idaho* at San Pedro, where he was assigned as first division officer. In April this crack battleship participated in fleet maneuvers off Hawaii, then joined the entire U.S. Battle Fleet for its grand cruise to Australia and New Zealand. The *Idaho* returned to San Francisco for overhaul on September 24. Later it would visit several other West Coast ports (Bremerton and Seattle, especially).

Under Gallery's coaching, the *Idaho*'s wrestling team won the wrestling championship among the battleships, and Dan was proud to report that one of his sailors won the All-Navy lightweight title that year. Gallery also edited the ship's weekly paper, the *Idaho Yarn,* a four-page issue set in linotype and printed on board, which featured all sorts of sports stories, many of which Gallery wrote himself. The paper regularly displayed cartoons as well, some of them also Dan's. He didn't limit his humor to those drawings, however. Once the ship was reassigned for a port visit from Seattle to a small Puget Sound town called Anacortes, which (everybody thought) would make for a dull time. So Gallery tried to cheer up the crew with a fictitious lead story featuring some invented escapades of the fictional mayor of that small city.

As it happened, the actual mayor of Anacortes made a courtesy visit to the ship's captain at the very same hour that a marine placed some copies of Dan's paper on the captain's desk. The mayor looked at the article, became highly incensed, and abruptly took his leave. The captain summoned Gallery to his cabin and fired him on the spot. Gallery later remarked, "I found out then and there that a lot of this stuff about freedom of the press, editorial license, etc., did not apply aboard first-line battleships of the U.S. Navy." However, Gallery was shortly rehired as the editor, and ran the paper until he left the *Idaho* in late 1926.[33]

However, all of this was collateral work. Gallery's primary responsibility aboard the *Idaho* was running Number One Turret. Gallery described this gunnery duty in his 1966 autobiography.

Number One Turret on the USS *Idaho*

On the *Idaho* I was the First Division officer and assigned to Turret One. A 14-inch turret in those primitive days was about the equivalent of a SAC bomber in these enlightened times. A young turret officer had frightening power under his thumb tip. One 14-inch shell could blow up an enemy battleship, as was demonstrated at the Battle of Jutland. Of course in this atomic age the battleships are in the moth-ball fleet. But it may be of interest to learn how things used to be in the pre-atom navy.

A well-trained main-battery turret was like a Notre Dame football team before N.D. went soft and began stressing education. Everything was done by machinery, but the shell hoists, upper and lower powder hoists, trays, and rammers were all run independently of each other, and the sailors throwing the switches needed split-second coordination to get the loading interval down and boost the HPGPM (hits per gun

Dan and a family friend stand on the bow of the USS *Idaho*. On a battleship, "turret officer" was a very important billet. Dan was in charge of the forward turret, seen here at his left shoulder. *Courtesy of Mrs. Daniel V. Gallery*

per minute). Speed and accuracy were the watchwords and only sissies worried about safety. When you fired a salvo the guns came back to loading position, the gun captains flung the great breech blocks open, and compressed air hissed into the powder chambers to blow the flaming gases of the previous salvo out of the bore. To save a little time the gun captains always hollered "bore clear," whether it was or not, because it was a hundred to one the bore *would* be clear before the powder charges were rammed home (That time on the *Mississippi* when a turret blew up and we damned near lost one battleship was the hundred-to-one shot.)

I had a chief turret captain who hated my guts and vice versa. He was a fine turret captain, but he resented having to take orders from a young-punk j.g.. He figured it was *his* turret and I figured it was mine, so we didn't get along very well. He got shot and killed some years later when he was a cop in Los Angeles. I often considered shooting him myself but never quite got around to it.

Despite this lack of cordiality we had a good turret. We could pump out salvoes of three 14-inch shells at ten-second intervals and put most of them through the target. . . .

In 1925 we were constantly training for the coming great naval battle with the Japs. We still thought then that it would be fought along more or less classic lines. We drilled at approaches and deployments of the battle lines, attacks by light forces of the van and rear, and mopping-up tactics. Some officers thought airplanes might be useful for scouting and for spotting main-battery salvoes. But the big show would be the fight between the two columns of battleships. The carriers would be kept well over the horizon on the disengaged flank, and the big ships would slug it out. Actually, it worked out just the other way in World War II. Carrier planes did all the heavy slugging, and the battle wagons never got closer than 100–200 miles from the action.

Once a year we would hold a regular Chinese New Year's out at sea and would run through the battle rehearsal using live ammunition. It was an awe-inspiring sight to see a dozen battleships, a couple of cruiser divisions, and several dozen destroyers all blasting away at the towed targets at once, with the tin cans darting in and out firing torpedoes too. . . .

From Pensacola to "The Gun Club"

OF HIS VERY FIRST experience with aviation, Dan Gallery tells a story that reaches back to his early childhood. It has to do with his "guardian angel," and Gallery's sliding down the banisters in his three-story house. "I knew, of course, as all Catholic kids do, that you have a guardian angel who goes around behind you trying to steer you straight. Up to this time I hadn't met mine, but I knew he was there." As the story continues,

This morning I got up a little late, and when I started downstairs nobody else was around.

Just as I was about to throw my leg over the banisters and start my let down, my Guardian Angel appeared behind me, put his hands under my armpits, lifted me up, and took off!

He spread his wings, nosed over, and glided down the stairs like a pelican.

At the bottom of the stairway he did what I now know was a wing over, pulling up in a steep *chandelle* to the left, and reversed course 180 degrees. Then he soared down the hall in level flight, made another beautiful *chandelle,* and glided down the next stairway to the ground floor. There he leveled off, made as nice a full stall landing as I've ever seen, and set me down on my feet so gently I wouldn't have cracked a wren's egg.

Looking back now after thirty-three adventurous years as a naval aviator, I still regard this as the most skillful bit of flying I've ever taken part in.[1]

After this, the Guardian Angel's interest in aviation slumbered awhile. Despite his having taken his first hop in an aircraft in Antwerp in 1920, the aviator bug didn't really bite Dan Gallery until four or five years after graduation from Annapolis.[2] Then it bit hard.

While en route the West Coast on the *Rappahannock* in June of 1924, Dan wrote home, requesting consent from both his parents to enter aviation. At first they both vigorously refused. Dan's mother remained opposed for some time, but his father changed his mind a month later, telling Dan to "go for it." In September of that same year all Dan's letters to his father were "full of his desire for aviation."[3] Despite Dan's admiration for the battleship *Idaho,* to which he reported in January of 1925, his interest in aviation increased. According to Gallery, practically all the young officers aboard that ship wanted to take up flying. However, they encountered firm opposition from the *Idaho*'s command, especially from the executive officer, Comdr. (later Vice Adm.) A. B. Cook.

As junior officers we would put in for aviation, [and] the request would go through the exec. He used to get each of us in there and give us a lecture about giving up our birthright for a mess of pottage. This was one of the watchwords of the ship, "Your birth right for a mess of pottage." And a lot of us gave it up.[4]

Not Dan, however—though he did delay his request until he had established a reputation on board. Gallery made formal application for aviation in September 1926 and was detached from the *Idaho* in December.[5] In May of the next year, while he was already in flight training in Pensacola, his mother was prompted by Charles Lindbergh's successful flight across the Atlantic to write Dan, saying she was delighted he had entered aviation.[6] And within a year or so after he had completed the course, to Dan's amazement, "who should show up down at Pensacola to learn to fly himself but A. B. Cook, giving up his birth right for a mess of pottage, too."[7]

In Pensacola, the eight-month course mixed ground school, flight instruction, and pilot tests or "checks." As Dan recollected,

We started off with seaplanes. We flew the old N-9, which was a Jenny really with an extra wing section put in and a pontoon on it. Then after going through the course in seaplanes, you shifted to land planes. The primary trainers were the NYs. . . .

Then you went to the so-called advanced training, which at that time was still at Pensacola. Then you learned to fly observation planes, big boats, and fighters. As I recall it, the course ran around 300 hours flying time then. Then you got your wings, and went out in the fleet.[8]

If you passed, that is. A bit over fifty percent of Dan's class didn't make it. This was apparently a pretty typical dropout rate.

For example, on February 27, Dan wrote his father that eight of forty-two original trainees had failed the first check, and three had failed the next one. The class was already down to thirty-one with twenty more checks to go. On March 6 two more had "busted," and April 4, four more "busted out." On April 15, twenty pilots remained.[9] This number would graduate in August.

Dan withheld news from his family that very early on he had had problems, too. He had failed his first two tests in the Primary Seaplane course.[10] In his father's log, we find the situation had been more critical yet. Dan had failed both on the first and second trial of the "First Solo Check," and the Flight Board had refused an additional three hours of instruction. But an Advisory Board on appeal granted the three hours, and Dan passed on his third (extra) try.[11] It had been a close thing. Dan might have been among that very first group to fail the program.

After this he had little trouble, and on the fighter portion of the program, Dan ranked first. He graduated seventh in a class of twenty,[12] a class that included three senior officers of some little distinction. In his autobiography, Dan explained the reasons for the presence of a few commanders and captains at Pensacola:

By law the carriers had to be commanded by aviators, but until war broke out most of our naval aviators were too junior to command a big ship. The Navy had got around this by training as flyers a number of older officers to fly who were senior enough to qualify for command. This worked out a lot better than you might think. . . .[13]

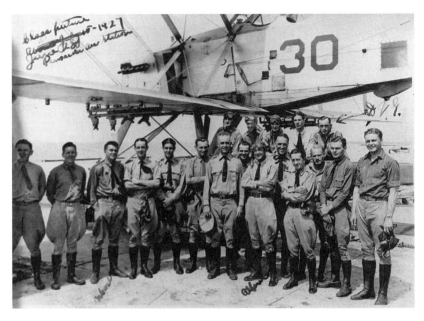

The officers in Gallery's Pensacola class included some famous World War II admirals: Ernest J. King (who ducked this photo) and Richmond Kelly Turner (front row, center, holding hat). Several enlisted aviators (not shown here) were also in Gallery's class. Dan is in the top row, far right. *Courtesy of Mrs. Daniel V. Gallery*

Commanders Alva Bernhard and Richmond Kelly Turner were in Dan's Pensacola class. Both had highly successful naval careers after this, Turner becoming especially renowned for his wartime leadership of the amphibious forces in the Central Pacific drive toward Japan. But the most eminent man in the class was a very senior officer, a captain who would guide the navy throughout the war years—future Chief of Naval Operations Ernest J. King. Captain King ducked some of the class photos, but otherwise (although some aviators have doubted this) according to Gallery he went through the same course as all the other pilots. "In primary seaplanes, I remember, there was one part of the course where you had to do stunts. They told King that they would excuse him from the stunt check, on account of his age. King said, 'Nothing doing. I'll take the stunt check the same as everyone else.' And he did." [14] Years later, Gallery recalled the Captain King he had known in Pensacola.

On May 22, 1927, two days after Lindbergh's historic flight across the Atlantic, Dan had written his father, "We all envy young Lindbergh down here now. Anybody on the station would gladly swap places with him." On October 9, Lindbergh posed with Dan and his fellow aviators at Pensacola while on a tour through the United States. *Courtesy of Mrs. Daniel V. Gallery*

He was a very austere and reserved sort of character. For the first month or so, while he was around down there living in the BOQ with the rest of us, nobody could get friendly with him at all. But then after about a month, he loosened up and he became one of the boys.

Then after we had finished the course and gotten our wings and went back in the fleet, he became E. J. King again.[15]

Gallery would see more of King in the years ahead. But some of his comrades he would not meet again. Six of his twenty classmates designated aviators on August 30, 1927, were dead from accidents within a year—two of those from a midair collision right over Pensacola.[16] This casualty rate, incidentally, seems to have been not at all atypical for these early days of naval aviation.[17]

Dan himself was not immune from danger. Right after he got his wings (but while still in training), he and another student crashed in a pontoon-rigged TM-3 some two hundred yards offshore of the commandant's office; they had to fight to the surface from the sunken aircraft. Oddly, the day before this accident, Dan's mother had sent him a religious medal, which he had sewn inside his flying helmet and was wearing for the first time. Dan joshed his mother about the coincidence, but in a habit characteristic of his religious commitment, he continued to wear the medal throughout his flying career. Concerning a later, equally daunting experience with possible religious or psychical implications, he expressed ambivalence instead of humor: he had a dream beforehand of a fellow pilot's spinning in and being killed while cross-country flying over a weekend, an event which then actually occurred. Gallery was stunned by the fact, but didn't draw any religious conclusions: "I have no idea how to explain a thing of this kind. I simply report it as an eerie fact and let it go at that." [18]

After postqualification training in observation and combat flying (courses in which he ranked second and first, respectively [19]), Dan's first aviation assignment was initially disappointing: instead of the fighters he craved, he was assigned to torpedo planes. His first squadron was VT-9, "sort of a bastard outfit. We were flying Tams, which was a carrier based torpedo plane but they had put pontoons on this thing. . . . So we were a torpedo plane squadron on pontoons." The planes could not operate off carriers because of the pontoons, nor could they land in anything except smooth water, and hence were not as versatile as true seaplanes. The planes were "trying to be a patrol squadron," as Gallery put it, and they trained in horizontal bombing and dropping torpedoes.

The squadron operated out of Hampton Roads up and down the East Coast, flew down to Panama and back for war games, and in the winters spent considerable time in Guantánamo, Cuba. The flagship of the squadron was the USS *Wright,* but on deployment two small "*Bird*"-class tenders also provided support. "Our cruise and radius was about 500 miles. We operated from little tenders like the *Sandpiper* and the *Teal.* They would go on ahead of us down the coast and anchor and put out buoys for us. Then we'd come along and tie up to the buoys and spend the night on [them]." [20] The long-range flying was absorbing. Gallery's letters show that despite the limitations of his aircraft, he was learning all along:

> . . . our gang are pretty seasoned pilots now . . . we have had experience that few others have had. We have cut loose from our base, flown down to Panama, done enough compass flying over open water to feel confidence in our ability to hit our objectives, and have weathered a couple of tough storms. There is a great deal of seamanship to be learned in handling planes on the water that you can get only from experience.

Gallery was also exercising his leadership qualities. While involved in bombing practice, Gallery was pleased to be "the boss of the show":

> . . . so far all the skipper has done has been to follow my recommendations, which is as it should be as a matter of fact. In a squadron where the heads of departments are on the job about all that the captain has to do is to answer the letters that busy bodies send in to the navy department reporting his pilots for blowing their wash off the line or frightening their babies.[21]

The skipper might have raised an eyebrow at this, for Gallery's own antics likely provoked such letters. In 1970, Vice Adm. Paul Stroop (retired) recollected his assignment in VT-9. Stroop recalled he had served with

> a number of very colorful . . . types, probably the most colorful one being Dan Gallery. Dan, as a matter of fact, was executive officer of the squadron and I was assigned to fly in his section, which turned out to be a very interesting experience because Dan was always trying to find something colorful to do like flying under a bridge or having the section zoom a ship or screaming down fifty feet over a highway, watching the tourists going to Florida in the winter time when we were heading south.

Stroop loved all his time in the squadron, and regarded Gallery as "a wonderful man to work for, [a] great leader and great fighter."[22]

In the summer, while Gallery was attached to this squadron, it flew graduates of the Naval Academy around at Annapolis, teaching them courses in aeronautics. The fliers also took part in several flying contests.

Gallery's plane practices dropping torpedoes at Guantánamo Bay in February 1928. According to Gallery, the torpedoes he trained with in VT-9 were the primitive ones with which the U.S. Navy started the war—they had to be dropped while the plane was practically touching the water. In contrast, Japanese torpedoes could be dropped from about 150 feet. *Courtesy of Mrs. Daniel V. Gallery*

At the Curtiss Marine Trophy Race at Anacostia in May of 1928, Dan won first in the Torpedo Plane competition, and in an aviation contest at Narragansett Bay held in August, he won Class B, the "Bombing Class."[23] All this time, Dan was very active off the airfield too, whether in sports like handball or baseball, by writing for the station newspaper, or by taking part in after-hours social activities. As we will see in the next chapter, it was during this tour that Dan would meet his future wife.

In May of 1930, Dan reported to Pensacola as an instructor. Years later, a fellow aviator offered an interesting view of Dan as an instructor pilot:

> Dan was quite an instructor. I remember when I first started, I got in a little two-piece seaplane on floats. He was sitting in the front cockpit and I in the rear cockpit. This was a bi-plane, with a ninety horsepower engine. He said, "There's nothing to flying, watch."

> So he put his hands on the cockpit sides, and taxied out. All the controls he had were a stick and a throttle. He would work the throttle with his one knee and the stick between his knees. He took off, did a loop, came down, and landed. It was kind of rough, you could see him sort of squirming around a bit. Then when he came to rest he said, "It's nothing to it, see, no hands. Now you try."[24]

Casual as Gallery made it appear, the instructor business did have a learning curve. In 1931, while explaining to his father the context of his brother Bill's (Onie's) having had to make four forced landings (Bill had also taken up navy flying), Dan commented on his own recent experience:

> I've had two crack ups myself since I have been down here due to a foolish policy of letting the student go too far before taking the controls away from him. . . . In both cases altho I let the student go too far to save the plane, I did take it away from him in time to make sure we weren't going to hurt ourselves and after all, in a training squadron, that is the main idea.[25]

Gallery's methods were apparently successful. In another letter he remarked that to date none of his students had failed, and that he greatly enjoyed seeing the students develop.[26] Here as elsewhere, Dan was obviously manifesting his unique combination of traits both in the air and while ashore: competence, ingenuity, leadership, quick thinking in emergencies, and an appetite both for skirting the regulations and for occasional high jinks.

While at Pensacola, Dan was assigned defense counsel for an enlisted student pilot named John A. Smith, a young man who had been accused of striking a rowboat and killing a mother of four while taking off in his seaplane during a training exercise. Gallery's long summary for the defense stressed that Smith had seen no one and only felt a slight bump; that Smith was cooperating fully with the investigation; and that there was only a small dent in one pontoon to tie Smith's seaplane to this severe accident.[27] Gallery apparently was quite persuasive, as the court acquitted the defendant. But authorities took a different view. On advice of the judge advocate's division, the assistant secretary of the navy took justice into his own hands, disapproved of the acquittal on the grounds that it "did not accord with the evidence,"[28] and ordered Smith to be "discharged as unfit," a relatively strong penalty, though less than that for the manslaughter with which Smith originally had been charged. In letters to his parents, Gallery expressed his dismay about this action. Although he acknowledged in the letter that Smith was probably guilty, Dan believed the accident was not only unintentional but probably unavoidable.

> We are sorry when a thing like that happens and we do all in our power to prevent it from happening again, but unless you stop flying altogether you are bound to have accidents. The Department's attitude in this case reminds me of the famous order issued five or six years ago by some non flying rear admiral to the effect that "forced landings are prohibited from now on."[29]

Gallery advised Smith to appeal his dismissal from the service.

After this trial (headlined in the Pensacola newspaper) Gallery was besieged by requests from other blue jackets to handle their cases. But believing "the majority of the court martials handed out are richly deserved and could only be beaten on technicalities," he turned down most such requests.[30]

During his instructor tour, Gallery applied for postgraduate school in "aviation ordnance engineering," and with the help of those letters from Halsey and King he was accepted. Gallery tells us why he was interested:

> The Ordnance P.G.'s were known as the "gun club" and were supposed to have an inside track on promotion. They alternated between shore duty in the Bureau of Ordnance and key jobs in the fleet at sea. . . . All the aviators that I can remember who managed to get into the "gun club" eventually made admiral, too.[31]

The first half of this three-year course of instruction was at Annapolis (where "P.G." school was then located); the second half at a series of corporations and technical institutions on the East Coast.

In this program Gallery had ample opportunity to exercise his substantial technical aptitude. While on instructor duty at Pensacola he had already designed a "Checksighting Device for Aeriel Gunnery Training," for which he won a special commendation from Rear Adm. William A.

Moffett, an especially far-sighted officer who was the first chief of the navy's new Bureau of Aeronautics.[32] This device of Gallery's was subsequently patented, then manufactured and used in bomber training, especially by the army. Now, while studying in P.G. School itself, Gallery won a similar commendation for a "Synchronous Anti-Aircraft Range-Keeping Device," useful in fire-control.[33] This commendation was signed by H. R. Stark, who would be chief of naval operations at the outbreak of World War II, but who was then chief of the Bureau of Ordnance. A bit later Gallery received a third letter, for designing an "Automatic Release for Arresting Hooks on Carrier Planes."[34] This letter of thanks was signed by Gallery's old acquaintance, Rear Adm. E. J. King, who had taken over Moffett's job at the Bureau of Aeronautics. Thus, several major naval figures had begun to notice Gallery's technical inventiveness and drive.

During this tour Gallery also began developing his public speaking skills by giving talks to civic groups on aviation topics. One undated talk among Gallery's papers, apparently written and delivered about this time, discusses several aspects of naval aviation of the 1930s. It includes an interesting description of a tightly-packed carrier flight deck:

> A carrier deck, when all the planes are aboard, has not a square inch of vacant space. It has always been a marvel to me that many people don't get cut to pieces by propellers, because when getting ready to take off all planes are turning up at the same time, the propeller of every plane is missing the tail of the next ahead by inches, and several hundred people have to move around all thru that mass of planes. During fleet maneuvers this has to be done before dawn at times, and you may have to crawl under a dozen planes to get to yours. I guess the only reason we don't have accidents is that everyone feels the same way I do about it—they are scared to death every minute they are on deck.[35]

Gallery was disappointed at the reception of a couple of these early talks, but he had better luck when he made them less technical. He was pleased to receive many compliments after an address to the University Club of Annapolis on February 8, 1934.[36] He was beginning to learn the public speaking business. He was also developing his writing style in technical papers, and starting to manifest a comprehensive vision of the field of naval aviation.

While in P.G. School, Gallery continued to put in his required flying hours. Once he made the newspapers when he crash-landed a land biplane in Long Island Sound after his engine stopped a thousand feet above Stamford, Connecticut. Unable to find a landing place ashore, he had turned the plane toward the Sound. He landed in the water a hundred yards from the shore, and he and his copilot scrambled out of the cockpit onto the tail. As the plane sank, a local resident who had seen the plane swinging about for a water landing with its motor dead fetched the two pilots off the plane and brought them to shore in his rowboat.

Gallery attributed the crash to the engine running out of fuel—though the plane still had a full tank! Bravely, Gallery faulted himself: "The cause of this forced landing was gross carelessness on my part in not checking up properly on the setting of the valves in the fuel system before leaving Boston." A mistakenly closed cutoff valve meant the engine could not receive fuel from the plane's second tank. Although technicians should also have opened the cutoff valve, Gallery realized that had he followed standard procedures, he could (and should) have rectified the problem,[37] and therefore he put himself on report. In doing so (rather than make excuses), Gallery manifested the forthrightness and honesty which were among his great strengths as an officer. Perhaps because he was up front about it, he suffered no professional penalty for this error.

Several years later, again while on shore duty in the "gun club," Gallery would make additional headlines by making two tight 180-degrees spirals to land in a farmer's chicken coops when his engine went dead directly over the Hudson River.[38] It was either those coops or the river—the rest was forest. In this case, the engine had simply failed.

In the meantime, between these two ordnance tours, Gallery had gone back to flying full time, this in duty which would culminate in his first two flying commands.

To begin with, in 1935 he was assigned to VS Squadron Four, a scouting squadron assigned to the carrier *Langley* (the navy's first carrier) in the Pacific Fleet. After a year as operations officer in this outfit,

Dan is shown in November of 1936 while commanding Scouting Squadron Four. His squadron was originally stationed on the navy's first carrier, USS *Langley,* but when that ship was decommissioned, they moved to the USS *Saratoga. Courtesy of Mrs. Daniel V. Gallery*

he fleeted up to squadron command. The *Langley* was an old converted collier with a top speed of about fifteen knots—an awfully slow platform from which to fly airplanes. Gallery later pointed out the kind of difficulty involved:

> *Langley* had no catapults, so every takeoff was a fly-off. Sometimes, with only 20 knots of wind over the deck, you would roll off the bow ramp, right on the verge of stalling speed. But the flight deck was about 50 feet above the water and, by judicious use of this altitude, you could pick up flying speed before you hit the water.[39]

In the 1930s battleships were still the capital ships of the navy, and the *Langley* scouted for the Battle Fleet up and down the West Coast. One

morning during a battle problem near the Canal Zone, Gallery was sent
out to hunt submarines. He found an oil streak, obviously coming from
a submarine, and heading at the battleships. He flew down the streak
several times to indicate the submarine's position—but when the sub
fired its torpedo it also shot up a flare-marking rocket which almost hit
Gallery's aircraft. As Gallery gleefully reported, he had barely missed the
unique distinction of being shot down by a submerged submarine.[40] On
another occasion, while scouting, he sighted a submarine on the surface,
stalked it while he rallied other aircraft, then "cracked down on her thru
the clouds without ever having been seen until I was about to knock the
skipper's hat off"—thus becoming the only aviator on his side of the
wargame to be credited with sinking a submarine.[41]

In all this flying duty, Gallery took note of the leaders who were especially innovative and vigilant. His friend Bull Halsey (who now qualified
as an aviation "observer") was commanding the *Saratoga,* on which Gallery's squadron and others would practice a few night landings (when
the moon was full).[42] Partly based on his VS-4 experience, Gallery was
to spearhead night flying in all degrees of darkness in the Atlantic while
commanding the *Guadalcanal* during World War II. Another commander who drew Gallery's notice was the commander in chief, Adm.
Joseph M. Reeves. Reeves was constantly preaching vigilance—and also
training to develop this virtue. Reeves believed the Japanese might begin
a future war with a sneak attack as they had at Port Arthur in 1904. So,
on one Saturday afternoon Reeves waited till most of the commanding
officers of the fleet were off on the golf courses, then sortied the fleet
with an urgent signal from his flagship in San Pedro. Captains and commanders (with 25 percent of their crews) were left at the docks as their
vessels frantically got underway, wondering if the Japanese fleet was just
over the horizon. The whole fleet made it to sea and to the ordered
rendezvous, ready to fight the enemy.[43] Gallery, who had sortied with
the *Langley,* would remember this event on hearing of Pearl Harbor. In
his opinion, Reeves would not have been caught napping.

Gallery went from this scouting duty to operate more closely yet with
the battleship fleet, specifically as commander of VO-3, a battleship
"observation squadron" attached to the ships of Battle Division Three:
Mississippi, New Mexico, and Gallery's old ship, the flagship *Idaho.* The
battleships and aircraft cruised from North Island to the Hawaiian

Gallery's squadron of SBVs flying over the Golden Gate Bridge, probably upon the bridge's dedication in May 1937. The navy concentrated all Pacific naval vessels at San Francisco at the time of the opening, and a mass flight of 500 navy planes was one of the major events of the five-day dedication ceremony. *U.S. Navy*

Islands and back, and participated in fleet problems and war games, too: "We flew seaplanes that were launched by catapult. Our job was to spot the fall of shot from the big guns so we could control the main batteries in the great battleship action against the Japs which the nonaviators still thought would be decisive in World War II." [44]

Gallery became the senior aviator on the BatDivThree staff as well as the squadron CO, but upon receiving his orders, Gallery thought he'd be "in Siberia so far as active flying is concerned." [45] He was right about that; the battleship aviators didn't fly nearly as much as the carrier squadrons. [46] He grew to enjoy the job anyway, partly because he so liked his fellow officers, and partly because he greatly admired Admiral Wainwright, a kind of kindred spirit. He did have some arguments with

Wainwright's chief of staff. By this time Gallery had been an aviator too long happily to be confined to typical battleship regs:

> In aviation the big idea is to get results. We don't stand on ceremony and if the regulation book gets in our way when we want to do something that will promote efficiency we wink at the book and go ahead and do it. Up here however it often seems that it isn't what results you get that counts so much as it is complying rigidly and at all costs with every silly damned article in the reg book—and the book has over a thousand pages.[47]

Gallery also complained in a letter to his father that he was squadron skipper in name only. Since each battleship captain tended to regard his planes as just another part of his ship, Gallery didn't have much say in the operation of the squadron's aircraft.[48] Hence, after some eleven months, Gallery welcomed orders back to the "gun club," especially since he was to receive an assignment of some consequence.

Gallery had received orders as head of the Aviation Ordnance Section of the Bureau of Ordnance. As he wrote his father:

> It is a big job and the people who get it are specially selected for it. The man I will relieve stood first in his [academy] class, and also the man who preceded him. It will be my job to supervise and direct the design, manufacture, and procurement of all the aviation ordnance equipment for the navy and also to direct the experimental programs undertaken to develop new weapons and to keep us ahead of foreign powers.[49]

Important people indeed had been selected for this position in the past: the commander Gallery relieved, "Red" Schoeffel, would soon make admiral, and Schoeffel had himself relieved Forrest Sherman, an outstanding officer who, some years after the war, was to become CNO. Gallery's work was quite weighty, as well. He began his tour managing a budget of some ten million dollars, but that amount rose quickly. One of the most important projects Gallery oversaw was the development and procurement of the famous Norden bombsight. Over Gallery's thirty-month tour, the commitment to the Norden Company grew from about eight hundred thousand dollars to something like eighty million

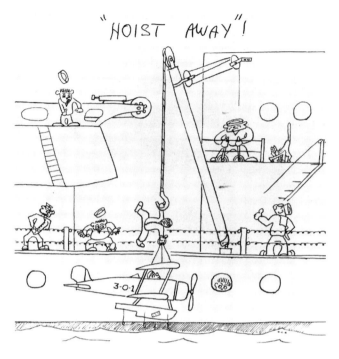

On the great battleships of the day, seaplanes were launched by catapult, then recovered by being hoisted aboard from alongside after landing in a "slick" created by the ship. During this "Cast Recovery," the rear-seat man sat astride the fuselage and tried to hook the ship's crane hook to the airplane's sling. If he was successful, the airplane was hoisted aboard. (Occasionally the airplane turned turtle and capsized during the evolution.) Gallery drew this cartoon in 1937–38 while aboard the USS *Idaho,* commanding Observation Squadron VO Three. *Idaho Yarn*

dollars per year. Although eventually every heavy bomber (navy and army air corps) got one of these bombsights, and it was an absorbing, top-secret project which required thwarting of Nazi espionage (among other things), Gallery later regarded it as ironic that dive-bombing tactics in the Pacific and area bombing in the European theater made the great effort that so many people had spent on this bombsight comparatively inconsequential.[50]

Gallery's section, of course, had other responsibilities, too—armor plating for airplanes, leak proofing of the fuel tanks, and changing from

.30-caliber guns to .50-caliber guns to 20-millimeter cannon, for example.[51] He also managed a great expansion of production facilities, as the beginning of the European war propelled a great growth of the U.S. Navy. As mentioned above, Gallery's section also had responsibility for experimental programs. In a 1939 letter to his predecessor, Gallery discussed projects such as a new fire control pan; the Mark II Aiming Angle Sight; a deck target; experimental armored pilots' seats; a cartridge release bomb rack; a miniature practice bomb to approximate the trajectory of service bombs; a "mechanical" wind vane sight for VP turret mounts; and so on.[52]

In this work Gallery's technical ingenuity again was personally exercised. In a memo to his boss dated March 1939, Gallery is seen supporting an idea far ahead of his time.

MEMORANDUM For the Chief of Bureau:
SUBJECT: Flying Bomb—Radio Controlled.
1. The Bureau has received numerous suggestions for rocket bombs, radio controlled gliding bombs, and bombs controlled by combinations of television and radio. Up to the present time, we have turned all those suggestions down as being impracticable. However, at the present time we have:
    (a) Automatic flight control (SBAE).
    (b) Radio controlled aircraft (Drones).
    (c) Television in every home "just around the corner."
2. I believe that if we wished to do so right now, we could produce a "flying bomb" which would be propelled by a small engine, have a limited wing span and be launched from a catapult. This flying bomb could, if we wish, carry SBAE, radio control apparatus, and television apparatus. Our attitude right now is "even if it was good we wouldn't like it," due to the fact that we think it would be too difficult to make it hit a precision target such as a battleship in a vulnerable spot.
3. I do not take any issue with this attitude at the present time. However, I believe that at some time in the future we will undoubtedly want such a flying bomb. . . . I recommend that we apply for a patent on a flying bomb controlled by radio. . . .
                                                        /s/ D. V. Gallery[53]

Two months later Gallery would write his predecessor that he was trying to get the admiral to buy a "flying torpedo," after which he would add, parenthetically, "They all think I'm nuts, but the Admiral is still on the fence." [54] And at the end of the letter he would go on to remark,

> I'm enjoying this job immensely—and it certainly gives you a wide field in which to operate. It's a liberal education, you learn something every day, and you are associated with a swell bunch of people. Until rather recently I've been working on the theory that newcomers in the Bureau of Ordnance should be seen but not heard. After June 1st, I figure I'll no longer be a newcomer. Don't be surprised if you hear that I'm in the little red house across the creek under observation some time after that date. [55]

It is characteristic of Gallery, even in the midst of the most technical discussions, not to take himself too seriously. His attitude was infectious. When Schoeffel returned to the bureau, he found "everybody around there was talking about what a hell of a fine fellow Dan Gallery was." [56]

So by the beginning of World War II, Dan Gallery has proven his worth in many different aviation billets, including squadron command. He has manifested an excellent flying ability in races, war games and aircraft emergencies, and as a leader he has shown himself not only competent and ingenious, but often inspirational. He's been assigned very important technical and managerial responsibilities as well— clearly, this last job at BUORD was a position reserved for aviators who showed early potential for flag rank. He has attracted the favorable attention of two future chiefs of naval operations as well as several other future wartime leaders. Above all, Gallery is a fighter. Soon the time will come to put this last talent to test.

WE'VE SEEN ABOVE how Gallery was quick to react in various flying emergencies. Below is Gallery's description of the occasion while assigned instructor duty at Pensacola when he literally almost fell out of his aircraft, an incident reported in newspapers throughout the country. Although some aviators of the era expressed doubt about the likelihood of this account, the details of the story and Gallery's background as a wrestler suggest it is true.

Hanging By His Toe

I had a close call one time when I fell out of a plane over Washington. I was practicing slow rolls in a Boeing single-seater and went into a roll with my left hand holding the throttle lightly and my right hand on the stick. We had just reached the inverted position and I was hanging head downward by the safety belt when the belt let go. My hands slipped off the throttle and stick and I took off head first for terra firma. As I was leaving the cockpit I instinctively kicked my legs apart, and the toe of my right shoe hooked on a projection up around the windshield. The only hold I had on that plane was with my right toe.

A plane won't stay on its back with no one at the stick, and this one promptly went into a vertical dive. I still had my toe hold but the air blast flattened the rest of me back over the turtle-back, with my head near the tail. I had a parachute so I could just kick my foot loose, get clear of the plane and pull the ripcord.

But we had started at seven thousand feet and I didn't *have* to bail out yet. The plane might hit in a populated area, so I decided to stay with it for a while.

I found that by bending my right knee I could pull myself forward, still flattened against the turtle-back, until my hands could reach the after edge of the cockpit. There I pulled myself to a sitting position on the rear of the cockpit, reached inside, got hold of the stick, pulled her gently back to level flight and got back into the cockpit. I must have looked silly as hell sitting there on the turtle-back like a cowboy riding a wild horse!

When I resumed my place in the cockpit I expected to find the safety belt was broken. There was nothing whatever wrong with it that I could see. The buckle of a safety belt is so designed that the harder you pull on it, the tighter it is supposed to lock itself.

Being of an inquisitive turn of mind I decided to buckle the belt again, try another slow roll and see what happened. But this time I going to be cagey about it. My left hand, instead of being on the throttle, would be under the bottom of the seat, ready to grab if the belt let go, so I would still be firmly attached to the airplane.

I did a couple more slow rolls, but I didn't find out anything. My left hand refused to cooperate in this project and wouldn't allow me to put any weight on the belt when we were upside down. Instead of just hooking under the seat ready to grab if the belt let go again, it took a firm hold and sank fingerprints into the metal of the seat bottom. I just couldn't get word down to it to relax and take it easy.

I've still got the shoe I was wearing when it happened, with a half-inch gash in the leather of the toe to show how strong the air blast was.

Private Life

NAVAL OFFICERS USUALLY find their friends in the service, but normally need support of family members to become successful. So we end our discussion of Gallery's early naval career with a glimpse at his personal life as an adult.

We have seen the closeness of his family, and we have noted the frequency with which he wrote home. Dan continued to write regularly to his father and mother once he became an officer, and he was writing his father long letters once or twice a month into the mid-1930s. After Onie and Phil were commissioned at Annapolis in 1925 and 1928, respectively, he corresponded occasionally with them as well, often on professional matters, and he wrote to John, Margaret, and Babe, too. Dan also visited home on leave when he could get away, sometimes on holidays, almost always between assignments, and in any case at least once a year. This included Christmas of 1924, the first Christmas dinner at which the whole family had been present since 1916, as his father noted in the log he was keeping about Dan.[1] The family gathered again on a more somber occasion in November 1927, when all the navy brothers took leave and traveled to Chicago. The family members shared day and night watches at Babe's bedside, until she passed away on November eighteenth.[2]

As the years went on, all had not been happiness at home. Dan's mother was said not to have been thrilled that three of her sons had joined the navy at her husband's urging. Although soon enough she became very proud of their service, Dan Senior's insistence on brother Phil's also going to Annapolis (along with Dan and Onie) was a particular occasion of distress. Perhaps revelatory of her feelings is an off-hand comment Mary once made. In writing about the suddenness of her parents' wedding (specifically, in mentioning the fact that her father had failed to cancel a date with another young woman on the wedding night itself) we hear Mary expressing just a bit of dissatisfaction with the male ego:

> . . . in after years [my father] loved to tease my mother with the
> suggestion that she had very nearly failed to "catch him." Men
> have ruled the world so long it is not surprising they harbor many
> delusions.[3]

At any rate, years of trouble between Dan's father and mother caused them to separate more than once. As we'll see, the parents did get back together (at least for a time) toward the end of the 1920s.

Meanwhile, Dan eventually became interested in forming a family of his own. Not that Dan hadn't been attracted to young women all along: he had dated regularly at least since his "youngster" year at Annapolis, when he took girls to various hops and balls whenever he could get away from duty. (He remembered being prepared for this by the academy's "dancing drill" in which, under the guidance of a dancing instructor from Baltimore, the plebes danced with each other.)[4] Dan wrote to his parents about looking up young women in ports from Norfolk to New York during his summer cruises; usually these were girls he had met at Annapolis the winter before. As to the intensity of Dan's interest in the female sex, the 1920 academy yearbook itself remarked Dan's quick transition from a completely innocent plebe to an upper-class man-about-town: "When Dizzums first got here Plebe summer, he was a model of innocence and purity, but aided by his well-known note book and associates over at the Barracks he has since become a true boulevardier."[5]

After graduation, as we noted earlier, Dan had a great time with the mayor's daughter in a small city in France, and the boat back from the Olympics was the site of additional social interaction. As for his social life while a blackshoe, when the *Delaware* voyaged to South America

Dan got "in thick" with a Peruvian girl, but found to his frustration that the date entailed the company of her parents, sister, and brother-in-law: "If the family would give you half a chance I think most of these senoritas could get into the spirit of these big full moons and inspiring nights they have here."[6] Back in the States, while the *Stevens* was undergoing repairs in New York's Navy Yard, he wrote that "a lady friend of mine who drives a big 1921 Packard took me out to show me the sights."[7] Snapshots taken in Egypt while Dan was attached to the *Pittsburgh* show him and a Lieutenant Eldridge in front of the Sphinx with two young Egyptian women[8]; he dated several other young women in various cities in Europe; and he later remarked that when the *Idaho* cruised to Australia, the entire ship's crew was "greeted with open arms literally as well as figuratively."[9] Although Dan headed the shore patrol in the ship's visit to Australia and thus had to manage associated problems, one assumes he met young women there like everyone else.

Photos suggest that as Dan became a naval aviator his social life continued. But quickly it moved to a conclusion. To this point apparently no one had long held his fancy. Then, while in Annapolis on a holiday sometime after he got his wings, Dan met a young woman named Vera Lee Dunn on a blind date. "Vee" was a U.S. deputy marshal for the District of Columbia—the first woman to hold this position—and Dan thought her very beautiful. He squired her to several baseball games (Vee was already a baseball fan) and took her flying in a two-seater around Anacostia. The couple soon hit it off.[10] For Dan and Vee the marriage would be a very happy one. But notice of the proposed match would greatly trouble Dan's father.

We saw earlier Dan's resentment at his father's riding him so much over his grades. Later, in the 1930s, Dan would become incensed over his father's doubt about Dan's ability to handle financial issues, such as his building a house in Coronado.

> In this case, if the housing venture were as foolhardy as you say it is no decent banking institution would touch it. Hence your prediction that in a few years I will be thrown out of the house and into the street and then courtmartialed must be based not on a consideration of this deal from a business standpoint but on a total lack of confidence in the individual undertaking the deal. . . .

. . . if I were as irresponsible and feeble minded as you seem to think I am I would never have gotten as far as I have in the Navy.[11]

Dan got angry about his father's reaction to the proposed marriage, too. But his father's distress over this marriage seems to have been more deeply felt than any of the relatively few issues over which the two were ever to quarrel. Indeed, given the elder Gallery's deep pride in Dan's whole career, it might have been more troubling to him than his separation from his own wife.

REPRODUCED BELOW are substantial selections from letters that Dan wrote to his father (primarily), to his mother, and to brother John (now a priest) over a period of some twelve months, from December 1928 to December 1929. These letters were written while Dan was flying in Torpedo Squadron 9, and deploying from Hampton Roads to the Canal Zone and back to the States, and they offer incidentally a picture of Dan's professional interests while in this assignment. They also discuss in some detail the good news of his father's and mother's reconciliation after a long and difficult period.

However, Dan's main concern here is to explain his love of Vee, and his intention to marry her despite his father's (and brother John's) strong objections, which include Vee's not being Catholic and her lack of social status. Although we have only one side of this correspondence (the letters from Dan), the strength of feeling on both sides of the controversy couldn't be more evident.

Two Tough-Willed Irishmen

UNITED STATES FLEET
AIRCRAFT SQUADRONS, SCOUTING FLEET
U.S.S. WRIGHT (FLAGSHIP)

Naval Air Station
Hampton Roads
Dec. 8, 1928

Dear Papa,

I've got some news for you in this letter that I've been trying to save until I got home but I just don't seem to be able to keep it to myself any longer. I think I'm going to get married next May when we come back from the cruise, to Miss Vera Lee Dunn of Washington. . . . In my letter to Mama, which I am mailing with this, I . . . gave you a little more dope on the girl. I told Mama to show the letter to you so I won't go into all that again in this letter. Miss Dunn is a fine girl and I'm sure you'll like her when you know her, so I hope that you'll consider this as good news. She is left handed, from the north of Ireland, but she is going to become a Catholic. . . .

Everything is still OK on the prospects for leave, altho it hasn't been officially granted yet. So I expect to be home in about ten days and can give you further dope on Miss Dunn personally, as you will undoubtedly want further dope.

> Dan

> Naval Air Station
> Hampton Roads
> Jan. 2, 1929.

Dear Papa,

Its sort of hard for me to write to you right now because I know that the thing that interests me most and means the most to me is an unwelcome subject with you and you would probably rather not hear about it at all. I know very well that you are taking the attitude that you do for what you think is my own good, but I disagree with you on it and I guess its just a stalemate, thats all. . . .

The squadron takes off Saturday for Charleston. I'll be leading the sixth section this cruise and as we always cruise in inverted order of sections I will also be leading the way for the whole outfit. About the only thing that that means though is that I will be responsible for passing the dope back by radio to the others about the weather and will have to use my own judgment about landing if we run into bum weather. We will spend Sunday in Charleston and will then proceed to Key West, where we will spend four days. Charleston to Key West is the longest hop we make on the cruise. The rest are all short jumps of about 350 miles with over night stops in between. Our tenders are shoving off tomorrow to get in their positions along the coast and guard the flight and everything is all set for us to take off Saturday morning at 8, weather permitting.

Happy new year to you Papa, and I hope that before long you'll give me credit for a little bit more sense than you do right now.
    Dan

USS Wright
Balboa CZ
Feb. 7, 1929

Dear Papa,

The best news I have received in many years was a letter from Mama yesterday telling me that you and she had gotten together again, patched up your differences, and that everything is fine at home. I certainly hope it will remain that way and can see no reason why it shouldn't. Because I've felt for the last five years or so that if the two of you would only get together and talk things over quietly and calmly for about fifteen minutes, that you'd both realize how useless it was to be on the outs all the time.

And so the news that you have done it means an awful lot to me. I thought when I got Mama's first letters about a week ago that there must be some mistake about the whole thing. And as it is now I'm just forgetting about them as if they were never written. And I certainly hope that this time the reconciliation is permanent. You and Mama have been together for too much of your lives, have gone thru too much together, and I know that you both think too much of each other to be able to get along without each other now.

We are still pretty busy with maneuvers down here. I put in 60 hours in the air last month, which I think is my biggest total yet with the possible exception of one month at Pensacola. So you can see that they are keeping us hopping.

I have seen Onie several times. He seems to be getting along fine on his ship and to be getting a kick out of life now. However, he has no ambitions about a naval career and altho he is doing well on his ship he just sort of laughs about it and says it doesn't worry him much one way or the other. So I advised him to resign, because unless he is going to stick to the navy for good and be serious about it, then the sooner he quits the better.

I think he has gotten rid of the flying bug. I wouldn't want him to go to Pensacola, and am pretty sure he would bust out if he did. He seems to have no appreciation of danger whatever and thats something that every flyer ought to have in a high degree. I flew him across the Canal to Colon last week.

Have had only one letter from you since we left the states.

Dan

Balboa CZ
Feb. 8, 1929

Dear John,

I can't tell you how much the news of the reconciliation meant to me. Fortunately your cable saying everything was OK and Mama's letter telling about the big blow up arrived the same day. I hope and pray that the reconciliation is permanent this time, and God knows it should be. When a man and woman have lived together as long as Mama and Papa, raised as many kids as they have, and stuck to each other, grudgingly though it may have been, thru the storms that they have, it would be a terrible misfortune to have them break up now. And down at the bottom of their hearts they both think an awful lot of each other too, I know. But they have been fighting against that feeling and repressing it for these many years. If this latest flare up has at last brought them both to see the light then God be praised.

I have always had a great feeling of affection and respect for Papa, and I never could bring myself to be bitter toward him or to say that he was willfully and maliciously to blame. That feeling has weathered some pretty hard knocks too and I hope and trust it will have no more to weather.

Now, about the "sad case" of your elder brother. . . . I'm twenty seven years old now and have never been in love before. And believe me John I am in love now. If I have to just chuck that love over the side this time as being rotten and unworthy then I doubt very much if I'll ever fall in love again. In the midst of all this waiting, worrying, and struggling against what seems to be everyone in the world that I care about, I have tried to imagine myself loving and marrying some one

Daniel V. Gallery, Sr., and four sons in uniform—Ensign Onie, Lieutenant Dan, Father John, and Midshipman Phil—on November 25, 1927. Dan makes sure viewers will note his seniority. *Gallery Papers, U.S. Naval Academy, Nimitz Library*

else. The idea is simply repellant to me and I can't do it. So I'm pretty sure that it will be Vee or no one, and for that matter I wouldn't have the crown princess of England if I could have Vee instead. I suppose you'll say that every young lad in love feels the same way, but remember that this young lad has seen enough of this world to know his own mind and that he was a damned tough nut for old cupid to crack. . . .

. . . This last month has been a pretty tough one for me on account of my own troubles alone to say nothing of those at home, which have now solved themselves thank God. I hope He will be as good to me. I've had only one letter from Papa since leaving home and I would rather not have had that one. Maybe his point of view on things has been softened by his own recent crisis. I hope so because as I said before, I have a great deal of affection and respect for him, and when I get letters from him such as this one was it has just the opposite effect from the one he intends and in addition puts foolish and reckless ideas in a guy's head for a moment or two. In this flying racket those sort of ideas are bad for the health, but of course they are merely passing flashes.

I hope you can see my point of view on all this because it means an awful lot to me. . . .

Thanks for the pictures. They came via the first air mail flight from Miami on the Pan American Air line, and were flown down by my old buddy Col Lindbergh himself. You gypped the P.O. dept. out of a lot of postage on that letter but somehow or another it got thru. I'm going to try to get this in on Lindy's return flight but I'm not sure that I can. I'll send you back your envelope via separate cover as envelopes of first flights, particularly Lindy's, are quite valuable from a collectors point of view.

Lt. (jg) Dan Gallery on the bridge of *USS Rappahannock,* September 1924. *Courtesy of Mrs. Daniel V. Gallery*

The *Miami Herald* published this photo on January 19, 1928, with the following caption: "Fliers in the naval air squadron VT9S, 12 planes of which have been in Miami since Monday afternoon, were guests of Mr. and Mrs. A. T. Ritchie of Coconut Grove estate, yesterday afternoon at a swimming party in the private pool." The planes were en route Key West and Cuba. Note Dan, front row, center. *Courtesy of Mrs. Daniel V. Gallery*

    Drop me a line again soon John, and remember the old slogan "Don't knock, boost! If you can't boost, say nothing."
        Dan

                                                    USS Wright
                                                    Balboa, CZ
                                                    Feb. 15, 1929
Dear Papa,
    Your letter dated Feb. 7 arrived today, the second I have received since leaving home after Christmas. I am very glad indeed to learn that everything is all right at home and I hope and believe that it will continue so now. Don't worry about anything that Mama said in her letter to me. I've got a very short memory for peoples *past* troubles and misunderstandings.

I don't see how any useful purpose can be served right now by any further discussion of what you regard as my impending troubles. It hasnt been easy for me to keep from busting loose with some hot retorts to what has already been said on the subject, and the only reason that I havent is that I realize that whatever you have said you have said because you thought it was serving my interests to say it. However, I'm on the wagon, for the duration of Lent at least, and am making a conscientious effort to save some money for the first time in my naval career, so I think you'll admit that the girls influence on me so far hasn't been wholly bad.

The maneuvers furnished a very striking example of the right and the wrong way to use aircraft. The Battle Fleet made monkeys out of our fleet because they used theirs properly and we didn't. The Saratoga got all her planes into the air and over the locks where they could have blown the canal to smithereens while all of our planes were still on the ground. Our hands were tied because our admiral in the scouting fleet didn't know how to use us and discarded the plan that we submitted telling him how to use us. The CinC of the fleet, who was the chief umpire and was a neutral observer, said in an address to the officers of the fleet afterwards that the Saratoga's attack was a masterpiece and was an epic in the history of aviation. I agree with him too. . . .

Dan

Naval Air Station
Hampton Roads
April 30, 1929

Dear Mama,

We went up to Baltimore last week end. . . .

I've asked all my friends if they know anything about getting special rates from the US lines for European trips or if they ever heard of anyone getting them, and all of them say no. The American Fruit Company, or rather the United Fruit Company, does give special rates to the families of navy people from New York to Panama, but that is the only such concession I know of. That will be a fine trip though, and I'm sure you'll enjoy it. I'm sorry I can't help out by getting a reduced rate as that would make it all the more enjoyable. . . .

. . . believe me Mama it has helped me a lot to know that there is someone who understood and had a little confidence in my judgment and who didn't condemn and slander Vee. And that will make it just a wee bit easier to bear the break if it does have to come. When Papa writes to me as he does about Vee it makes me so damned mad. . . . . . . believe me some things hurt, and hurt so much that it will take more than a day or so for them to heal.

    Love,
    Dan

                                         Naval Air Station
                                         Hampton Roads
                                         May 9, 1929

Dear Papa,

    I'm certainly glad to hear that Onie has realized his ambition and has made chief [engineer]. I'm almost as glad to hear it as you were, and I think he will make good. I say "almost" because I know that the welfare of us kids is the greatest concern of your life and so naturally I can't be as elated as you must have been. I will write to him and give him whatever good advice I can.

    Now—concerning my own welfare—as I have said before, I realize that whatever you do, you do for what you believe is my own good, and I appreciate your motives as much as I can under the circumstances. I'm glad you think that I have displayed a certain amount of self control under what you call the trying circumstances of "this affair." It has been the hardest thing I have ever had to do, and the temptation to cut loose and say things that I know are nothing in the world but Gods truth, but which would hurt a lot, has been very great. The only reason that I haven't done it is because I know that you think the world of me and are conscientious in your desire to further my best interests.

    However, I think you realize by now that this is not an "affair." . . . I wish for your sake that Vee did have a lot of money and social position (whatever that is), and that you did approve of her. (Please don't say that I'm apologizing for her when I say this. That cut deeper than anything else you have ever said, and if you think I could want to marry a girl that I have to apologize for then we are so far from understanding each other that we might as well call everything off between us—and God forbid that).

The whole thing in a nutshell is this,—I know and Vee knows what all the objections to our marriage are. We knew them before we ever loved each other, and we fell in love in spite of them. . . . . But we are not fighting against *all* the rest of the world, because almost everyone in the squadron has met her and they all love her too.—What I am leading up to is this—if you continue in your opposition until *after* we are married. . . . then it will be too late to change. If you are ever going to change you've got to do it *now,* because if the change came afterwards we would both feel that it didn't really mean anything. All I ask is that you put just a little bit of confidence in my judgement. After all I'm 28 years old and many people in the navy with whom I have served place quite a bit of faith in my judgement. . . .

Any further discussion of this matter along the lines of the last four months can not alter the final outcome in the least, and can do nothing but deepen wounds that are already deep enough. Believe me Papa, you are the only one in the world who could have carried it this far without causing an irrepairable breach.

   Dan

          U.S. Naval Academy
          Annapolis, Md.
          July 22, 1929

Dear Papa,

I'm so sorry I forgot about your birth day. There was no excuse for it, especially when it came so soon after I received the ties from you on my own. All I can say is that it was unintentional and that I'm very sorry.

I realize more and more as time goes on how much you have my interest at heart and how much you did in the early years to advance my interests. I guess the only reason we ever clash now on what can best serve my interests is that you have difficulty in realizing that the youngster you drilled and worked on 15 years ago has grown up in the meantime, which is I suppose quite a natural feeling for a Dad to have. But anyway, even tho it hurts me very much when we do differ on some important matters as widely as we have, I realize that your motives are certainly the best anyway, and so I can usually hold my peace about it. . . .

Our detachment has been augmented by two more planes so I now have 8 planes, 8 pilots, and 20 men. Things are still running very smoothly, we are carrying more than our share of the load, and have helped out several times by being ready for hops we were not scheduled to make when planes of the other outfit went out of commission unexpectedly. The funny part of it is too, that ordinarily a squadron of eight planes will have around 80 men in it instead of 20 as we have, but so far we have done everything we have been called upon for and have kept the planes in A number one condition. Besides that the officers and crew are all quite contented, we have had no disciplinary troubles at all, and we have all gotten along so well that at times I'm afraid that its just too good to be true.

     Dan

                                            U.S Naval Academy
                                            Annapolis, Md.
                                            Sept. 23, 1929

Dear Papa,

Miss Dunn and I were married on Aug 9th in a civil ceremony in Washington. Up to yesterday it has been a secret from all but a few and we have been living in Washington. We have announced it now and she is coming down here to live.

I know that you have very high ambitions for me and that your objections to our marriage have been based on the fact that it would jeopardize those ambitions. Time alone can settle that point definitely. My ambitions for myself are just as high as those you have set for me, and I expect to realize them all the better now.

I realize that under the circumstances you may not wish to hear from me any more. Hence I will await your reply to this, if you make one, before writing again.

     Dan

U.S Naval Academy
Annapolis, Md.
Nov. 4, 1929

Dear Papa,

   Your silence for the last month leaves me pretty much in the dark as to what I should or *can* say now. . . . If you feel that your opinion is better left unexpressed then I appreciate your consideration of my feelings in keeping it from me. If such is the case then I'm afraid that there can be no further correspondence between us.

   However, I know very well that your main concern in life has always been the welfare of us youngsters, and I flatter myself to the extent of believing that you have always been especially solicitous about mine. And so I believe that your silence (and disapproval) is based on the fact that you believe that my marriage is going to injure my prospects and handicap my career in the navy. It is because of that assumption on my part that I am writing this letter. If I am wrong in it then simply ignore this letter and we can both try to forget.

   However, if I am right, as I think I am, then allow me to say that I think you are jumping to conclusions, and that by doing so you are hurting the very cause that you are trying to serve, and *have* served for some twenty seven years.—Vee and I love each other, and we are married now—regardless of whether we should be or not. As I see it, the only chance for either of us now to make a success of anything is to make a success of our marriage. And *so far,* at least, we have. We love each other more after three months than we did before, all our friends in the navy are enthusiastic about the new addition to the circle, and I'm saving money now for the first time in years. Therefor, I haven't been hurt *yet,* and there's no immediate prospect of it either. That's why I say that you are jumping to conclusions.

   Now—you are the only one left who hasn't sent us their good wishes. It would mean a lot to us to have you do so, and I don't see how it can hurt anyone to do it. As things stand now you are simply adding another handicap to those that you already visualize for us without serving any good purpose by doing so. If, by any chance, it should turn out later that your original opinion was correct, then even so, the only purpose that your present course can serve will be to make me feel that I have one less friend to turn to when the crash does come.

However, I *know* that there will never be any crash of that kind, so—why not at least give us the benefit of the doubt and drop me, or better still, Vee, a line and wish us luck?

　　　Dan

　　　　　　　　　　　　　　　　　　　　　U.S Naval Academy
　　　　　　　　　　　　　　　　　　　　　Annapolis, Md.
　　　　　　　　　　　　　　　　　　　　　Dec. 22, 1929

Dear Papa,

Things have changed a lot since the days when the starboard watch used to help you decorate the tree on Christmas Eve. Those were happy days that I'll never forget, and I'm sure you won't either. And so, on account of the merry Xmasses we had together in those days, I wish you another merry Christmas this time and happiness for the New Year.

　　　Dan

Coda

Although the correspondence between father and son eventually resumed (and continued until the elder Gallery's death in 1938), still, according to Mrs. Vee Gallery in a 1997 interview, Dan's father never really accepted her into the family.[12] One other item perhaps is especially suggestive in indicating some kind of continuing strain between father and son. As mentioned above, Dan Senior's vicarious involvement in his son's achievements was intense: from Dan's early childhood his father had been keeping a detailed typed log about events in his eldest son's life, a log that recorded events beginning with Dan's birth and continuing on well into Dan's professional naval career.

In that log, a penned-in note announcing the marriage is the very last entry.

Camp Kwitcherbelliakin

WHEN WAR BROKE OUT in Europe in September 1939, Gallery was still serving in the Bureau of Ordinance in Washington, D.C. Eventually he volunteered for "observer duty" in England, where he reported in January 1941.[1] Gallery's official duties there involved visiting Royal Air Force (RAF) bases and naval stations, gathering technical information, and searching into subjects like early warning and fighter defense. He was also active in unofficial ways. For example, although he turned down numerous offers to ride bombers on night raids over Germany—"I couldn't see much future in it"[2]—he volunteered to fly for the Air Transport Corps Auxiliary during off hours, and so he flew newly built Hurricanes or Spitfires from factories to RAF fields.

Like most Americans, Gallery was not entirely convinced that the British could succeed in fending off the German threat. His experiences soon made him think twice about that. For instance, during weekends in London he visited tube stations in the East End.

> The tube stations were full of standee bunks for those whose homes had been blitzed. Those for whom there were no bunks slept on the concrete platforms. They slept with their feet toward the tracks, leaving a narrow passageway between their heads down the middle of the platform, and also at intervals between their bodies, where the car doors would open when the trains stopped. The air was foul

from sweat and overwhelmed toilet facilities. Lights glared in the sleepers' faces and the trains ran all night. Babies learned to sleep through it.

None of these people seemed to have the slightest doubt that England would win the war.[3]

From such informal experiences as this one, Gallery not only began to understand something about civil defense, but also learned to doubt his original assumption that England was flat on its back, utterly demoralized. Gallery's conversations (on his cross-Atlantic plane ride) with Lord Louis Mountbatten, whose destroyer had sunk under him off Crete without injuring his fighting spirit, and his observation of the soft-spoken pilots (many of them nonprofessionals) who quietly went about defending Britain in the crucial early days of the war also impressed him.[4]

In March of 1941[5] Gallery came back to Washington, D.C. to join the staff supporting the Navy's London office, and to tend to family members. In the 1930s Dan and Vee had adopted three children—James J., Daniel V. III, and Beatrice Constance (Connie). Earlier, when Dan had returned to the "Gun Club" in Washington in 1939, the family had moved from their Spanish bungalow in Coronado to Arlington. However, on getting orders for England—and in his ordnance work having heard of an astonishing new weapon with a potentially very large blast—Dan decided to buy a farm far west of Washington, near Fairfax, Virginia, to keep the family out of harm's way. Dan would be overseas through most of the war, and Vee would hold down "Harmony Farm" on her own. The children would board at nearby schools.

Having settled these matters, Dan returned to Great Britain in October 1941 with orders as the prospective commanding officer of a large new seaplane base, which the U.S. was building in Loch Ryan, Scotland.

This job in Scotland was one of the very best available for an officer of my rank. It promised command of a large shore base and the patrol squadrons assigned to it when we got into the war. I would be in one of the key spots in the Battle of the Atlantic, based in Scotland, where the bombing wasn't so bad, and close enough to London to get down there as often as I wanted to. It was a choice billet for a captain and I was only a commander. I considered myself very lucky.[6]

In letters back to his boss in Washington, Gallery described difficulties in projected seaplane operation—troubles in hauling the planes out of the water, problems in getting their wheels on and off, tendencies for the planes to tear up the ramps—and outlined possible solutions. He also pressed for completion of the seaplane base ahead of U.S. destroyer and submarine bases, which were also being constructed. Gallery proposed establishing U.S. patrol wings both in Ireland and in Loch Ryan, arguing that these two wings could

> take over the whole job of convoy and antisubmarine patrol from the British forces now engaged in this work (15 group) and would do a much better job at it than they are doing. . . . [The British] do a tremendous amount of flying, drop lots of bombs and depth charges, but they don't get any kills. All they do is worry the submarines.[7]

In an out-of-channels letter to Rear Adm. W. H. P. Blandy, chief of the Bureau of Ordnance, Gallery also suggested several ways to improve British tactics for bomb and depth charge attacks.[8] Later, Gallery would find killing submarines a distressingly difficult job for his own planes. But his long engagement with the problem would eventually bear fruit.

Dan was enthusiastic about his assignment, and so it came as a shock when a friend alerted him in early December that he would shortly be ordered to Iceland instead, to become commander of the Patrol Plane Base Detachment at Reykjavík. Instead of commanding a base which housed several squadrons or even a patrol wing, Gallery would control a mere sixteen planes. And rather than being a hop-scotch from London, he would be in the "arctic boondocks."[9] On receiving the actual orders on December 6, 1941, he reported in his diary, "I'm still hanging over the ropes from the blow."[10] But quickly he received an even greater shock. At 1:00 A.M. on December 8, Gallery was awakened and called into the embassy to be given the news of the Japanese attack on Pearl Harbor. Later that day he recorded his reaction in his diary:

> We had to wear uniform today but I wish we hadn't. Never in my wildest dreams did I ever imagine that I would be embarrassed by my US Navy uniform—but I was today. That Pearl Harbor show is a stinking disgrace. . . . Some heads had better roll.[11]

Actually, Pearl Harbor made his personal situation somewhat more palatable. Whereas it would originally have been months before his Scottish base was completed, now Loch Ryan was immediately turned over to the British, and Gallery moved to an operational assignment where he would quickly be able to engage the enemy.

When he arrived in Iceland on December 30, aircraft and personnel were already being delivered for his base. There were immediate problems, however. On January 15 a great storm blew up (with consistent winds of 80–90 mph, and gusts to 110), so that not only did many ships go around in the harbor, but five of Gallery's seaplanes (two PBMs and three PBYs) sank at the buoys, leaving him only the four "amphibs" moored on the field and a few seaplanes that had not yet

One of several Catalina seaplanes that were wrecked by a gale in Iceland while moored at buoys. Gallery blamed himself for not having crews man the planes during the storm. *Courtesy of Mrs. Daniel V. Gallery*

been offloaded from the transport ships. In his diary, Gallery blamed himself for the loss.

> I am convinced after watching the 2 PBMs and 1 PBY fill gradually, nose up, and sink at their moorings, that if we had had the crews aboard we would have saved those three. We might have lost the crews of the other two, but cest la guerre. I blame myself, and it's a hell of a poor beginning for [Fleet Air Base] Iceland.[12]

Gallery also owned up his perceived fault to his superiors, but he was relieved to find that they didn't seem to blame him.

In Iceland, rather than being his own boss, Gallery had to report to five different authorities—"two U.S. admirals, one U.S. General, a British admiral, and the R.A.F. Air Commodore." Long after the war, Gallery would make light of his complicated command obligations.

> It says in the Gospel that "no man can serve two masters," and I agree that serving two is a very difficult job indeed. But I soon found that serving five is easy. All you have to do is to exercise a little judicious stupidity and get your bosses debating among themselves. . . . The situation becomes confused and to avoid any high-level rhubarbs about it, they finally let you write your own ticket.[13]

At the time, however, Gallery had been far from happy about the situation. At least one of Gallery's bosses was very troublesome, even professionally dangerous to him. For one thing, Adm. J. L. "Reggie" Kauffman, the "black-shoe" commanding officer of the Naval Shore Base in Iceland and the senior naval officer present, exercised his traditionally ample S.O.P. privileges by confiscating for his own surface forces many shipments and personnel Gallery had gone to great trouble to order for his air base, and Kauffman didn't appreciate Gallery's complaints about the confiscation.

But that wasn't their only clash. As Gallery later explained to a friend:

> Two months ago when we were just getting started and before we got the old peace time complacency of the new gang uprooted, several officers made stupid blunders that smacked of the pre–Pearl Harbor Navy. So I tossed them in their huts for ten days. They saw

my point, are doing their stuff and to my definite knowledge are 100 percent loyal to me. Well, the Admiral got me in and delivered me a long harrangue on leadership, and on not being too tough on the boys.[14]

This incensed Gallery, who recorded his reaction in his diary:

Well, if I'm going to get bawled out I don't know of any things I would rather get it for than—
1. Standing up for my own gang.
2. Making my gang toe the line. . . .
That business with the admiral was funny as hell. I decided some time ago I would rather be an SOB and help win the war than be a swell guy and help lose it. . . . So the upshot of it all is that all my gang are thriving on my view of running the station and the only guy who thinks I'm an SOB *is the guy I am working for!!*[15]

Gallery recognized the potential seriousness of the conflict. He wrote several colleagues back home in Washington for support, pointing out that in late March Kauffman had called him in and informed Gallery he "was seriously considering sending a despatch requesting immediate orders home for me."[16] According to the autobiography, Kauffman eventually recommended Gallery be relieved "as unfit to command an advanced base in wartime."[17] However, apparently with the aid of the complicated command arrangement, Gallery's friends were able to protect him until Kauffman was reassigned.

Gallery saw a sign of his leadership success in the spontaneous actions of his own troops, as he wrote to a friend on Easter morning:

Last night I noticed that the plan of the day for Easter Sunday called for reveille an hour earlier than usual. I thought it was a mistake and asked Pat Henry about it. He said it was done at the request of the crew. The boys had been discussing the possibilities of invasion by parachute troops, and had decided that Easter Sunday morning would be the best time for the Nazis to try it. So they wanted to be in the machine gun emplacements at sunrise waiting for them, just in case. It was colder than hell this morning—but the boys were out there . . . ready instead of asleep as the U.S.N. was on another Sunday morning.

> I admit that in a way it was just a gesture as the possibility of attack was remote. But it was a gesture from below that made me feel pretty damned good after what I've been getting from up above.[18]

In contrast to his appreciation for his troops, Gallery's final judgment on his difficult boss is probably the one he wrote in his diary the night after Kauffman told him he was thinking about sending Gallery home: "Kauffman is very definitely pre–Pearl Harbor. The selection board that passed him over was right."[19]

It should be remarked that this strong negative expression toward a fellow officer is highly unusual in the Gallery papers. Although he regularly expressed very strong views and frequently quarrelled greatly with others' opinions, Dan was seldom personally judgmental and never vindictive. He was remarkably free from such tendencies.

Gallery would confront other management difficulties, although more minor ones. At one point some junior officers were offended that he let four chief petty officers be patrol plane commanders, making the JOs fly for awhile as copilots or navigators. Gallery pointed out to the newly minted officers that the chiefs were far more familiar with the Catalina aircraft than they were, and that they also had two or three times the flying hours that the young officers did. In another momentary morale crisis a bit later on, Gallery's troops were seriously discomfited by a navy message stating that one hundred troublemakers had been "given the choice of general court-martial or being sent to Iceland"[20] from the States, and that they had chosen the next convoy east. The fact that Iceland was considered the rough equivalent of a Siberian prison camp naturally upset the whole outfit, and Gallery spoke to the crew at the movies that night. He explained that the facts were less severe than reported (only forty malefactors were actually assigned to Iceland, and not all of them to the Fleet Air Base), then suggested that the whole episode had been a big mistake. Finally, he said he had made an official protest.

> . . . when I left the Admiral's office he was spouting steam, fire, and smoke from his eyes, ears, nose and mouth. I got out of his office just in time to avoid being caught in the explosion. A despatch went back to the States last night which burned up the air and blasted the hide off the people responsible for this business. . . . I'll guarantee

you that if they ever should try to make a penal colony of this place they will have to put a ball and chain on my foot before they get very far.[21]

His quick action calmed the storm.

On another occasion, Gallery was disconcerted by the terrible language of the hundred marines assigned to his station, and felt he had to catch them up short. In a speech he began by cursing them all voluminously. Then, "while they were still stunned by this [unprecedented] blast from a commissioned officer to enlisted men, I said, 'I'm only calling you what I've heard you calling each other ever since you got here.'"[22] Gallery also kept the marines on their toes by swiping three rifles that he saw some off-duty marines stack in the entrance to the recreation hall as they went in to see the show and hiding them in his own Quonset hut. The whole marine detachment searched the camp for three days for these precious rifles before Gallery turned them back over to the marine major. Later, Gallery personally witnessed the robbery of his own base's ship's store in broad daylight by a soldier from an adjoining camp—the army commanding officer's own orderly! Gallery dealt with this by ribbing the army, refusing to prosecute on account of the audacity of the soldier.

However, the main difficulties of the tour were those posed by the job itself—"the little problem of helping to guard the North Atlantic convoy lanes in the worst flying weather in the world."[23] His aircraft had to search far to the west to find in-bound convoys, then patrol over them until they were picked up by planes based in Britain. Since the convoy routes passed some five hundred miles south of Iceland, Gallery's "lumbering PBY's" typically had to fly five hours just to get over the convoys, then fly four hours of escort, and finally fly five more hours searching for home through the regularly terrible Arctic weather. A description of patrols flying out of Scotland found in one of Gallery's prewar letters probably applies to conditions in Iceland as well:

This morning was one of the most dismal and dreary ones I have ever seen—cold drizzling rain, visibility 500 yards, ceiling from zero to 300 feet, and a nasty wind blowing. . . . So no pilot has any business going out on long flights in this part of the world unless he is fully qualified to spend a couple of hours on instruments coming back and to let down on the beam through a 300 ft. ceiling with visibility about $\frac{1}{4}$ mile on the surface.[24]

When he talked to his people, Gallery stressed the importance of "mental toughness" ashore and in the air:

> You have to be mentally tough about doing irritating extra jobs, standing extra watches on which nothing much has ever happened —yet!—and getting out into the machine gun pits when it is cold and dark, on false alarms. Mental toughness enables you, for instance, to keep coming at a submarine which elects to open up with a machine gun instead of diving. It enables you to pretend that the tracers you see coming aren't there and to shove home your attack and get him just the same as if you had surprised him sound asleep.[25]

Gallery thought his pilots should see their CO taking his chances with them and about twice a month he served as copilot on flights to, from, and over the convoys. By this habit, he almost became involved in one of the few operational crashes of his Iceland command. A plane in which he originally had been scheduled to fly, but shifted out of to help a less-experienced pilot, crashed and burned with two fatalities after flying into a violent Arctic storm.[26]

While in Iceland, Gallery prepared extensively for one major event— the possible breakout of the great German battleship *Tirpitz* through the Denmark Strait. He was determined to be prepared to prevent any more German warships to get to the open sea (several had broken out from Brest not long back), but knew that although his squadron's torpedoes were the only ready weapons sufficient to disable the German battleship, his planes were far too slow to attack her successfully by themselves. (In fact, by attacking alone his planes would be decimated, just like the torpedo planes at Midway.) So he cajoled commanders from the RAF, the U.S. Army Air Corps, and the U.S. Navy into forming a combined attack group and letting him command. Afterwards, when any U.S. or British battleships came into Reykjavík he ordered "*Tirpitz* drill," and organized combined attacks by bombers, fighters, and (finally) his own torpedo planes. In its own way, this unusual scheme was quite as audacious as some of Gallery's more well-known enterprises, manifesting his great enterprise and habitual preparedness.

By all accounts, Gallery's Iceland command was a success. He was praised by Ernie King for getting the base into operation quickly,[27] his planes kept the U-boats down through extensive convoy patrols, and despite an initial lack of success, Gallery's small outfit reportedly accounted for six confirmed U-boat kills over Gallery's sixteen-month tour.[28] Although the breakout of the *Tirpitz* (for which his men had prepared so extensively) never occurred, Gallery's club of "FBIs"—"Forgotten Bastards of Iceland"—did its job, and even had a relatively good time doing it.

WHILE STATIONED at the Pentagon in 1948, Gallery wrote up the lighter aspects of his Iceland experience in an article meant for publication. He sent it to Comdr. William J. Lederer, then public relations officer in charge of the navy's "Magazine and Book Section," and later of course author of *All the Ship's at Sea,* coauthor of *The Ugly American,* and author of many other books. Lederer sent a draft of the article on to Marty Somers of the *Saturday Evening Post* with this comment: "The article is chock-a-block with delightful anecdotes; the thing has quite charmed me. It's in no shape to be published the way it is now—it being too loose and too long. But I believe if it were compressed to around 3500 or 4000 [words] it would be a natural."[29] Somers accepted the article (after revision and substantial cuts), and so began a long and fruitful relationship between Gallery, Somers, and the magazine.

Below is a condensed version of the *Post* article, which illustrates both Gallery's characteristic humor, and his engaging style of leadership.

From "Our Hot War for Iceland"

I arrived in Reykjavik late in December, 1941, and found the situation grim. Our Navy fliers, eking out a miserable existence knee-deep in mud, were waiting for their supply ship to come in. All that came in was me!

The Navy's Iceland contingent had taken refuge in dilapidated Nissen huts abandoned by the British, through which the Arctic winds howled with glee. The well-dressed young man about camp wore long flannel drawers and at night he closed himself up in an eiderdown sleeping bag.

The galley was equipped with salvaged junk and the food was terrible. The principal plumbing necessities were of the Chic Sale variety, and you couldn't take a bath even if you wanted to. While struggling to stay alive under these conditions, we also had the little problem of flying the North Atlantic convoy lanes in the world's worst weather.

My first job obviously was to keep the planes flying and help get the convoys through; next to get decent living conditions established; and third, I thought, to prevent the boys from blowing their tops after six months in that godforsaken hole.

It seemed as if the top brass in Washington had forgotten us. But soon the long-awaited supply ship arrived. From her holds she discharged one naval air base complete with spare parts.

We turned to with a will to set it up. Everybody helped build the new camp. One day I caught the dentist, paymaster and chaplain dynamiting rocks out of the frozen ground. They were making a foundation trench. From that day I knew the United States couldn't lose. This was really total war.

Quonset huts go up fast and, while there is nothing luxurious about them, they do provide adequate shelter, even in Iceland. Our planners back in Washington sent us a lot more than the bare walls and frames; every hut had electric lights, automatic phonograph and radio.

We made our own electricity with Diesel generators designed to run at a constant speed. At first, the boys who stood watch in the generator hut suspected me of being either a mind reader or a magician, because I often called up from my hut to bawl them out for running the generators a little too fast or too slow. Sometimes the machines differed so little from the correct speed that you couldn't tell it by looking at the lights, but the dials on the control panel always showed that my beef was justified. The secret was my electric record player and an album of records by Toscanini. When the music sounded sweet, I knew the generators were exactly on the right speed. When it came out sour, I knew it wasn't Toscanini who was off the beam.

A few of Gallery's squadron members in a Quonset hut at the Fleet Air Base, Iceland. Once a crewman served 100 days, Gallery gave him a certificate as an "FBI"—a "Forgotten Bastard of Iceland." *U.S. Navy*

Each hut had fourteen bunks and lockers, a card and checker table near the stove, and writing desks near the door. As time went on, easy chairs made out of discarded shipping crates, homemade lamp shades and rugs began to appear. One hut even had a makebelieve grandfather's clock standing by the stove. Of course, every square inch of wall and locker space was inevitably plastered with lurid reminders, clipped from magazines, of the one missing comfort of home.

Complaints about the lack of home cooking soon stopped. I wish you could have seen the galley equipment they sent us—excellent ranges, ovens and steam kettles, automatic dishwashers and driers, freezing lockers and fine butcher-shop equipment. When I brought the British air commodore over to inspect it, his eyes bugged out like a tromped-on toad's. He went away muttering to himself about the hardships the poor colonials have to put up with.

After our new ovens began roasting, we received daily tribute to the excellent work of our cooks. Every day at noon and suppertime a dozen or so British and United States Army truck drivers found excuses for stopping at the Fleet Air Base and bumming a meal off us. I never objected, because as long as all those vehicles lined up on our main street at chow time, I knew without going any further that our cooks were doing all right.

Our Navy chow attracted visitors from all over Iceland—after we got our camp built, rats overran the place. Although we welcomed our hungry brothers-in-arms in the Air Force and the Army and our Allies in the RAF and British Navy, we had to draw the line someplace. I put a bounty of one dollar a head on rats. Catching and shooting rodents became a profitable and exciting pastime. Large bounties were collected at first, and after a couple of weeks I saw no more rats nosing around our streets. However, our "game warden's" office continued to do a brisk business, and it took me some time to find out that I was paying bounties on rats killed all over Iceland. My boys paid two bits apiece to their friends in the adjacent RAF, Norwegian and United States Army camps for dead rats, and smuggled them in to collect a nice profit. However, our soda fountain made money for the welfare fund so fast that we decided to ignore the rat racket. By cleaning out the surrounding camps we were helping ourselves anyway.

During the long Arctic nights we held grave discussions about the name for our camp. We finally adopted one with an Icelandic or Eskimo air about it, which on close inspection contains some good American advice to all hands: KWITCHERBELLIAKIN.

One thing our logistic planners back home forgot was the need for a recreation hall and gymnasium. They sent us plenty of recreational gear, but no place to use it. We remedied this oversight by "misappropriating" two of the supply officer's big storehouses. I figured that, if necessary, I would rather try to justify leaving some of our equipment out in the weather than to explain why the boys were going nuts. Admiral King put a terse "Okay" on that decision when he stopped in at our place some months later, on his way home from a conference in London.

The arrival of our first shipment of recreational equipment from the United States led to an incident which helped us by-pass protocol, break the ice and get acquainted with the British. Opening up the boxes in this consignment like a bunch of kids on Christmas morning, we found, among other things, a pushball, which we promptly blew up to its full five-foot diameter. Exploring the boxes for more loot, we left the pushball sitting outside the gymnasium unattended.

You should never leave anything as big and light as a pushball unattended in Iceland, because the wind comes along and blows it away. I came out of the gym just in time to see our pushball bounce down the hill, over the bluff and into the water. It sailed rapidly across the inlet and grounded on the opposite shore, where a British antiaircraft battery had its camp.

We wanted that pushball, so I picked up my field telephone to call the commanding officer of the antiaircraft battery and ask his help. Strange things often happened on the labyrinth of wires forming our field-telephone system. Very often connections got crossed—as they did this time. I heard my friend across the way calling British Admiralty Headquarters and reporting, "The biggest bloody mine you've ever seen in your life has just washed ashore at our camp, and will you please send a bomb-disposal party over to deal with it?"

I hung up without saying a word. A few minutes later I called Admiralty Headquarters and reported that we, too, had seen this mine wash ashore, that we had a qualified bomb-disposal squad, and if the Admiralty wished us to do so, we would be glad to deal with this situation. Of course, the Admiralty wished nothing in the world more than to have somebody else take this nasty job off their hands. They promptly replied that this would be "quite satisfactory."

So I rushed around to the adjoining huts, rounded up about a dozen helpers, explained the pitch to them, and we organized a bomb-disposal squad on the spot. We all knew enough about bomb disposal to have a pretty good idea as to what equipment we needed and how to go through the proper motions. We commandeered a half-dozen rifles, scrambled around the camp and grabbed a portable field-telephone set, a couple of voltmeters, a stethoscope and some small toolboxes. Dumping this equipment into jeeps, we roared over to the

British camp, where we found a crowd of our Allies all standing back at a respectful distance, casting nervous glances at the "mine."

The arrival of our businesslike group of American experts obviously relieved the tension. We immediately stationed our sentries and pushed the crowd back to a safer distance. Leading out our field telephones, we placed one of them at the "mine" and the other about 100 yards back, so that our mine-disposal boys could phone back every move they made—to be recorded in a notebook—for the guidance of future mine-disposal squads, in case we made the wrong move and blew ourselves up.

After a few minutes of hocus-pocus with the stethoscope and voltmeters and much telephoning back and forth, we finally gave the signal that the big moment was at hand. As the crowd watched in awed silence, we unscrewed the valve, let the air out, and with our deflated mine, got the hell out of that camp as fast as we could.

Although there was plenty of this kind of horseplay and monkey business on the ground, we were playing for keeps out over the convoy lanes. Flying through stinking weather, at night and in fog, when the low-lying clouds around your airdrome have centers of solid rock and your wings load up with ice, is bad for your blood pressure. To keep enthusiasm for this kind of flying at a proper level, the skipper has to take his regular turn out over the convoy lanes too. I often wondered, during some of my all-night hops, whether there was any worthwhile future in the business.

We worked hand in glove with the British covering the convoys, and Air Commodore Lloyd of the RAF turned out to be a grand teammate. He and I saw eye to eye on every operational question, though at first inclined to be somewhat skeptical of each other. After we became close friends, he confessed he had feared that anyone whose ancestry was as obviously Gaelic as mine would necessarily make things as difficult as possible for His Majesty's representative.

I assured him that I bore no ill will whatever toward the British. "In fact," I said, "I am eternally grateful to your ancestors for persecuting my ancestors, so that I was born in the U.S.A."

Through association with the air commodore I acquired a unique honorary title, the Order of the D.D.L.M. I am the only officer in the

United States military services so honored. As a matter of fact, I created the title and bestowed it on myself. This came about as follows:

Co-operating with the British on a common job, I naturally had frequent exchanges of official memoranda with the air commodore and the British admiral. Whenever a high-ranking British officer signs a letter, he puts a long string of initials after his signature—DSO, KCB, CBE, and so on—indicating the orders and decorations which he holds. When I replied to such letters, I had nothing to put behind my name except "junior," and that made no impression whatever upon our gallant Allies.

So, after I got to know my correspondents pretty well, and found that they were regular fellows with twinkles in their eyes, I began putting DDLM after my signature, knowing full well that sooner or later they would ask me what it meant. Sure enough, one morning I met the air commodore in RAF Headquarters, and after saying "Good morning, Dan, old man" and discussing various matters, he asked, "I say, old boy, what does that DDLM that you put after your name mean?"

"Why," I said, "that's the American equivalent of your KCB."

Of course, KCB—Knight Commander of the Bath—is one of the highest and best decorations the British have. So the air commodore was duly impressed. He said, "That's splendid. That's fine. I didn't know you Americans had any such thing." I could see the wheels going round inside his head as he tried to puzzle out the meaning of the cryptic initials.

Finally he gave up and asked, "Just what does it stand for?"

I said, "It means Dan Dan the Lavatory Man."

Concurrently with the international leg pulling, our camp construction moved along, the Seabees performing their usual miracles. The last thing to go up was the officers' club. By this time we proudly exhibited our place to sight-seers.

Showing some American nurses around the camp, one of our boys gloatingly pointed out what we had already done and described future plans. Having seen our ultramodern galley, well-equipped recreation hall and gymnasium, the gals were about ready to believe that anything was possible for the Navy. Going through the nearly finished officers'

Even the normally austere Adm. Ernest J. King (wartime chief of naval operations) relaxed a bit and grinned when he saw these "palm trees" in Iceland; later he had the photo hung in his office. The palm trees had been created by a chief metalsmith. Gallery is third from the right, two spaces to the left of King. *U.S. Navy*

club, my gallant young gentleman pointed out the window at the forbidding rocky beach in front and said "The next convoy is bringing us a shipboard of white sand from Miami, and we'll have a regular beach out there by summer." The nurses believed this story and spread it through all the Army camps on the island, causing great indignation and some threats to write to congressmen.

Even though we never got our beach, we did have some almost equally improbable things. Our proudest possession was a pair of palm trees near the main entrance of the camp. Trees do not grow in Iceland. So when the leading chief from our metalsmith shop came into my office one day and said, "Captain, we ought to have some palm trees around this place," I thought to myself, *Now it begins—here's the first man we have to ship home in a strait jacket.*

However, I humored him and listened to his proposal. When we got through outlining his plan, I quoted Joyce Kilmer—"Only God can make a tree."

The chief replied, "Yeah, we know that, captain, but we'd like to have a shot at it anyway."

Within a week, two authentic-looking palm trees had grown on our main street. The trunks were steel pipes about six inches in diameter which we wrapped with burlap to give them a tapering and rough appearance. The stems of the leaves were reinforcing rods for concrete runways, bent to the proper curvature, and we cut the leaves from tin obtained by flattening out five-gallon kerosene cans. A coat of green paint plus worn-out softballs for coconuts completed the horticultural wonder. . . .

For the official opening of our recreation hall we put on a gala event and we invited all the top brass in Iceland. There were three Army hospitals with nurses in Iceland, and it was obviously my duty as commanding officer to stand in well with the chief nurses, so they would be favorably inclined to date my boys from the Fleet Air Base. I invited the three chief nurses to the grand opening, sent my car to pick them up and instructed my driver to stand by at the OOD's shack to take the ladies home after the show.

When the *premiere* was over, all the official guests adjourned to my hut for coffee, sandwiches and "one for the road." At this gathering, one of the generals graciously offered to take the nurses home. In the midst of all the social activity, I forgot to pass this word along to my driver. So, after speeding the last departing guest into the night, I crawled into my sack and slept soundly until seven o'clock the next morning. On the way to breakfast I stopped in at the OOD's shack and there sat my driver, heavy-eyed and sleepy, but with an accusing smirk on his sassy face.

He was carrying out my orders and waiting to take the three chief nurses home! He had spent an all-night vigil in a place where everybody who happened to be up and around in the camp saw him and wondered what he was doing. Every four hours during the night a new duty section of about thirty men mustered in the OOD's office before relieving the watch. Naturally, they all wanted to know why the captain's driver was up so late. All night long he spread the happy word, "I'm waiting to take the captain's gal friends home—he's got three of 'em down in his hut."

I noted a marked increase in the deference with which I was treated by all hands from then on.

In the meantime we hunted Nazi submarines amid icebergs, sleet and arctic gales. I encouraged my crews to relax at our recreation centers. I had no trouble getting the order obeyed. Soon after the opening of our officers' club we fumbled our first three opportunities to sink subs, due to buck fever, bad luck and inattention to seemingly minor details. I read the riot act to the boys and announced that our recently opened club was hereby closed until we got our first kill. This was cruel and unusual punishment. But my platform was that I would rather be a Son of Brotherhood and help win the war, than help lose it and be thought a swell guy.

During the era of the closed club, one of our pilots, Lieutenant Hopgood, caught a sub surfaced about fifty miles from a convoy. He crippled her so she couldn't submerge, but could still limp along on the surface. All his depth charges expended, Hoppy circled and watched the sub go alongside a near-by Icelandic fishing trawler and commandeer it. The Nazis abandoned and scuttled the U-boat, and laid a course toward Germany.

Hoppy duly reported all this by radio and spent the next couple of hours shuttling back and forth, coaching an oncoming British destroyer which broke off from the convoy. This was an exciting three hours in all the RAF and Royal Navy operations rooms in England, as well as in ours up in Iceland. Hoppy's first electrifying message that he had a cripple on his hands, but couldn't finish it off, brought everybody in England to the operations room. For the rest of the morning vice-admirals, air marshals and their staffs sat with the ears glued to the radio, following the dramatic developments at sea.

All Hoppy's radio reports up to the final one were masterpieces of correct official phraseology, giving a terse, clear and complete picture of events in the North Atlantic. Finally he came through with the big punch line that we were all waiting for: "Destroyer is alongside trawler and has taken off fifty-two prisoners." Then shifting from code to plain

English, he continued: "Personal message for Commander Gallery. Sunk sub, open club!"

We opened the club all right. We damned near blew the roof off the joint. But Coast Command Headquarters and the Admiralty were a bit puzzled over that final message, and even after the Air Commodore, Iceland, explained it to them, they considered it "most extraordinary."

Command of the USS Guadalcanal

IN MAY 1943, GALLERY was ordered home from Iceland to take up the ultimate job of a naval officer: command of a fighting ship. After a month's leave with his wife Vee and their three children at Harmony Farm, he headed for Astoria, Oregon. Just up the Columbia River at Vancouver, Washington, Henry J. Kaiser was turning out some fifty escort carriers on an assembly-line basis. These *Casablanca*-class "jeep" carriers were identical physically, but Gallery wanted command of a particular one—the *Guadalcanal*. He had been originally assigned this vessel, but when the navy asked him to take a carrier that would come off the ways earlier, Gallery vehemently refused. He figured that any ship with the name of the Pacific Island sanctified by the heroism of U.S. Marines was going to be special. Here, as elsewhere, Gallery showed the deep-rooted instinct for spiritual and psychological values that served him so well as a leader. Meanwhile, in his workup of his ship and crew, he would display a lively interest in his crewmembers as individuals, and exercise the forehandedness, imagination, and good humor that made him both a memorable and an outstanding commanding officer.

At 7,800 tons displacement, the *Guadalcanal* was small for a carrier, without such features as the sort of watertight compartmentation that one would expect to find on a warship. Aside from a scattering of 40 mms and 20 mms, she had a solitary five-inch gun pointed backwards from her stern. Gallery called her captain's quarters "the most primitive I've ever seen on a ship this size."[1] Her crew would be young and mostly inexperienced. Still, she was a carrier, she was Gallery's first ship command, and he expected she would be assigned to the Pacific. There, unlike in the Atlantic, heavy fleet action remained to be fought.

In the months prior to commissioning, Gallery had plenty to do. Still, when required to send part of his crew through the navy's tough new Firefighting School, Gallery went, too—deciding to "lead by example" from the very start. He got somewhat more than he bargained for.

> I was the first four-striper to appear at the school, and those professional smoke eaters gave me a worse hazing than I got as a plebe at the Naval Academy. . . .
>
>   They put me on the nozzle end of the hose and smack in the hottest part of every fire they set. . . . Time and time again the only sensible thing to do was to throw that damned hose away and run. The only trouble was that my whole crew were right there watching me, and you can't throw away a hose and run in a dignified manner when the seat of your pants is practically on fire. So I just had to sweat it out. . . .[2]

The reader will recall Gallery's playing baseball and coaching wrestling in his earlier tours; firefighting served the same general purpose. One reason for Gallery's great success as a leader was his habit of establishing close personal contact with his men, this in situations where competitiveness and bravery could be easily scanned.

Of course much of Gallery's work in precommissioning days was administrative, but here he paid close attention to extra morale items, like starting a ship's newspaper and getting recreational equipment. Finding the five hundred dollars the navy allowed for the latter a bit skimpy for his nearly eight-hundred-man crew, Gallery put the touch on his corporate friends. He had a very specific shopping list. Lion Manufacturing in Gallery's home town of Chicago coordinated the contribution of an intercom system, eight record players, a library of over four hundred records, and plenty of checkers and playing cards. C. L. Norden, Inc., with which Gallery had worked on the famous Norden bombsight, provided thousands of dollars in cash to buy, among other things, athletic equipment and a hotel-sized pressure cooker ("Feed 'em well and the battle is half won," said Gallery). Gallery also wanted instruments for a ship's orchestra, of all things—and got them (and set up the orchestra, too). He apparently felt he was stretching the rules in all this. He wrote one donor, "For God's sake promote it as being your own idea, not mine. The Navy Department would flay me alive for proposing such a thing, because their story is that all that sort of thing is adequately taken care of by the Welfare Section of the Bureau of Personnel."[3]

Gallery's first official regulation, Ship's Order Number One, made morning prayer part of the ship's daily routine. Gallery believed "it is poor psychology as well as poor theology, to wait until you are looking down the enemy gun barrels before you admit that you may need a little help from on high."[4] Though shipboard devotions were not uncommon, this was apparently the first time in the U.S. Navy they were the subject of the commanding officer's first written order. But after all, Gallery pointed out, "one of the four main objectives we say we are fighting for is Freedom of Religion."[5] In ordering this morning prayer, Gallery took care to respect the crew's religious preferences. Though a devout Catholic, he told his chaplain, "We should be careful to select a prayer to which everyone can say amen, Jews as well as Christians (and we may even have some Mohammedans among the Filipinos)."[6] So every morning at the bosun's word, the *Guadalcanal*'s crewmembers doffed their white hats, faced the bridge, and listened to a nondenominational prayer.

Gallery put the *Guadalcanal* into commission September 25, 1943. He gave a series of speeches to the chiefs, the officers, and the whole crew, letting them know who he was and what he expected of them. At the actual commissioning ceremony, he repeated much of what he had published two months earlier to men reporting aboard:

> 1. The motto for the GUADALCANAL will be "CAN DO," meaning we will take on any tough job that is handed to us and run away with it. The tougher the job, the better we'll like it.
> 2. The ship's major mission in life will be—to kill Japs.
> 3. Before a carrier can do its big job of sinking enemy ships several hundreds of small and unspectacular jobs have to be done and done well. One man falling down on a small job can "bitch the works" for the whole ship. Whether you are in the Flight

USS *Guadalcanal* (CVE 60) rides down the ways into the Columbia River at Vancouver, Washington, on June 5, 1943, while shipyard workers look on. The ship was commissioned on September 25, and reached Norfolk in December. *U.S. Navy*

Department, Gunnery Dept., Engineering Department, or Supply Dept.—whether you are plane captain, gun captain, or captain of the head—remember that some day the fate of the ship may depend on YOU. So, learn everything you can about your job during this precommissioning period. In a few months we will be out where it rains bombs and it will be too late to learn then. We will have to KNOW.

4. NOTE: This ship will be employed on dangerous duty. We will either sink the enemy or get sunk ourselves, depending on how well we learn our jobs now and do our jobs later. ANYONE WHO PREFERS SAFER DUTY SEE ME AND I WILL ARRANGE TO HAVE HIM TRANSFERRED.[7]

There were no takers for the offer, and *Guadalcanal's* men began referring to their ship as the *"Can Do."*

By commissioning date the assignment of the ship had been switched
from the Pacific to the Atlantic. Her skipper's disappointment with the
assignment, but also the importance to him of the ship's name, show in
his letter to a contact at the Pentagon: "How about getting the *Guadalcanal* switched back to where the good Lord meant her to be? But don't
get me switched to any other ship, because *Guadalcanal* is *my* baby and
I wouldn't swap that name for anything except possibly the *Saratoga.*"[8]

Gallery took his baby to sea in October 1943. A preliminary local
cruise northward to the Strait of Juan de Fuca and into Puget Sound
shook down his crew of neophyte sailors with heavy rolls and green
water over the bow. Gallery got ammunition aboard and dispensed with
degaussing and other prelimaries in five days rather than the scheduled

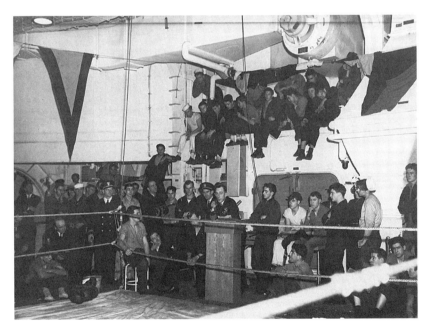

Gallery at the mike at the "New Year's Eve Happy Hour" smoker aboard the
Guadalcanal, December 31, 1943. Boxing and wrestling matches were the main
events. *U.S. Navy*

ten, before the mandatory blimp was ready to escort him south. Braving the anger of naval authorities (some of whom were furious), Gallery left anyway.[9]

The Air Group came aboard the ship in San Diego. The carrier then left for Panama (planning to exercise while en route), but when the scheduled time for the first take-offs and landings approached, group commander Joe Yavorsky told Gallery there wasn't enough wind to fly his planes. Gallery (who had flown off the *Langley* a decade earlier with hardly a breath of wind to help him) played along for a moment.

> Then I went aft on the flight deck, climbed into my plane, took off, made one trip around the ship, and landed. Yavorsky met me rather sheepishly as I got out of the plane, and said his boys were ready to go.[10]

Gallery thus made the *Guadalcanal's* first landing. (Seventeen years later he would make her last, flying aboard as the rusting ship was being

Gallery makes the first landing on the USS *Guadalcanal* in an SNJ trainer. Note the LSO (landing signal officer) with the paddles, and the arresting cables on the deck. *U.S. Navy*

Gallery plays with his dog "Flairby" on the deck of the *Guadalcanal*. Gallery had
acquired the dog in Iceland and after relinquishing command of the carrier
took it home to Harmony Farm. *Alex Zar/U.S. Navy*

towed to Japan to be sold as scrap. It was a less than inspiriting occasion.) Then the carrier headed south in company with sister carrier *Mission Bay* and two destroyers. Their track took them down the coast past
Mexico and through the Panama Canal to Norfolk.

The *Can Do's* captain was a distinctive figure on the bridge. Slender
and of medium height, with prominent ears, he learned only years later,
to his considerable amusement, that his crew had nicknamed him "Full
Flaps."[11] (After the war, a German magazine described him as "Admiral
Gallery, of whom his comrades say: 'His protruding ears shorten the
voyage when he stands on the bridge.'")[12] But the crew spoke with
respect and admiration.

Gallery himself was taken with admiration of a different kind. Reminiscing later about the otherwise uneventful run south and east, Gallery commented on how even ordinary days and nights at sea can have a profound impact on a thoughtful person. Specifically, in his case, they strengthened an already powerful religious orientation:

> Keeping the night watches at sea under a clear sky is good for your soul. On a ship's darkened bridge the full grandeur of the heavens soaks into you as it never can ashore. When you watch the majestic procession of the constellations across the sky, you can't help thinking of the millions of light years that separate us from the stars, of how long they have been there, of their infinite extent and uncountable numbers, and of their vast bulk dwarfing our earth into insignificance. It helps you to put this puny planet of ours with its wars and conquests in proper perspective.
>
> It does a lot more than that. It is better than a sermon in St. Patrick's Cathedral to make you *know* beyond possibility of doubt that there is an almighty and all-wise God who controls this universe and that the only reason you were born into it was to serve Him and be rewarded for it, if you deserve it, when you die. . . .
>
> Near the horizon astern you can see Polaris, the hub of our universe. It shows true north to all seafaring and flying men, be they Americans, Russians, Nazis, or Jap. You ask Polaris, "Don't you know there's a war on?" Polaris simply goes on announcing to all impartially, "Here is north." . . .
>
> I admit it is hard to grasp the concepts of eternity and life after death. But I string along with the unknown philosopher who said, "I would rather govern my life by belief in God, die and find out there is no God—than to live refusing to believe in God, die, and meet Him face to face."[13]

WHEN THEY REACHED Norfolk, Gallery and his ship would be assigned the job of hunting U-boats. Gallery's enthusiasm for this task quickly overcame any letdown at being left out of the Pacific war. In fact, he later regarded this change to the Atlantic as "one of the luckiest breaks I ever got."[14] As it turned out, jeep carriers in the Pacific were often used merely to ferry aircraft to the big carriers in the great task forces, and even when they got to operate their own planes they usually were small cogs in a very large machine. In the Atlantic, *Guadalcanal's* assignment was an important one and Gallery was his own boss, indeed the boss of his own task group. Calling his job "the best one in the armed forces of the United Nations," Gallery told a friend:

> The Guadalcanal is a honey of a ship and the way we operate is almost too good to be true. Cinclant gives me 5 destroyers, a set of orders which limit my operations to the Atlantic Ocean, and as soon as I get out of sight of land I turn off the radio and I'm the Lord High Admiral of as much ocean as my planes can reach. It's really a hell of a come down to get back into port again where there are a dozen admirals who can push you around and tell you what to do.[15]

Now, along the way to the Atlantic, the "*Can Do*" crew practiced all the various skills they would need later. Though most such drills were pretty straightforward, Gallery did not explain the reason for one exercise that was, for a ship like the *Guadalcanal,* quite unusual. This involved passing astern an inch-and-a-quarter wire cable and towing one of the destroyers behind the carrier. Gallery's reasons for this were "so visionary that I didn't care to explain them."[16] They would become clear enough later, after the capture of the *U-505.*

Approaching Panama, Gallery was asked by the general commanding the defenses of Panama to test those defenses by staging a mock air attack on the Canal Zone. Typically, Gallery responded with full zest and ingenuity, as the following account (taken from Gallery's book *Clear the Decks!*) attests.

Attack on Panama

The *Mission Bay,* a sister ship, accompanied us on our cruise from San Diego to Norfolk. On the way to Panama the Army asked us to play war with them and challenged us to test out the air defense of the Canal. I don't think the defenders of the Big Ditch took our little jeep carriers too seriously when they arranged this game. The things we did to their radar warning net, their interceptors and bombers were as illegal as piracy.

Their far-flung air scouting line picked us up five hundred miles from the Canal, just before sunset, and they kept a shadower over us all night. By prearrangement, we parted company with the *Mission Bay* right after dark. She made a beeline for the Canal, while we backtracked to the north for Salinas Bay in Nicaragua. The shadower, unfortunately, elected to stay with the *Guadalcanal,* but, by judicious skullduggery, we made that plane think we were steaming south all night when we were actually running north. You have to behave very dishonestly to do that.

We got our shadower's navigation so badly fouled up that the plane sent out to relieve him, just before sunrise, found nothing but an empty ocean several hundred miles to the southward of our actual position. I am sure that no one in the Air Force who was on duty in Panama at that time will ever trust the Navy again, even under oath.

You understand, of course, that this deception was a bit complicated, otherwise we couldn't have fooled our brothers-in-arms as we did. However, I will try to explain it so that even an Air Force pilot can understand it.

It all hinges on two simple facts: First, that on a dark night you can't tell looking down on the rectangular flight deck of a carrier whether she is headed north or south. The only way you can tell is by spotting the bow wave at one end and the wake coming off the other. Second, that an aviator flying a complicated pattern over a ship, which is making good a known course and speed, bases his navigation on this "known" course and speed of the ship rather than on an independent plot of his own gyrations.

When our friend found us at sunset we were headed south and he knew and reported our exact position, course and speed. Then he began flying a clover-leaf pattern over us, keeping track of us by radar. We soon found that this clover-leaf pattern brought him back over us only once every half-hour.

I knew that if I had been in that plane I would not have attempted to lay down this complicated clover-leaf pattern on my chart and to keep a dead reckoning plot of my position. I would have started from the known fix at the first contact, and every hour during the night, while the ship held the same course and speed, I would have moved her twenty miles further south on my chart. So I made the conservative assumption that our Air Force pilots are no smarter than Navy pilots.

The problem was to make him think we were running south all night when we were actually going *north!* We did this by tampering with the bow wave and the wake.

The carrier escort USS *Guadalcanal* (CVE 60) with planes embarked, May 15, 1944. The torpedo bombers (TBMs) forward were employed as antisubmarine aircraft; FM-2 fighters can be seen aft. *U.S. Navy*

Shortly after dark, when our friend was out of visual contact and just after *Mission Bay* sheared out, we reversed course and steamed north the rest of the night. Every time the shadower's clover leaf brought him back over us we backed full speed. This put the "bow" wave on the south end of the ship and made a "wake" coming off the north end, indicating that we were still running south at twenty knots. In the phosphorescent waters around Panama this was "unmistakable" from the air.

We couldn't actually turn south and then north again because two 180° turns require about five minutes, and would have left a conspicuous S-shaped trail in the luminescent water showing exactly what we were doing.

(Do you "follow" me so far? . . . So did our Air Force friend, who escorted us all night.)

He simply moved his charted position ten miles further *south* every half-hour. Actually we were making good about seven and a half miles to the *north* every thirty minutes, but homing on us by radar it was very easy to miss this.

Just before daylight he had to leave us, but he confidently radioed our position to his relief before shoving off. His "relief" hasn't found us yet because the position was about three hundred miles in error.

Next day we pulled a Statue of Liberty play on the Canal defenses. *Mission Bay* launched her planes with orders to climb way up in the air on the Pacific side, where the Canal Zone radars would be sure to "see" them. Simultaneously the *Guadalcanal*'s bombers cut across the Isthmus of Nicaragua, above the Canal, stayed down low, and hit the Gatun Dam coming in from the *Atlantic* side.

The play went for a touchdown. All the fighter defenses of the Canal tackled *Mission Bay*'s decoys on the Pacific side, and our bombers went the length of the field to the Gatun Dam unopposed. I could write a chapter about how this proves the Navy's case for mobile carrier bases—but I won't.

The Canal Zone scouts didn't find the *Guadalcanal* again until near the end of the afternoon watch that day. By that time we were committed to arrive in Panama at a definite hour, so we held our course and speed all night with no hocus-pocus.

We knew that after sunrise the guardians of the Canal would lower the boom on this troublesome little insect of ours, which had fouled up their defenses.

Just before sunrise, we met an angry rain squall about five miles in diameter. I sent for our aerological officer and said, "Riggs, for the next few hours you are the skipper of this ship. Put us right smack amidships of that squall and keep us there."

Riggs did a scientific job. For the next three hours weather conditions on our flight-deck were zero zero, although it was clear and unlimited a few miles away all around us.

Two squadrons of B-17's came out from Panama shortly after sunrise to beat the daylights out of us. They had our exact position, but that rain squall was a little too rich for their blood.

For three hours we watched them circling on our radar scope as they went round and round the mulberry bush waiting for us to come out. It was the most beautiful rat race I've ever seen in my life.

Finally we heard the two squadron commanders cooking up a deal on the radio to "get this damned thing over with," and to have their planes make individual instrument approaches by radar at one-minute intervals.

That meant that the jig was up—except that there had been a great deal of uninhibited chatter on the radio during the previous three hours. We had been listening in on this party line and by this time we knew all the radio call signs, authenticators, and procedure.

We simply called the two squadron commanders, using the "phone number" of their home base in Panama, and told them: "Exercise completed, return to base."

It so happens that both squadron commanders missed our transmission. But somebody *always* gets the word to knock off a tedious exercise. The number two and three planes promptly relayed the message to their skippers, thus making it seem all the more authentic. They all buzzed off and went home.

After we anchored in Panama the next day there was a critique of the exercise in General Brett's Headquarters. Adding insult to injury, I brought to this gathering a wire recording of all the radio transmissions, climaxed by our phony about returning to base.

As soon as the critique was over, I slipped my cable and beat it right back to the ship. I'll never go ashore in Panama again as long as I live without a bodyguard. Some of those Air Force people might still be on duty there.

"Away Boarders!"

THE KEY OPERATIONAL moment of Gallery's naval career took place during his command of the *Guadalcanal:* the capture of the *U-505.* This first American capture of an enemy vessel by boarding at sea since 1815 was the direct result of Gallery's combination of personal qualities: innovative thinking, careful planning and attention to detail, technical expertise, and superb leadership. Ultimately, too, it led directly to his second career—as a writer.

The idea had first emerged long before the event, one evening around the fireplace in the Officer's Club in Iceland. Why, he and the other PBY fliers around the fireplace speculated, couldn't they try to *capture* a sub with a PBY, instead of just sinking her? A PBY could land in fairly rough water, though it would be unable to take off. Landing near a disabled sub, it could put a wing over her, keep the crew below and cowed with machine gun fire and a grenade or two tossed down the conning tower. A chain down the hatch would keep the crew from closing it and submerging. Then the PBY could radio for ships to come and take over. The scheme never developed further. As Gallery later remarked, "By the time we got that far in the planning it was about one o'clock in the morning and we all decided to go to bed and sleep it off. So that was that."[1] Still, the idea of capturing a sub remained in the back of his head.

As commanding officer of the *Guadalcanal,* Gallery also commanded Task Group 22.3, composed of the carrier plus five destroyers, dedi-

cated to hunting and killing submarines. Early in 1944, on their first
sally from Norfolk, they drew blood. The previous year, Admiral King
as Commander in Chief, United States Fleet (COMINCH) had set up
the "Tenth Fleet." A fleet only in name but vested directly with King's
full authority, it consisted only of a couple hundred people in Washington, whose collective purpose was to counter the U-boat threat. A major
component of the Tenth Fleet was devoted to tracking U-boats by radio
direction finding and decryption.[2] Informed by this outfit of a scheduled refueling rendezvous involving two attack boats and a tanker submarine, Gallery sent the *Guadalcanal*'s aircraft. The planes caught the
U-boats on the surface in the midst of refueling, sank the tanker and
damaged one of the others. Ironically Gallery was to discover later that
another submarine had somewhat earlier passed undetected "almost
between my legs." It was the *U-505*.[3]

With their aircraft ranging the entire Atlantic, jeep carriers like the
Guadalcanal made life a good deal more difficult for the German submariners. However, because the carriers did not conduct flight operations at night, the U-boats could stay below during daylight and surface
to charge their batteries in the dark. Gallery soon changed that. Beginning his second cruise, he told the air squadron commander, Lt. Comdr.
Dick Gould, that he wanted to start developing night landing capability.
They would begin on nights when the moon was full and get the pilots
gradually accustomed to greater darkness. Gould, who had already
practiced night landings ashore, readily agreed. As Gallery put it, "It was
scary business. . . . But it worked. We busted up a few planes, but
nobody got hurt."[4] The second night, a *Guadalcanal* plane spotted a
surfaced U-boat (it turned out to be the *U-515*), which crash-dived
under attack. Twice in the night the sub surfaced, low on battery charge
and air; each time it quickly dived again to avoid aerial attack. Meanwhile the destroyers closed in, and shortly before sunrise began their
own attack. The submarine skipper was wily, and the pursuit continued
for hours, but by midafternoon the end came. He blew tanks to surface,
and ordered his crew to scuttle and abandon ship.

Brought aboard the *Guadalcanal* with forty-five of his crew (ten were
killed by gunfire as the destroyers sank their ship), *Kapitän-Leutnant*
Werner Henke, Knight's Cross of the Iron Cross, had sunk over 160,000
tons of Allied ships. He was, said Gallery, "husky, blond and eagle-

eyed," looking like "an All-American halfback whose team has lost a close game and who is beaten but unashamed."[5] He irritated Gallery by complaining about Gallery's shooting his men as they were abandoning ship, and by arguing about treatment of prisoners of war under the Geneva Convention. Gallery's chief master-at-arms began conversing with Henke. After a few days the chief told Gallery that among the U-515's victims had been the British ship *Ceramic,* from which Henke had rescued a single survivor for intelligence reasons, leaving seven hundred others to die. Though Henke had acted no differently than American submariners in the Pacific, the German captain was worried, said Gallery's chief, that if the British got their hands on him they would hang him and his crew.

Gallery tried a ruse. Showing a faked message purported to have been received from his own commander, Gallery indicated he was on his way to Gibraltar, where he might turn Henke and his crew over to the British. (He actually was on his way to Norfolk and had no intention of taking Henke anywhere else.) Gallery's price for keeping the Germans in U.S. custody was that Henke sign a pledge to answer all questions truthfully when interrogated. With some reluctance, Henke signed. He later reneged, as Gallery expected him to, but meantime his crew, having seen a copy of Henke's pledge, signed pledges of their own. Gallery afterwards claimed that when interrogated after transfer to a U.S. prison camp, the crew "sang like canary birds." The ruse was a clever one, though a close study indicates the crew of the *U-515* actually "told no more and no less than the average U-Boat POWs for the 1944–5 period."[6] When Henke himself refused to talk, preparations were made to send him from the camp to Britain by way of Canada. Just before his scheduled departure, Henke ignored a sentry's order to get back from a fence and was shot, essentially committing suicide.

Two decades later, Gallery wrote an article on the episode for the U.S. Naval Institute *Proceedings.* Although in the 1950s *Proceedings* editors had gone out of their way to ask for something from Gallery's pen, the journal's board of directors refused this article, saying "its conclusion—with the U-boat commander in effect taking his own life because of the pressures that had been brought to bear on him—was distasteful."[7] Gallery, infuriated, resigned from the Naval Institute. In subsequent correspondence he said that he never regretted his actions with Henke and had "no qualms" about the suicide.[8] He had, however, felt badly about how he treated his next German captive.

During the "hold-down" of the *U-515,* another possible contact had been noted some sixty miles away. Once the action with the *U-515* was over, attention focused on that area.[9] Just before dawn on Easter Day, Gallery's night-flying aviators spotted a surfaced U-boat. Its skipper crash dived with such desperate speed that he left three lookouts behind on the ocean's surface. To no avail—the submarine was blasted apart and went down with all hands except the abandoned lookouts. The planes dropped flares and rafts and circled to vector in the ships. By the time the task force arrived, one wounded German remained alive in a welter of oil and wreckage, grasping a rubber raft with one arm and with the other supporting the body of a dead comrade.

This sole survivor of the *U-68,* whose name was Kastrup, was brought to Gallery's cabin. In what years later he called "my only unethical shenanigan of the war" (although it is unclear how Gallery's actions here differed morally from his actions with Henke) Gallery also attempted to get this German to talk. Speaking through an interpreter, Gallery told Kastrup that he had been abandoned by his own captain, while he, Gallery, had gone to some risk to save him. Kastrup's reply was to look Gallery in the eye and say, *"Ich bin deutsche Soldaten."* He averred that the captain had done the right thing in abandoning his lookouts to save his ship, and gave no further information. Gallery was immensely impressed (as he had not been with Henke) and stopped the interrogation. Some time after the war Gallery and Kastrup began to exchange cards every Easter.[10]

Parenthetically one should point out that Gallery's eventual friendship with this enemy sailor is characteristic of his respect for former opponents, generally—whether in sports or at war. As Gallery had insisted that Worth Bagley Daniels shake hands with him after Gallery had first knocked him out, so in combat Gallery was highly aggressive in the heat of battle, but afterwards paid respect to the shared humanity of his combatants—especially those who had first put up a good, fair fight.

Clearly now, in the spring of 1944, Gallery's task force was learning to fight and kill submarines, thanks in some measure to the innovation of night flying. However, with the sinking of the *U-515,* the idea first conceived around that fireplace in Iceland reemerged. When the *U-515* had surfaced, Gallery's task group had thrown everything they had at it to destroy it—"everything but the galley sink," said Gallery later. "I was beginning to think we'd have to ram her."[11] Suppose the effort had not been to sink her, but to board and capture? If another such opportunity presented itself, Gallery decided, he would be prepared. The results are told in "We Captured a German Sub."

UNLIKE MANY POPULAR accounts of battles, this one was not told to a journalist and was not pieced together from records; nor was it recalled many years afterwards by an aged participant. Rather, Gallery began writing it immediately after the event, while towing the captured submarine to Bermuda: "I knew that I had a hell of a story at the end of the tow line there and I also knew that I would not be able to talk about it to anybody, including any ghost writer when I got back. So I thought, well, I'll try to write it up myself."[12] Gallery's account of the action was deposited under "TOP SECRET" classification with the Navy Department. After the German surrender in May 1945, Gallery got the classification lifted and sent his manuscript to the *Saturday Evening Post.* The August 5 issue of the *Post,* with Gallery's article, was in the hands of readers just days before the bombings of Hiroshima and Nagasaki brought an end to the war.

    The *Post* article, from which the following selection is taken, was a very slightly edited form of Gallery's original "Top Secret" account. Note that the *Post* editor did not change Gallery's undifferentiated wartime reference to "Nazis" (and "krauts") vice "Germans," which distinction was later to become a matter of some sensitivity.

    Gallery's first step as a professional writer, this article was to make him nationally known.

From "We Captured a German Sub"

The story of this battle, without parallel in American naval history, really begins on April ninth of last year, when the task group I commanded was making its first antisubmarine cruise near the Azores. The action seems to me all the more remarkable because all the ships of the task group—the baby flattop *Guadalcanal* and her five escort destroyers, the *Pillsbury, Pope, Chatelain, Flaherty* and *Jenks*—were less than a year old and 80 per cent of the crews were landlubbers from our inland farms and cities, serving on their first seagoing vessel. Fools rush in? Well, maybe.

During that first cruise, our task group engaged in a long game of hide and seek with an ace of the U-boat fleet, Kapitän Leutnant Werner Henke—Knight's Cross of the Iron Cross, with Oak Leaves—in the *U-515*. After the *Guadalcanal's* planes from VC Squadron 58 did their spotting job, the destroyers got on the scent, tracking the deeply submerged U-boat by sound indications. The *U-515* was brought to the surface with depth charges in the middle of a group of three cans. The sub surfaced in perfect position to sink one or more of our destroyers by torpedoes or gunfire before she was hammered to pieces. But she made only a feeble effort to fight. The *U-515's* crew swarmed on deck and leaped overboard as fast as possible. We poured rockets and shells into the sub for five minutes before she upended and sank.

After we picked up Henke and survivors of his crew, it struck us that here was an ace of the U-boat fleet, a man of proved courage and skill, yet when cornered he didn't fight. He didn't blow up his boat. He and his crew of veterans, with him for two years, abandoned ship in confusion. The startling conclusion was that if we had ceased firing and had called away boarding parties immediately, we might have boarded and captured the *U-515*. Of course, the call "Away, boarders!" had never been used in any modern navy—boarding parties went out of fashion 100 years ago with the advent of long-range guns.

But there was the fact staring us in the face: If we had had sufficient imagination to foresee our opportunity and be set for it, we might have made modern naval history. We determined then and there to be set the next time. So, before our next cruise, at a conference in Norfolk attended by the commanding officers of all vessels of the task group, we agreed to make capture our objective. All ships were directed to organize boarding parties and prize crews, and to draw plans for capturing and towing a submarine.

We decided that if we brought a sub to the surface we would immediately stop firing weapons that could sink her, such as torpedoes, depth charges or armor-piercing shells. We would encourage the crew to abandon the sub by smothering her with fire from small weapons. At the time we drew up this plan, I'm sure most of us thought it was visionary—shooting the moon. But anyway, the boarding parties were organized and instructed . . . as best they could [be] in view of our very limited knowledge of the interior of a Nazi sub. The *Guadalcanal* was to furnish the prize crew to man the submarine after capture. . . .

There couldn't have been a nicer Sunday morning, bright and clear, with a good breeze blowing. All night Saturday, June third, we spent in a fruitless search, which stretched our fuel supply to the limit. So we reluctantly abandoned the hunt and headed for Casablanca. We cruised along behind the destroyer screen and all was serene. I had just come up on the bridge after attending divine services when the radio loud-speaker announced: "U.S.S. *Chatelain* to task-group commander. I have a possible sound contact."

That was nothing startling. "Possible sound contacts" were routine. However, our doctrine was to treat them all with respect. The *Guadal-canal* swung away from the contact and put on full speed, while the two nearest destroyers broke off to assist the *Chatelain*. A carrier right smack at the scene of a sound contact is like an old lady in a barroom brawl. She has no business there, and can do nothing but get in the way of those who are going to need elbowroom for the work at hand.

So far, this was no different from the many other doubtful sound contacts. But now Lt. Comdr. D. S. Knox, skipper of the *Chatelain,* reported: "Contact evaluated as sub. Am starting attack." He immediately dropped his depth charges.

Our two Wildcat fighters from VC Squadron 8, which had streaked over to the *Chatelain*'s position, were just starting to circle overhead like hawks ready to pounce on their prey. As the *Chatelain*'s depth charges hit the water, both fighter pilots sighted the long dark shape of the submarine running fully submerged.

Ens. J. W. Cadle, flying one of the Wildcats, sang out on the radio, "I've sighted sub." Lt. W. W. Roberts, in the other fighter, confirmed.

At this point the sub first spotted us and reversed course, jamming her diving planes to the down position to shake off the *Chatelain*. But the planes promptly reported this to the *Chatelain,* advising her to reverse course, too, and fired their machine guns into the water to indicate the spot where the sub was disappearing. The *Chatelain* swung around, following the directions from the air and the indications of her sound gear, and delivered her Sunday punch of depth charges. This, incidentally, is one of the few cases in which an aircraft has actually directed the attack of a surface vessel on a submarine.

By this time all eyes were on the *Chatelain*. Cheers went up as the depth charges exploded. As the first depth-charge plumes were subsiding, Ensign Cadle jubilantly shouted, "You've struck oil! Sub is surfacing!" At $11:22\frac{1}{2}$, just twelve and a half minutes after the *Chatelain's* original report, all doubt was dispelled. The sinister black hull of a submarine hove itself up out of the water less than 700 yards from the *Chatelain*. As she broke surface with depth-charge plumes still rising all around her, the *Chatelain, Pillsbury* and *Jenks* opened fire with their small-caliber antiaircraft guns, and the two fighter planes went to work on her, strafing her decks with their .50-caliber fixed machine guns. The *Guadalcanal, Pope* and *Flaherty* had itchy trigger fingers too, but held their fire because the other destroyers were in the way.

Hundreds of men lined the decks of our carrier and crowded to topside positions on the destroyers for ring-side seats. The three destroyers firing on the U-boat formed a rough crescent around her and hammered streams of shrapnel shells into the U-boat's conning tower. From above, the Wildcats swooped down, sending torrents of hot steel ripping across the sub's deck and ricocheting through her superstructure.

As soon as the sub surfaced, it flashed through my mind, *Here is exactly the same situation as the U-515 all over again.* This was indeed the situation we had hoped for. So I grabbed the mike on the bridge and broadcast, "I want to capture this buzzard if possible—I want to capture this buzzard if possible."

The Nazis scrambled out of the conning-tower hatch and, finding themselves in a hail of bullets, dived over the side as fast as they could. After a few minutes the sub appeared to be abandoned, and fifty or sixty heads could be seen bobbing around in the water astern of her. Comdr. F. S. Hall, the destroyer division commander on the *Pillsbury*, ordered, "Cease firing. *Chatelain* and *Jenks* pick up survivors. *Pillsbury* is going to board. Away, boarders! Lower away whale-boats!"

By this time, the *Guadalcanal* had launched her ready killer group of planes with orders not to use any weapons that could sink the sub,

The *U-505* from the stern of USS *Guadalcanal* as the carrier makes ready to pass the tow line. Men on the bow of the sub are fishing for the heaving line seen in center foreground, which will be attached to a messenger line, which in turn will bring the large towline aboard. Other members of the boarding team are rigging a pump on the conning tower, while still others are down below. Ship's boat from *Pillsbury* stands off, awaiting orders. *U.S. Navy*

unless she started to submerge. They circled the crippled U-boat, shooting a series of pictures.

The sub was still running at about seven knots and making a very tight circle to the right. As she cruised by, with her curious aerial escort and pursuing whale-boats, the *Pillsbury,* commanded by Lt. Comdr. G. C. Casselman, took off after her in the wildest seagoing chase I've ever seen. The boat with the *Pillsbury's* boarding party cut across inside the circle, while the *Pillsbury* herself was darting around outside of the circle trying to overhaul the runaway. From the carrier's bridge it looked for all the world like a cowboy trying to rope a wild horse. So I broadcast, "Hi-yo, *Pillsbury!* Ride 'em, cowboy!"

Meanwhile the boarding party of eight men under Lt. (jg) A. L. David had leaped aboard the sub from the *Pillsbury*'s boat as it plunged alongside. There was no one on the sub's deck now except one dead German—miraculously, the only man on either side killed during the entire engagement. However, there was every reason to believe that there were still Nazis below, opening sea cocks and getting ready to blow up their vessel. The very fact that the sub was running at good speed, surfaced, indicated that she was not totally abandoned. But this didn't give David any pause. Without hesitating, he and A. W. Knispel, torpedoman's mate, third class, and S. E. Wdowiak, radioman, second class, plunged down the conning-tower hatch, ready to fight it out with any krauts below.

As soon as they hit the floor plates, one ran aft and one ran forward with tommy guns, and found, to their amazement, that the boat was all theirs.

However, they also found that the Nazis had done a job of scuttling; the sub was rapidly filling with water. As soon as they pulled the switches on the main motors, she went down so far by the stern that they had to start the motors again to keep headway and hold the stern up.

The rest of the boarding party now were busy closing the valves which the Nazis had opened. In the main control room they found a stream of water six inches in diameter pouring into the hull through a large strainer in a sea connection which had the cover knocked off to make certain that the boat went down, even if all the other scuttling measures taken should fail. This stream of water would have sunk her in a few more minutes, but the boarders found the missing cover, slapped it back in place and stopped the water.

Boarding parties from the *Guadalcanal* were now swarming aboard. One party literally arrived with a bang when its boat was picked up by the sea and deposited bodily on the deck of the sub. This crash caused some concern to the stouthearted lads from the *Pillsbury,* who were busy down below and didn't know what was going on up above. Only a few minutes earlier the sub had received a bad bump from the *Pillsbury* when she finally got alongside. This bump drove the submarine's port bow diving planes clear through the paper-thin plates of the destroyer, and when the *Pillsbury* sheered out again, she wrenched off the diving planes. The *Pillsbury* was then obliged to haul clear with water pouring into her forward engine room and her sound room, both of which were soon flooded to the water line.

As the *Pillsbury* limped clear of the arena she signaled to us that the submarine had to be towed to remain afloat. So the *Guadalcanal* signaled back, "Have submarine stop engines and we will take her in tow." The crew of the *Guadalcanal* had been kept informed of each new development in the battle by the ship's public-address system.

Right after this electrifying announcement a conscientious boatswain's mate on the bridge, carrying out the checkoff list for routine daily announcements, boomed out over the loud-speakers, "Now, the name of the movie for tonight will be————" That gave us a laugh to break the tension.

When the sub stopped, she again settled with her stern down, coming to rest with about twenty feet of the bow and three feet of the conning tower remaining above water. We pulled alongside and put our stern close aboard the submarine's bow. The U-boat's ugly snout, with its four loaded torpedo tubes, was almost touching our side. I said a fervent prayer, "Dear Lord, I've got a bunch of inquisitive young lads on that submarine. Please don't let any of them monkey with the firing switch."

No time was lost passing a one-and-a-quarter-inch tow wire to our lads on the forecastle. In a short time we were under way with our prize in tow. As we gained headway the sub's stern came up again— and with it the spirits of the whole task group.

One group of men, now in the task group, watched the proceedings with different emotions. The *Chatelain* had picked up about forty survivors from the sub, and had herded them on her forecastle, where seamen armed with tommy guns kept them covered. They looked on grimly and silently from a distance of 500 yards while we took their ship in tow.

Just before the *Pillsbury*'s boarding party got aboard the sub, three cheers went up from the Nazis, who were then in the water. We found out later that the captain of the U-boat had ordered his men to give "three cheers for our sinking boat." He was convinced that his craft was clearly on its way to the bottom.

Though our maverick was securely roped, she was not yet broken to the halter. She still wanted to circle to the right instead of towing meekly astern, the way tows are supposed to do. Before she would go our way, she sheered way out on the starboard quarter, drawing the towline as taut as a fiddlestring.

Now we sent a dispatch through channels to the Navy Department and British Admiralty, stating that our task group of the Atlantic Fleet requested aid in towing an enemy U-boat to port. Later we learned what excitement and incredulity that message stirred in Washington and London. Everybody there knew that you don't capture enemy ships or submarines in the twentieth century. You either sink them, or, when they can't fight any longer, they scuttle themselves.

Then we took stock of our situation. Our sub was in nearly sinking condition and it was doubtful whether we could save her. The *Pillsbury* had one engine room flooded to the water line and wasn't certain whether she could prevent further flooding and possible sinking. We had barely enough oil to make Casablanca if nothing else happened. We were right in the middle of the lane used by U-boats bound to or from the Cape of Good Hope and the Gulf of Guinea.

The sinking of the *Block Island* [an escort carrier similar to the *Guadalcanal,* sunk by a U-boat two weeks earlier.—eds,] was still very fresh in our minds. So I decided that we would get the hell out of that area and head for the nearest friendly port, Dakar, which was more than 400 miles away.

We then shot in another dispatch to our boss, Commander in Chief, Atlantic Fleet, giving the number of the U-boat, stating we had it in tow and requesting permission to take her to Dakar. While waiting for the answer, the boarding parties were working fast and furiously, disconnecting electric leads from demolition charges, looking for booby traps and passing up on deck all secret papers and documents, so that we would have something to show for it in case the U-boat blew up or sank.

The papers and documents removed at this time were of inestimable value. The sub had been abandoned so hastily, with the crew so sure she was going down, that nothing had been destroyed. We thus got possession of every chart, publication, general order and code book that an operating submarine carries. From the point of view of Naval Intelligence it was the greatest windfall of the war. . . .

I then went into conference with Comdr. Earl Trosino, our chief engineer, who had been in charge of salvage operations aboard the sub. He reported that the pressure hull was intact, with the possible exception of the after torpedo room. Conditions back there were unknown because the watertight door to that compartment was closed and there was what looked like a booby trap on it. The prisoners said that the after torpedo room was flooded.

It was good news that the pressure hull was intact. But the pressure hull of a submarine does not have sufficient buoyancy to float the boat if the ballast tanks are flooded. It seemed highly probable that the depth charges had ruptured some of these tanks. The only thing we could do was to watch carefully and see whether she was settling any lower in the water. Since we had taken her in tow, the water line had remained at about the same level.

Just before the boarding parties returned to their ships, we had sent over the biggest set of United States colors we could find. This set of colors was left proudly flying from the top of the periscope. As the sun went down I stood on the flight deck and looked back at Old Glory flying above our prize, recalling the hoary joke, never so apropos, of the man who spent fifteen minutes contemplating the circus giraffe with the conclusion: "There ain't no such animal."

During the first night that we had her in tow, the sub acquired a new name. She was christened "Can Do, Junior," later shortened to "Junior." The *Guadalcanal* had been known as the "Can Do" ship almost since the day she was commissioned. The first order I issued to our crew when it was organized, less than a year previously, stated that the motto of our ship would be "Can Do," meaning that we would take on any sort of a job no matter how difficult and would run away with it. This bit of wishful thinking a year previously resulted in a new name for one of Adolf Hitler's U-boats. Proving once again that if you hitch your wagon to a star almost anything can happen, even to finding an enemy U-boat hitched to your wagon by a one-and-a-quarter-inch wire! . . .

[Gallery personally boarded the sub to disarm any booby trap, and opened the door into the after torpedo room, which proved to be watertight. The crew could now put the rudder amidships, which helped straighten the tow. But the drama was not over. It was decided to tow the submarine to Bermuda instead of Dakar, and the fleet tug *Abnaki,* dispatched to assist the task group arrived on the seventh of June. When the *Guadalcanal* hove to so as to pass the tow, the submarine sank lower and lower in the water, stopping with the conning tower just barely above water level.—eds.]

The *Abnaki* took over the tow, hove in to short stay and went ahead to help hold the stern up. Commander Trosino and Lieutenant David took the salvage party over to the sub, and a race against time began. Electric submersible pumps from the *Guadalcanal* were connected to power leads from the *Abnaki,* and several tons of bilge water were pumped over the side. There was a little air left in the U-boat's air flasks. After careful tracing of lines and comparing of notes over blueprints found on board, this air was expended in blowing the after ballast tanks. The salvage party was really working under pressure, because they knew that Junior had very little reserve buoyancy left and was gradually losing that. At times they simply had to gamble that the valve they were opening or the switch they were throwing was the right one. The penalty for being wrong would be losing the sub and maybe themselves with it.

But these lads never were wrong, thanks to the brilliant direction of Commander Trosino. When it was touch and go whether the sub would remain afloat, he spent hours down in the bilges, crawling around in the oily water under the engines, tracing pipe lines and closing valves to make the boat watertight. He risked his life many times by squirming into inaccessible corners under the floor plates where he wouldn't have had a chance to escape in case the sub started to sink. . . .

At the close of that weary day, our salvage party had a brilliant inspiration. They threw the switches connecting the submarine's motors to her batteries—practically run down by now. They also released the clutches which connected the main motors to the Diesels and held the propeller shafts from turning. That night the *Abnaki* towed her at nine knots. This high speed turned over the propellers. They, in turn, turned over the main electric-propulsion motors, which now acted as generators and charged the U-boat's batteries.

Next morning we were able to run all the electric machinery in the sub, including air compressors, bilge pumps and ballast pumps, and to bring her up to full surface trim. My airplane mechanics were rapidly becoming qualified submarine experts. . . .

During the long tow across the Atlantic we broke out naval history books to do some research on captures at sea. To find the most recent case of the United States Navy boarding and capturing a foreign, enemy man-of-war on the high seas, we had to go back to June 30, 1815, when the U.S. sloop *Peacock* boarded and captured H.M. Brig *Nautilus* in the Strait of Sunda, East Indies.

That was 129 years ago. Naval warfare has been revolutionized since then. In the old days, one surface ship used to board and capture another surface ship. Now an aircraft-carrier task group had boarded and captured a submarine. If any of the old-timers of the old Navy of 1815 could have been present at the action of June 4, 1944, they would have been nonplused by most of the things they saw. Strange-looking steel ships maneuvering at high speed without a sail in sight, roaring mechanical birds being catapulted from the deck of a flattop frigate, and an enemy ship heaving itself up from the depths of the ocean. They would have been puzzled by many of the things that were done, but when the call, "Away, boarders!" was sounded, they would have understood that, all right. And when the United States colors went up on the *U-505*, I'm sure they would have concluded that the current generation of American sailors is living up to the traditions of the old Navy in grand style.

In fact I think they would have made an admission that would be regarded as almost sacrilegious among old sailors—"that the U.S. Navy is still as good as it used to be."

Coda: The Last Secret of the *U-505*

The capture of the *U-505* had to be kept secret. The most valuable part of the prize was the German cipher keys. Possession of the keys used to set Enigma codes, plus the grid plot code used by the German navy to identify positions, enabled the Allies to read German naval messages as quickly and completely as the Germans could. Arriving in Washington on June 12, only a week after D-Day, the *U-505* materials also freed cryptanalysis assets for use on German army and air force messages.[13]

Ironically for Gallery, one of the great secrets of the war was how successful American and British cryptographers had already been in breaking German codes. So although the *U-505*'s cryptographic materials were very valuable, the possible damage if the Germans learned one of their submarines had been taken intact was severe. Not only would they have switched codes, rendering the captured codes useless, but, as Clay Blair notes, they might have made other "'major changes' to improve U-boat Enigma security, perhaps temporarily blinding Allied codebreakers on the eve of the postponed Overlord invasion." For this reason, Blair reports, when Admiral King learned the *U-505* had been captured rather than sunk, he was at first so upset that he threatened to court-martial Gallery.[14]

Though unaware of the full ramifications of capturing the *U-505*, Gallery took great care to make sure none of his sailors revealed their feat, even requiring them to turn in their many souvenirs from the U-boat, which largely they did (despite his assurances, they never did get the souvenirs back). He was later immensely proud that all three thousand task group sailors faithfully kept the secret until it was published after the German surrender. However, neither the sailors nor Gallery revealed another, deeper secret, despite Gallery's own tireless publicizing of the *U-505*'s capture for the rest of his life.

In 1956 the Hamburg tabloid *Kristall* ran an article titled "U-505: The Secret Around Felix."[15] The article, apparently based on interviews with Captain Lange and *U-505* crew members, mentioned that "there was one man, someone from the machinist's crew, who did not come back. We shall call him simply 'Felix.'" The article suggested that Felix had helped the Americans keep the *U-505* afloat. For forty years there has been no confirmation of this story. But, based on newly declassified documents and interviews with the leader of the American salvage party, we are now able to piece the story together, verifying that, while the *Kristall* article is not without error, it is substantially correct: a member of the *U-505* crew was intimately involved in keeping the captured vessel afloat.

None of Gallery's men had ever been aboard a submarine, much less operated a U-boat. They even had trouble opening the conning tower hatch until they got advice from a rescued German (he pointed out a small valve that let air into the pressurized hull, equalizing the pressure

German crewmembers from the captured *U-505* climb a Jacob's Ladder to board the carrier. They bring along the body of the one casualty of the operation, a German sailor killed by strafing. *Alex Zar/U.S. Navy*

and enabling the boarding party to open the hatch).[16] Engineer's Mate Zenon Lukosius then quickly secured the gushing six-inch sea-chest line the Germans had left open, and the rest of the *Pillsbury* boarding party, later replaced by Commander Trosino's larger group from the *Guadalcanal,* did what they could to keep the sub afloat, but it still rode very low in the water. Every effort was required to keep the sub from foundering. (Trosino's part did not begin auspiciously; the waves careened his boat onto the sub's deck, leaving Trosino clinging to the U-boat's decking. Most of his gear sank, so for a brief while his salvage equipment was a camera and a first-aid kit.)[17]

Meanwhile, after being taken aboard one of the destroyers, the sub's crew had been transferred to the *Guadalcanal*. The enlisted captives were locked into a large storage cage beneath the flight deck. There, located right next to the ship's broiling hot engine exhaust uptake, they sweated their way to Bermuda, except for a daily hosing-down topside. (The seriously wounded captain was kept in sick bay, and the other officers in the brig.) On the first day aboard, the prisoners noted that a fellow crewman struck up a conversation with one of his guards—neither in English nor in German, but in Polish![18] The Polish-speaking American was Coxswain Leon Bednarczyk; Gallery eventually put him in for a Silver Star, noting that, *as a Polish interpreter,* he "played a very important part" in the *U-505* episode.[19]

The U-boat sailor, *Maschingefreiter* Felix Ewald, was twenty-one years old and one of the most junior men in the crew. He seems not to have been formally interrogated like the others, who were brought in one by one in front of a group consisting of Gallery; Trosino; the executive officer, Commander Johnson; and (serving as German interpreter) the ship's physician, Doctor Monat. Ewald apparently already had met privately with Gallery the day of the capture.[20] In their meeting, as Gallery wrote later, Ewald told Gallery he was not German at all, but a Pole. He "had been conscripted into the German Navy, had no sympathy for the Nazis, and . . . was willing to assist [the Americans] in keeping the *U-505* afloat."[21]

Ewald was put back with the other prisoners, but there he had other conversations in Polish with Bednarczyk, even—the other prisoners noticed—when Bednarczyk was off-duty.[22] The next day, Bednarczyk came to get Ewald, who departed with his few possessions (toilet articles issued by his captors) wrapped in his handkerchief. His crew mates did not see him again. However, they noticed that very shortly after his departure the *U-505* began to float higher in the water. The submarine's own pumps were now being used to bail her out.

The third day after the sub's capture, the German prisoners were told that Ewald had died suddenly of a stomach ailment, and had been buried at sea. He had seemed in perfect health when last seen by the Germans, and it also struck them as odd that none of them were asked or permitted to be present at the ceremony.²³ But then, of course, odd things happen in war.

In fact, though, as Gallery later stated, Ewald's knowledge was helping to save the foundering submarine:

> While the *U-505* was being towed to Bermuda, Ewald went aboard the submarine about a dozen times with salvage parties in their efforts to keep the submarine afloat. Without this expert advice and direction from Ewald, I am convinced that the submarine would have sunk.²⁴

Gallery wrote this letter some years after the fact, with the specific intention of making Ewald's contribution look as important as possible, because he was then trying to help Ewald emigrate to the United States. Following the custom of bureaucratic correspondence, he may have purposely magnified Ewald's importance. Earl Trosino in a 1998 interview said he felt confident at the time that he could keep the submarine afloat. Still, Ewald's help, freely given, was extremely valuable and may have been crucial. While going to and from the submarine during the first two days, Trosino spoke with Ewald (with Bednarczyk as interpreter) to obtain details of operating various systems on the *U-505*. On the third day, he wanted to take Ewald back aboard the sub. Gallery at first demurred, but agreed after Trosino not only insisted he trusted Ewald "with my life," but noted that, after all, Bednarczyk and others would be there as well. After that Ewald was a regular member of the salvage party that Trosino led to the *U-505* every day (no one went aboard after dark until the night before coming to Bermuda). Felix, his guard/interpreter "Benny" (as Trosino called him), and the others traced lines, adjusted valves, cleared waste and debris, and set up pumps and other equipment. (When on June 7, the fleet tug *Abnaki* arrived to take over the tow, with the oiler *Kennebec* to top off the task group's nearly empty tanks in preparation for the trek to Bermuda, there also came from Casablanca an experienced U.S. Navy submariner and salvage expert, Comdr. Colby Rucker. According to Trosino, the successful work that Clay Blair credits to Rucker was already in hand when Rucker arrived, and after Trosino showed Rucker what had been done, Rucker simply agreed, "That's what I would have done," and left the ship.) Trosino and his crew continued their work all the way to Bermuda, occasionally refreshing themselves from large cans of captured German dill pickles.[25]

As a Pole who had been drafted aboard a German submarine (one of a number so conscripted during the later years of the war), Ewald could hardly be called a traitor. Indeed, Trosino recalls Ewald saying that one or more of his family had been killed by the Germans. Ewald also told Trosino that once the *U-505* left port he was never allowed topside for fear he might signal someone. In contrast, once he had been separated from the other captives aboard the *Guadalcanal,* he received very special treatment. He was given a regular U.S. Navy dungaree uniform, and (presumably accompanied by Bednarczyk) bunked and ate with the American crew, who all seemed to like him. He was surprised when Trosino first handed him a cigarette, saying a German officer would never do that. Before leaving the *Guadalcanal,* he said he wanted to join the U.S. Navy—for no pay, just for the freedom.[26]

Aboard the *U-505* with the Americans, Ewald not only explained how equipment worked and helped carry out various adjustments, but was given sufficiently free rein that at one point he briefly terrified Trosino by turning off all the ventilation while working on his own initiative to get the bulkhead fans going.[27]

When the *Guadalcanal* and the now buoyant *U-505* reached Bermuda, the captives were held there for a while, then sent to the United States, eventually to a prisoner of war camp in Ruston, Louisiana. To avoid any risk of revealing the intelligence coup, the United States broke the Geneva Convention by not reporting the crew's capture. Indeed, when a Swiss International Red Cross team came to inspect the camp, the *U-505* crewmen were trucked out into the country until the Swiss were gone.[28] Meanwhile Felix had been sent separately to the United States on a destroyer, and was not imprisoned with the others. Gallery got news about him from time to time, to the effect that he was "getting along fine and is quite happy."[29] After the war, all the prisoners (including Ewald) were repatriated, getting home after Christmas 1945 to a Germany now divided into four zones of Allied occupation. Felix went to Hamburg and then wound up in the Russian Zone. Correspondence with Trosino, who had worked with him so closely in keeping the sub-

Just before coming into Bermuda with his trophy, Gallery poses atop the conning tower with Lieutenant David (to Gallery's left), who led the boarding party that made the initial capture, and Commander Trosino (to Gallery's right, in garrison cap), who led the salvage party that kept the sub afloat. The enlisted members of the salvage party pose below. Felix Ewald sits front and center, with Bednarczyk sitting to his left. *U.S. Navy*

marine afloat, encouraged him to try to emigrate back to the United States. Initial efforts failed, and Trosino enlisted Gallery's help. Gallery lined up things with the State Department and provided the letter quoted earlier emphasizing Ewald's crucial contribution in saving the *U-505*. Trosino was prepared to get him a job with the Merchant Marine, and Gallery planned to offer him one on his Virginia farm. Unfortunately, by this time Ewald had been driven by necessity to join his parents on their farm back in Poland, where things were also very harsh. When he wrote Trosino in 1948, it was to ask for some second-hand clothing for himself and his parents. Trosino's wife and her church group sprang into action and sent some packages. Ewald never emigrated, but eventually made it back into Germany, where he lived with his son. He maintained an irregular correspondence with Trosino until the early 1990s.[30]

The *Kristall* article suggests that a German who was killed in prison camp by fellow POWS after being accused of being an informer may have been Felix. This is an error caused by confusing Felix with a captive from another submarine.[31]

In 1957 Maj. Lenox Lohr of the Chicago Museum of Science and Industry sent Gallery a translation of the *Kristall* article with the comment, "Of course, you and I know who 'Felix' was and what he did."[32] The secret apparently was known to few others, and indeed some pertinent documents, though long forgotten, retained their "TOP SECRET" classification until 1998.

Gallery and "The Revolt of the Admirals"

GALLERY RETAINED COMMAND of the *Guadalcanal* for some three months after he captured the *U-505*. Then, in September 1944, he reported for ten months of duty in the Pentagon, doing logistics work and champing at the bit to get back to the war. In June of 1945 he was ordered to the carrier USS *Hancock* as its prospective commanding officer. You won't find Gallery in photos of the Japanese surrender ceremony in August of that year, unless you find one showing the sky above it. While MacArthur and Nimitz signed the surrender documents, Gallery flew in the review of fifteen hundred planes that thundered over the battleship *Missouri* (and tried to avoid hitting each other in the process).[1]

Gallery commanded the *Hancock* until the end of that year. In his short time aboard, the *Hancock*'s major employment was as part of "Operation Magic Carpet," in which the ship transported thousands of U.S. servicemen home, first from Okinawa, and later from Manus in the Admiralty Islands. We have little more than a snapshot of Gallery during this period, but it is an interesting one. A letter found in the Gallery collection was written by a young sailor to his father, an individual who himself somehow was already a Gallery fan. A passage in the letter is worth quoting at length for the picture it provides of the effect of Gallery's leadership on his men.

Undersecretary of the Navy Ralph Bard awarding Dan the Distinguished Service Medal for the *U-505* capture, probably in late 1944, while Vee and daughter Connie look on. Gallery's task group was awarded the coveted Presidential Unit Citation (the award board's recommendation for a lower award was overruled by Admiral King). *U.S. Navy*

Aboard USS Hancock, 5 October 1945

Dear Dad,

We are at anchor still in Buckner Bay, Okinawa. I came aboard yesterday with about 1700 Marines and CB's. It was like stepping from hell to heaven. Before I knew who the skipper was, they passed out mimeographed sheets of instructions to passengers and it immediately reminded me of some of the mementos of other Gallery commands of which you have a cross section. The ship was, and is a model of quiet efficiency and courtesy. . . . Since then I've found out what a well liked skipper [Captain Gallery] is. In most cases it came into the conversation automatically in talk about the ship, there were no reservations, everybody says he's the best they ever served under. He's gotten up twice since we've been aboard, to talk to everybody. It's been straight, good natured welcome aboard talk. The guy is one of the men and they know it. One boy said that he was the first skipper to give them the straight dope as he got it. When he got the news that the ship was destined to stay out on patrol—he told the men and when he found out that they were bound for home—he told them again. And as this kid put it, "It's the first time we've ever known anything, always before it was scuttlebutt." This morning after the skipper spoke, while the applause and cheers were dying down, a negro Sea Bee turned to me and with awe in his voice he said, "That's a fine man. Why that's the best we've ever been treated, this ship is wonderful."[2]

It's no surprise that many enlisted men repeatedly did their best to get reassigned to Gallery's commands.

On selection to Rear Admiral, Gallery reported for duty as commander of Carrier Division Sixteen, three active jeep carriers—but the frantic postwar demobilization meant the ship's crews were too small to operate the vessels, and the three of them spent a year alongside the pier in San Diego.[3] Gallery's promotion and past success, however, assured that before long he would return from sea to a major managerial assignment. Although a book jacket claim that Gallery was the youngest man ever to be promoted to rear admiral is in error, still, by any measure he was young for the rank, and very much a rising star. It was no surprise, then, that in November of 1946 Gallery reported back to the Pentagon.

It was no doubt with great happiness that Dan could return to Virginia, after most of the previous five years away. For a while, the family could live almost normal civilian lives together, time in which (except for official visits here and there and frequent speaking trips) Dan would be at work during the day, and back at home at the farm at night. He was happy to take part in farm life—driving the tractors (as did Vee) and chopping the firewood, while Vee bred both horses and dogs and also taught riding. With the kids now attending public high school, for pretty much the first time Dan could help oversee their homework. If not quite the constant companion/schoolteacher his own dad seems to have been, he was just as formidable; son Danny remembers hating Dan's checking his homework, for Danny was not the "math slide rule" that his old man was.[4]

The Gallery brothers—Phil, Dan, Chaplain John, and Bill—meet in 1946 on Bill's ship, the seaplane tender *Siboney* (AVG 112) in San Diego. Dan has recently made rear admiral, while Phil and Bill, captains at this point, will become "tombstone" admirals (they both made admiral upon retirement). *U.S. Navy*

At the Pentagon this technical whiz had been chosen as the first occupant of a newly created position—Assistant Chief of Naval Operations for Guided Missiles (OP-57). In an era that had just glimpsed some of the great potential of missiles in the terrifying German V-1s and V-2s, this assignment was potentially a very important responsibility, and eventually it had impressive results. Although some of his department's development efforts were not especially successful—such as the spectacular but impractical launching of a captured German V-2 from the deck of an aircraft carrier—others were to bear much fruit. During Gallery's tour, missile work began with projects like the LOON, and then the REGULUS; other work eventually would lead to the fleet standard surface-to-air missiles TERRIER, TARTAR, and TALOS,[5] missiles which would hold their place on surface ships through the 1960s.

However, when one held rear admiral's rank in Washington, the job title itself indicated only a portion of the job. Admirals usually were encouraged to speak in public (after first taking a public speaking course, as Gallery did). His spectacular wartime success assured that Gallery would become a highly sought-after speaker, and by delivering nearly seventy speeches or lectures from 1946–49 he now began to make something of a figure on the national scene. Gallery arrived on that scene during a critical period. As it turns out, probably more important than his missile work (and certainly more gripping to him personally) was his outspoken advocacy for naval aviation, at a time when it was under severe attack.

Rear Admiral Gallery at the controls of an FH-1, an early twin jet fighter, in August of 1948 (during his tour in the Pentagon). He and two other admirals flew three of these jets in formation at various air shows as the navy's "Gray Angels." *U.S. Navy*

After World War II, American military planning focused largely on (1) how our forces should be allocated between strategic (atomic) bombing (sometimes understood as a quick, inexpensive road to victory in any future conflict) and other missions; and (2) who should do the bombing. The debate crystallized into one between the navy and the newly independent air force, and focused on two weapons systems: the navy's carriers and the air force's strategic bombers. To the air force the navy's carriers, especially an envisioned new class of 65,000-ton carriers, threatened infringement on the air force's strategic nuclear mission. For that mission, the air force had been developing the B-36. If the air force took care of strategic bombing, proponents argued, *who needed big carriers?* The navy could focus on escorting convoys and transporting troops and equipment.

Under Secretary Stuart Symington, the air force's position was consistently and vigorously pushed. Tough bureaucratic maneuvers were coordinated with a strong public relations effort, including speeches, official documents, communications to congressmen, letters to the editors of prominent newspapers, articles in national magazines, even an occasional book. Newspaperman Steve Leo, whom Symington hired as his director of public relations, was tops in the business. Because the navy hierarchy had small regard for public relations or its practitioners, the navy's side was less cohesive and had no equivalent to the team of Symington and Leo. In fact, according to Leo, navy public relations at the time was amateurish or worse—"a fragmented and irresponsible operation."[6]

One document representing the air force position was the "Final Report" of the War Department Policies and Programs Review Board, which the CNO, Fleet Admiral Nimitz, circulated within the navy in early December of 1947, about a year after Gallery had arrived in the Pentagon. That report omitted any requirement for navy offensive capability.[7] Gallery's boss, Rear Adm. "Jocko" Clark, asked Gallery to write a response to the "Final Report,"[8] maybe because Gallery had sent him earlier memos on the navy's strategic role. Before Gallery's memo appeared, Fleet Admiral Nimitz delivered at his retirement ceremony on December 15 what came to be called the "Nimitz Valedictory," wherein he affirmed the importance of the navy as a strategic offensive force, rather than merely a transportation and escort service.

Gallery's memo (which became known as "The Gallery Memorandum") began circulating two days later, and also supported the navy's strategic capability. But it went further than Nimitz had. In his "Remarks," Gallery urged that the navy "start an aggressive campaign aimed at proving that the Navy can deliver the atom bomb more effectively than the Air Force can." Gallery went so far as to argue that the navy's primary mission should be strategic attack ("the delivery of an atomic attack on the capital and industrial centers of the enemy"), while the air force's primary mission should be "the defense of the United States against air attack."[9] In essence this suggested a complete reversal of the air force position and probably went much farther than the navy hierarchy would ever have been willing to go. Moreover, whether its ideas were good ones or not, the document was bound to upset air force proponents, should they ever see it.

Despite its "secret" classification, Gallery apparently shotgunned this memo relatively widely within the upper levels of the navy. Perhaps as a result, in March a copy reached Air Force Secretary Symington, who protested to John L. Sullivan, secretary of the navy.[10] To placate the air force, Nimitz's successor as CNO, Adm. Louis Denfeld, suggested in a memo to Sullivan that Gallery be given a private reprimand for "uncontrolled distribution," despite the fact that (as Denfeld also told Sullivan) the CNO personally admired Gallery's initiative in preparing the memo, and thought it showed "constructive thinking."[11]

By then, however, the memorandum had been leaked to columnist Drew Pearson, who published key portions. Though Pearson did not name Gallery, his authorship was sufficiently known that Sullivan had to make Gallery's reprimand public, and the navy published a statement acknowledging the air force's primary claim on strategic bombing. Moreover, Sullivan announced that the memorandum had "fallacious reasoning" and "erroneous conclusions."[12] Because leaking of the Gallery Memorandum stiffened air force opposition to naval aviation, it was even speculated in some quarters that Pearson had gotten it from an air force sympathizer. Gallery himself said he had no idea who had leaked it,[13] and the person's identity remains unknown.

Gallery's partisanship was specifically for naval air, rather than the surface navy. Indeed, with tongue slightly in cheek, he later privately proposed giving some crown jewels of the surface navy—five U.S. battleships—to the Soviet Union, saying that such a gift would cripple Stalin militarily by soaking up "a large part of Russian industrial effort and manpower."[14] But whether serious or joking, Dan's main opponent always remained the air force. About this time he sent a memo to his boss suggesting that the air force might be more amenable to the navy's planned 65,000-ton carrier if it were named the *General Billy Mitchell.*[15]

Secretary of Defense James V. Forrestal tried to get his two wrangling services to agree. After a conference at Key West in March 1948 proved inconclusive, he held another at Newport that August. At Newport, the air force conceded that the navy would have nuclear weapons for tactical use and even, as needed to assist the air force, strategic purposes. However, the navy continued to find the air force as uncooperative as before, its practice not living up to the Newport Promise.

Having appeared in print both with official blessings (with his *U-505* article) and with official disapproval (with the Gallery Memorandum), Gallery was now seriously working at his writing, using aides to do some of his basic research. December 1948 saw the publication of an article on guided missiles in *Aero Digest,* acceptance of another on "The United States' New 65,000 Ton Carrier" by *Science Illustrated,* and the arrival at the *Saturday Evening Post* of what would become "Our Hot War for Iceland." In addition, Gallery was quite visible as a public speaker to official and civic audiences. He not only spoke on such topics as guided missiles and the *U-505,* but also on the importance of naval aviation. For instance, on October 31, 1948, Gallery gave a Navy Day weekend address in Grosse Isle, Michigan.

In that speech (the substance of which he had delivered several times before) Gallery voiced support for the 70-group air force and argued that the armed services were cooperating fully with each other—but also contended that the special pleading of unofficial groups was handicapping the services themselves. Specifically, Gallery was responding to a resolution the Air Force Association had passed a month before, a typically incendiary proposal on its part that "Naval Aviation should be removed from the Navy and placed under the Air Force,"[16] in Gallery's paraphrase. With this headline as his starting point Gallery used the Navy Day occasion to examine whether there was indeed a future need for the navy, and to consider the advantages of carriers vis-à-vis ground-based air. For example, in defending carrier forces against the charge that they were highly vulnerable to attack, he cited the navy's good damage control record during World War II, and also pointed out that a task group has substantial active protection in its fighters, guns, and escort vessels. Then he pointed to a fleet's great mobility, which, according to the admiral, made it one of the most difficult bombing targets in the world.

> . . . a task group which is at Kansas City today can, within twenty-four hours, be anywhere inside a circle centered on Kansas City which extends from the Gulf of Mexico to the Canadian border and from Denver to Knoxville.[17]

He contrasted this great mobility with "land-based air power," which

> is like Jack Dempsey with his feet embedded in concrete. There is nothing in the world more immobile than a 10,000 foot concrete runway.[18]

Gallery's speech was effective at making a very strong case for carrier air, especially that represented by the planned new attack carrier.

However, a couple of Gallery's own comments were themselves pretty inflammatory, at least when taken out of context. When *Science Illustrated* published Gallery's article "Don't Damn the Carriers" in its February 1949 issue, it headed the article with large-print blurbs under the comment, "Fighting Admiral Dan Gallery stirred up a hornet's nest at Grosse Isle." In those blurbs, *Science Illustrated* accurately quoted Gallery as having said, "It would be cheaper and easier for carrier-based Navy bombers to reach the heart of any continent in the world," by which statement Gallery seemed to be repeating his "Gallery Memorandum" theme of the desirability of a navy (instead of an air force) strategic attack mission. The journal also quoted Gallery arguing against a recent remark of "One of the greatest airmen of our times," to the effect that the navy must be prevented from saddling the country with two air forces. According to Gallery, this comment showed "an amazing lack of understanding as to what the Navy can contribute toward survival in the air age."[19] The original remark had been made by former Air Force Chief of Staff Carl Spaatz—so here Gallery was attacking the intelligence of the just-retired head of the air force.

It seems not to have been the speech itself but its reporting in *Science Illustrated* that led to Gallery's receiving from Admiral Denfeld, the CNO, this memo:

> The Secretary of the Navy directs that until further notice you make no public statements, written or oral. This includes articles for publication on any subject whatsoever. You are further directed to withdraw any such articles or statements now outstanding for release or publication. The Office of Public Information will assist you in complying with this last directive.[20]

Gallery at once obeyed by asking the navy's director of public information to withdraw his innocuous Iceland article from the *Post*. Either sensing embarrassment if the gag memo became known, or realizing that it was simply going too far, Denfeld's office immediately asked to have the memo back. Gallery returned it (but kept a copy). He then weighed in even more heavily in the battle with the air force. A speech in Michigan or a somewhat reportorial article in *Science Illustrated* was one thing, but an article in *The Saturday Evening Post* was an address to the whole country. Gallery sent the *Post* a manuscript titled, "Gambling with the Future." In it he "undertook to show that reliance on the atomic bomb and nothing else could smash the way of life of everybody on this earth"[21]—a direct public attack on the standard air force position as was then being publicly expressed in *Reader's Digest* in a series of articles by William Bradford Huie. Huie, incidentally, was writing with the strong approval of the air force–sympathizing *Digest* editors (who refused to give the navy equal time) and under the direct promotion of the air force inspector general, Maj. Gen. Hugh Knerr.[22]

In his response to Huie, Gallery characterized wholesale dependence on an atomic blitz as narrow-minded foolishness: "It is a desperation concept which holds good only for a war of the United States versus the rest of the world." Interestingly, he attributed its attractiveness to isolationism:

> How . . . comfortable it is to think of simply lobbing atom bombs across the ocean until the misguided enemy sees the error of his way. But this sort of wishful thinking is really the last vestige of die-

hard isolationism. Since it is now apparent that we cannot actually isolate ourselves from European wars, we are seeking a way to participate only from the side lines at long range.[23]

Gallery always considered single-minded reliance on atomic weaponry a great delusion, a simplistic and lazy answer to a very complicated and especially dangerous problem. Several years later he commented on the air force's overreliance on the Strategic Air Command (SAC) in this way:

> . . . when we over emphasize SAC, we are in the position of a guy who is bothered by neighbors walking across his lawn. . . . So he sets up a machine gun on his front porch to keep them off. It will be a damned good lesson to the neighbors if he ever cuts loose with that gun, but maybe if he also had a sign, a hedge, and a dog, he wouldn't have to use the gun. Maybe he doesn't really mean to use it but some day a neighbor gets half crocked and walks across the lawn thumbing his nose at the gun. What does he do then???[24]

Some of Gallery's strength as a writer lay in the clarity of his down-to-earth comparisons.

That in such arguments as the one in the "Gambling" article Gallery was attacking a vulnerable point was later implicitly admitted by the former air force P.R. man Steve Leo in his 1982 oral history:

> . . . you see, the Air Force had been regarded as an irresponsible bunch of kids who were talking about, don't worry about the next war, we'll take care of it. We will have push button warfare, we'll send a missile over (boom boom) the war is over, or we will take off shortly after breakfast and bomb the enemy out of existence and we will be home for supper so don't worry about it.
>
> . . . This is what we had to get harnessed. The Air Force was full of bright people. They knew better then—but that was the stuff that was getting currency and getting headlines and headlines were important.[25]

Leo and Gallery, incidentally, greatly respected each other. Leo regarded Gallery as "a very colorful, very decent guy, very adroit, very manipulative,"[26] while Gallery thought Leo "one of the most expert poisoners of the wells of public information I have met."[27] Paradoxically the two opponents became very good friends. While the Air Force–Navy fight was going on, Gallery enjoyed disconcerting casual observers by lunching frequently with Leo in the Pentagon VIP dining area.

In March 1949, Secretary of Defense Forrestal, who had for some time been seriously troubled emotionally and who would shortly commit suicide, left office at President Truman's behest. Forrestal's replacement, Louis A. Johnson, abruptly cancelled the new carrier (to have been named not *General Billy Mitchell,* but *United States*). Furious that neither he nor anyone else in the navy had even been consulted, Secretary of the Navy Sullivan resigned in protest.

Gallery too was infuriated. He had delayed giving the *Post* permission to print his article while showing the draft to friends in the Pentagon and asking their advice. Reading Gallery's draft just after the cancellation of the carrier, Adm. Richard E. Byrd called the article "splendid," then warned, "in spite of your willingness to sacrifice yourself I still advise against it," but concluded, "We all appreciate your willingness to sign it yourself." [28] Another Pentagon friend who signed himself simply "W" (possibly Capt. Walter Karig) was even more direct: "I discussed this with Ad. Radford [then Vice CNO] and with Joe Bryan [a reserve lieutenant commander, formerly a *Saturday Evening Post* editor]. I agree with both—it wouldn't do the Navy as much good as it would do you harm, which was my original estimate." The writer suggested the article go out under the name of Rear Adm. Luis de Florez, a reserve officer not on active duty, who thus could not be hurt. "It is a swell piece and must be told, *but for Christ's sake, Dan, not at the expense of your neck. Give it back to Ad. Radford for Luis* [emphasis added]". [29]

However, Johnson's scrapping of the *United States* determined Gallery's mind. Despite the serious threat to his career, he felt compelled to speak up. At home at Harmony Farm, he told his wife Vee, "My gold braid is on the line. . . . I'm going to do this if it costs me my uniform." Then, "What do you think?" She answered simply, "Where you go, I go." [30] Though Johnson had recently promulgated a "Consolidation Directive No. 1," forbidding Defense Department personnel to publish anything without prior approval, Gallery was able to squint at this apparent order, as the directive had not actually reached him before he mailed his article. Acting under *navy* policy, he submitted to his superiors a post-acceptance copy of his article. [31] This was seen, as he apparently intended, as a direct test of the directive, which in fact was rescinded before the article was printed.

Releasing the article to the *Post* under his own name, Gallery sent another article two days later with a letter saying, "Don't believe anything you get from me unless it is signed "Dan" (D. V. Gallery is no good) or unless I come up and talk to you (without an F.B.I. man standing behind me)."[32] Two weeks later, under pressure from Johnson, Gallery wrote the *Post* (with a copy to Johnson) asking them to withdraw "Gambling With the Future."[33] Since Gallery had signed what he later ironically called his "pusillanimous letter" as "D. V. Gallery," the *Post* refused, responding that the article was so important they were billing it on the cover, of which a million copies had already been printed.[34] Though the secretary of defense reportedly flew personally to Philadelphia to try to prevail on the editors and then to New York to appeal to the publishers, too, he was unsuccessful both times,[35] and the article, now titled "An Admiral Talks Back to the Airmen," appeared on June 25. Johnson's efforts to kill the article were quickly known and reported in the *Chicago Daily Tribune* and elsewhere, under headlines like "Johnson's Gag Order Defied by Adm. Gallery." In the *New York Times,* Hanson W. Baldwin wrote that Gallery, "one of the most popular of the younger admirals, was . . . threatened with 'banishment.'" However, Under Secretary of the Navy Dan Kimball, always one of Dan's great fans, spoke up for Gallery, and the threat of retaliation waned.[36]

Meantime *Life* magazine published a substantial article on the "Navy–Air Force feud," citing the Gallery Memorandum as the "first flare-up," and remarking that as a result of being scolded publicly, "Poor Admiral Gallery was nearly embarrassed to death."[37] Reading that remark, Gallery sent *Life* a telegram, which they soon published:

IN 22 YEARS AS A NAVAL AVIATOR IN PEACE AND WAR THIS IS THE CLOSEST BRUSH WITH THE GRIM REAPER I'VE EVER HAD EXCEPT FOR THAT TIME UP IN ICELAND WHEN I FLEW WITH AN AIR FORCE BRIGADIER GENERAL.[38]

When that same month Under Secretary of the Navy Dan Kimball proposed Gallery for a job as liaison with the air force's Strategic Air Command, it was hardly a surprise that the air force said no. Gallery put in a formal application for the job anyway, apparently just to needle the air force.

The navy had Gallery slated to testify at the Unification and Strategy hearings being held that October by the House Armed Services Committee, but decided he would be too controversial. Admiral Radford, now commander in chief of the Pacific Fleet but also one of the navy's leading aviators, was back in Washington for the hearings. At his suggestion, Gallery's prepared statement was given to Captain John H. "Savvy" Sides (who a few years later, with flag rank, would himself head the Guided Missiles Division) to present as his own, thus keeping Gallery away from the likelihood of some "very pointed questioning."[39]

Those hearings proved controversial enough, even without Gallery. The new secretary of the navy, Francis P. Matthews, owed his appointment directly to Johnson. With Johnson, he fully expected navy testimony to support the Defense Department's pro–air force party line. What happened instead became known as "The Revolt of the Admirals." Beginning with Radford, one naval officer after another, including Captain Sides, testified against the position espoused by the secretaries of the defense and the navy. Radford later recalled that Captain Sides's presentation (which Gallery had drafted) "had made a great impression on all of them, particularly those who tended to favor the Air Force side and who were usually aggressive in follow-up questioning."[40]

At last (on October 20) CNO Denfeld also testified against the pro–air force view. The result was that on October 27 Denfeld learned from the news media that he had been fired. Gallery's latest *Saturday Evening Post* article, "Don't Let Them Cripple the Navy!" in the issue for October 29, must have been on the newsstands that very day. In it, Gallery defended sea power as necessary for shipment of material, and as a way of keeping any enemy "an ocean's length" away. Carriers' mobility, he said, made them poor targets. On the other hand, "within a few years we will have guided missiles, both shipborne and airborne, which will make sitting ducks out of *jet* bombers now on the drawing board."[41] By implication the propeller-driven B-36 was a waste of money.

Gallery, who had just left the Pentagon for an operational assignment, was dismayed at Denfeld's downfall, wondering if all his efforts were merely shoveling feathers against the wind. In response to a query for information to navy flag officers from Congressman Sterling Cole, a House Armed Services Committee member who had strongly defended Denfeld, Gallery wrote, "In view of events since Admiral [Denfeld] testified consider it too dangerous to express any opinion."[42] As required by a new ALNAV message, he defiantly sent a copy of this document to the secretary of the navy.

Also as required by regulations, in late December he sent the Navy Public Affairs office a copy of his forthcoming article, "If This Be Treason," prior to its publication. In this piece, Gallery strongly attacked recent actions of the secretary of the navy, and defended the right of senior officers to speak their minds to Congress. This article had been rejected by the *Post,* but was accepted by *Collier's,* whose editor, Louis Ruppel, was incidentally a marine reservist.[43]

When he saw it, Secretary Matthews thought the article pretty much *was* treason (readers can judge for themselves; see the end of the chapter). Gallery received the following memo:

> From: The Secretary of the Navy   10 Jan 1950
> To: Rear Admiral D. V. Gallery, U.S. Navy
> Subj: Your proposed article entitled "If This Be Treason"
>   1. A draft on an article entitled "If This Be Treason," written by you and intended for publication, has been received and examined.
>   2. The proposed article I consider to be not only inflammatory and inaccurate, but contemptuous of and disrespectful to both the Secretary of Defense and to me. Its publication would constitute conduct to the prejudice of the good order and discipline of the Navy.
>   Francis P. Matthews[44]

Gallery was well aware that the phrasing in paragraph two alluded to grounds for court-martial. Shortly afterwards, Gallery (who had been summoned back to Washington from Norfolk) was in Matthews's office, essentially under orders to stop the article.

Picking up a phone in the secretary's office, Gallery called Ruppel and asked him to stop the press and pull the article. As Gallery explained the situation to Ruppel a few days later:

At the time I phoned you I had just received official notice that publication of the article would result in general court-martial proceedings, and I also was *certain* that the article could not be stopped no matter what I did or said. In making the call I was simply going through the motions of attempting to comply with what I took to be a direct order, in order to protect myself against a possible additional charge of refusal to obey orders. I was in the Secretary's office with his aide sitting at my elbow and listening on another phone when I made the call so I couldn't say much more to you than I did at the time.

. . . for a while it looked like they were going ahead with a court. However, I think that wiser counsel has prevailed.[45]

Ruppel had perfectly deduced the situation, and played his part exactly as Gallery had expected. He refused the request, and "If This Be Treason" appeared in the million-plus copies of the January 21, 1950, *Collier's*. Gallery wrote later that Admiral Forrest Sherman, the new CNO, "squelched a [general court-martial] and gave me a letter of admonition."[46]

In late January Gallery wrote Capt. John Crommelin, another outspoken advocate for naval aviation. Gallery said he had "had a long talk with Forrest Sherman," and that at Sherman's request, he was going to "pipe down," and urged Crommelin to do the same.[47] Crommelin did not pipe down and was forced into retirement. For Gallery, although he was to know more controversy later, this particular episode had essentially ended.

In his autobiography Gallery touches only briefly on his involvement in this controversy, though he mentions the Gallery Memorandum, his articles, and his almost court-martial. Others, however, have given him even less credit. Jeffrey Barlow's indispensable book, *Revolt of the Admirals,* discusses only the Memorandum. And Jocko Clark's silence about Gallery in his autobiography, *Carrier Admiral,* caused Gallery to send Clark a letter exclaiming, "My nose is out of joint. . . . *I was there too.*"[48] Indeed, repeatedly over a two-year period, he had put his stripes on the table for what he deeply believed was right for the navy and for the country. In taking the navy's case to the American public, he incurred a direct personal order to shut up, a public reprimand, and very nearly a general court-martial. Partly because of his outspokenness here, he not only failed to be selected for several important billets later on in his career, but jeopardized a chance at a third star. Was it worth it? And what was the value of his intervention? Was Gallery's effort well-meaning but ineffective, or even counterproductive?

In the case of the Gallery Memorandum, one notes his enthusiasm and conviction, primarily. Surely point papers suggesting unconventional positions must be allowed to circulate relatively freely within government circles, and the degree of their influence may be in partial relation to the breadth of their circulation. If Gallery erred in broadcasting his memo too widely, it was surely a venial error, and in fact was treated as such. Almost certainly, too, the memo was far more widely distributed than Gallery intended.

His speech at Grosse Isle was, overall, simply an effective presentation of the case for carrier-based air. However, the two statements the media picked up on were in fact somewhat inflammatory—especially the attack on Spaatz. Spaatz, however, was sometimes pretty extreme in his own views.[49] Gallery may have felt that somebody had to put him to rights, and if no one else dared to speak (which often seemed to be the case), Gallery would. Nevertheless, this kind of willingness to say exactly what he thought (and the political danger in that) may have been the reason Gallery was not allowed to present his speech to Congress in person.

However, as for the articles he wrote (by far Gallery's most important contribution and most sustained effort), though very strongly expressed, they were pretty carefully measured. Gallery had most of them vetted widely by friends in the Navy Department, and they spoke what most naval aviators and naval veterans believed. Besides his okays from senior colleagues ahead of time on their substance, Gallery received kudos after the fact from such respected figures as J. L. Holloway, Jr. (superintendent of the Naval Academy), former CNO Ernest J. King, and even renowned British historian B. H. Liddell Hart.[50] Thus, in writing his articles, Gallery proved a "loose cannon" only to Secretaries Symington, Sullivan, Johnson, and Matthews—who, one might argue, at certain times were all either proponents of or tools of the Air Force.

How effective were those articles? Of course, in the absence of modern polls and surveys and vote counts, the effectiveness of public relations is difficult to measure. However, Barlow in his fine book stresses again and again the importance of the extremely well-planned, large-scale, and continuous air force public relations campaign, attributing to that campaign (and the navy's ineffective responses) much of the air force's success in the period. If Barlow is right about the importance of public relations, then maybe Gallery's P.R. fight on the *other* side *was* worth the risk to his career, and those who advised him against signing his pieces were wrong about their potential impact. In any case, Gallery certainly succeeded in doing what nobody else on the navy side had done: in three or four of his articles putting the navy's view on the coffee tables of millions of readers (and into the *Congressional Record,* too, for the articles were read into that document) at a very critical time.

But in any final assessment of the effectiveness of his public relations efforts, one should ask *how the public itself* perceived Gallery. It is of course impossible to offer here more than the slightest anecdotal sketch of this subject, but it seems relevant to quote briefly from three relatively long letters written to Gallery, some of the most interesting of all the correspondence Gallery received during his Pentagon tour.

Gallery's "Airmen" article in June of 1949 prompted a Mrs. Mary Dockstader of Charleston, South Carolina, to write the admiral in thanks for his "courageous stand." Her comment on her own interest in the Defense Department controversy suggests the kind of arguments that were being made around the dinner tables over much of the land:

> With one son a B-29 pilot in the United States Air Force and the other a fighter pilot in the Naval Air Corps, in the training command at Pensacola, I have heard plenty of discussions on the subject of whether we shall win our next war with airplanes alone, or if it would not be advisable to add a few ships of the Navy and some divisions of ground troops, just in case. I am happy to say my two young men agree in entirety with your stand.

Mrs. Dockstader went on to tell Gallery of some promotional problems of her naval reserve son, but (as she said later) she really didn't expect a response. She was astonished (and moved with gratitude) when Gallery filled several pages with a detailed personal reply. Mrs. Dockstader wrote a second time to thank the admiral, beginning by mentioning her relief at even seeing his address on the envelope in which his letter came:

> Because even before reading the contents I was able to assume that the Post article hadn't, as might have been feared, separated you from the service of your country and that you and the Navy were still simpatico. And your neck still intact.

But now toward the end of a third letter, in which she promises not to write again—"You have NOT gotten involved in a reciprocal correspondence with an elderly female in Charleston"—she makes this very interesting comment:

> The press carries the news that Admirals Denfeld, Bogan, and Radford have joined with you and Captain Crommelin in an outspoken stand for the future of the Navy. Long may you wave! [51]

Note the crucial perception here. For Mrs. Dockstader, and no doubt nor much of the country, too, Admirals Denfeld, Bogan, and Radford *are following Gallery* (and Crommelin) to the fight; for her, neither the CNO nor the navy's senior aviators but *Dan Gallery* leads the way.

It is not our purpose to suggest that such public statements of opposition to the air force as occurred in the "Revolt of the Admirals" would not have been made without Dan Gallery. Certainly none of the navy principals in this engagement give him credit for their inspiration, and many of them were very determined men on their own. Great courage can accompany the quiet work of diplomatic maneuvering and political infighting (such as Barlow deftly depicts), and work hidden in offices can be much more important than what is open to public view, where prima donnas prefer to perform.

Still, who knows how much effect Gallery's arguments and his personal example actually had—at the immediate moment, or in the future; in the admirals' testimony (which came after the "Airmen" article), or in the perceptions of Congress—for, after all, the navy eventually did get its carrier.[52] At least this much seems to be true: Dan Gallery's was the only substantial voice to reach the entire public on the side of navy air at a critical point in American naval history. Late in the day, seeing virtually no one answer the air force, Dan Gallery stepped onto the rickety bridge that was navy public relations, and like his favorite Roman character Horatius, single-handedly did his best to hold back the tide. As a result, it was clear to the public and to his colleagues, as well, that whatever the circumstances and whatever the cost, one man at least would fight for the navy—and that man was "Fighting Admiral Dan Gallery."[53]

ADMIRAL DENFELD'S ouster as chief of naval operations—an apparent reprisal for his outspoken support of naval air—greatly offended most of the naval community. The freedom of senior American officers to speak their minds on issues critical to the national defense seemed endangered. When Secretary Matthews then struck the name of Arleigh Burke off the promotion list to rear admiral, apparently violating not only the selection board's unanimous decision but also his own authority, things seemed to be getting even worse. Gallery appears to have felt (once again) that, despite everything, *somebody* simply had to speak out.

Gallery originally included in the article a scathing attack on Burke's deselection. Before it was published, however, President Truman was persuaded to put Burke's name back on the list, and Gallery scrubbed those paragraphs. His case was strong anyway. Among other things, his defense of Capt. John Crommelin as recorded below was right on the money, for at a critical moment and at great danger to *his* career, Crommelin had leaked information to the press that virtually forced Congress to let the admirals testify.[54] Otherwise the "Revolt of the Admirals" might not have occurred—and again, that revolt laid the ground for an eventual reconstitution of naval air.

That Gallery's position was substantially sound in these pieces is perhaps evidenced by the fact that despite all the enormous heartburn he repeatedly caused the navy and defense secretaries, for the most part, astonishingly, he got away with it. After all, he served for over ten more years. As Gallery put it in that letter he wrote to Crommelin in January 1950 in the aftermath of the "Revolt," urging that Crommelin back off from his adamant stance (a letter that Forrest Sherman may have asked Gallery to write), "The very fact that you and I are not now in jail indicates that the conditions we were criticising are being corrected."

On the other hand, a fair assessment of the following article also requires putting oneself in the place of Secretary of the Navy Matthews, who finds this article from a junior admiral on his desk one day, and (no doubt getting madder and madder) reads all the way through to the implicit challenge issued in the very last line.

From "If This Be Treason—"

The recent stormy hearings before the Armed Services Committee have produced a much bigger issue for the American people than the merits of the B-36 or even the fate of the Navy under "unification." The real issue, which has finally emerged, is the right, or more accurately the obligation, of military officers of *all* services to tell the truth as they see the truth when summoned before the Congress of the United States.

Up to now, Americans have subscribed to Voltaire's statement: "I disagree with every word you say, but I will defend to the death your right to say it."

The very fact that this has now become an issue is a portentous sign of our times. We are presently engaged in a cold war to prevent the spread of Communist dictatorship and to make possible the continued existence of democratic government on the earth. Yet, while we are pouring billions into Europe to stop the Communist advance abroad, we have seen fit to adopt their thought-control tactics in the United States.

We must now decide whether or not national security and our democratic system of government are incompatible in the Atomic Age. Up to now, the great chasm which has separated our system from Communism has been called "Rights of the Individual." We certainly cannot long preserve our cherished individual rights by using the tools of the police state. It will be the height of futility if, on the plea of defeating Communism abroad, we are forced to scrap our democratic system at home.

The recent "cold purge" in the Navy is a grim symptom of this danger. That purge was directed not against men accused of treason, but against officers who proved their patriotism and valor in the war fought to preserve the Four Freedoms. These men were accused of no greater crime than having the courage of their convictions and refusing to conform to a party line.

Last October, on the date which was formerly Navy Day, Admiral Louis Denfeld, after 40 years of distinguished service to the country in peace and war, was kicked out of his job as Chief of Naval Operations.

The admiral learned of his firing from an aide who read about it in the newspapers. In the reshuffle which followed, all the other top admirals who supported Denfeld were swept into the deep freeze.

So far the Navy is the only service which is feeling the iron heel of thought control. But I think that the implications of the purge are even more ominous to the country than they are to the Navy. The handwriting on the wall can now be plainly seen by military officers in the Army, Air Force and Marine Corps as well as the Navy. It says, "Conform or be liquidated."

Modern warfare, whether on land, sea or in the air, is a highly specialized and technical profession, one to which men devote lifetime study. The survival of our country in the Atomic Age depends upon the wisdom of military decisions which will be made in the next few years, and under our form of government the basic decisions of military policy should be made by Congress. How can these decisions be made wisely if Congress is to be denied the honest advice of the men whom the taxpayers have trained to be their experts?

Sometimes even the experts disagree. At the very least, Congress is certainly entitled to know about it when they do. But from now on it's hard to see how Congress can expect anything but a party-line unanimity of opinion from the military officers who appear before it.

Today the Navy's advocates of the so-called supercarrier are being "liquidated." At some future date, it is conceivable that the best professional opinion in the Air Force might swing away from huge, transoceanic bombers and favor more adequate jet fighters and fast medium-range bombers for defending the United States. Suppose that, when this happens, the party line of the Defense Department still is "Cheap and Sure Victory at Bargain Rates." In view of what has happened to the Navy in recent months, how will the Congress find out about any such change in professional opinion?

Perhaps the memory of Billy Mitchell is still sufficiently green in the Air Force to call forth the necessary martyrs. But some valuable men will have to sacrifice their further usefulness to the country, if events since October 27th are any criterion.

It may be possible for a good lawyer to make out a case for the firing of Admiral Denfeld on grounds other than his testimony under oath before the Armed Services Committee. But no amount of pettifoggery can obscure the fact that other admirals were ruled out as Denfeld's successors because they appeared before this committee and told the truth as they saw it.

The unanimity of opinion among the top admirals who testified was quite remarkable. One of the dramatic high lights of the Congressional hearing occurred when Admiral Arthur W. Radford completed the opening statement setting forth the grave issues which were at stake. During the tense pause which followed, Chairman Carl Vinson peered skeptically over his spectacles and inquired, "Admiral, is there anybody else in the Navy who feels as you do?"

Admiral Radford replied, "Yes, sir. Fleet Admirals King, Halsey and Nimitz, Admirals Blandy, Conolly, Kinkaid . . ."

"That is sufficient, sir," said Mr. Vinson. "We will proceed."

The last three admirals named, as well as Radford himself, would normally be the logical candidates to fill a vacancy in the office of Chief of Naval Operations. All four were passed up in the upheaval following their testimony.

Of course, in any organization the boss man has a right to the loyalty of his senior advisers. In a narrow sense a "yes" man exhibits loyalty to his boss. You can get that sort of loyalty from small men simply by appointing them to high office. But an adviser who is worth his salt and who is really loyal to his boss in the larger sense, must have the guts to disagree with the boss when his conscience tells him to.

A press release issued by the Navy Department to justify the firing of Admiral Denfeld said:

"A military establishment is not a political democracy. Integrity of command is indispensable at all times. There can be no twilight zone in the measure of loyalty to superiors and respect for authority between the various ranks."

This is a difficult statement for the ordinary citizens of a political democracy to swallow. At least, I'm sure it would have been difficult for the founding fathers of this country to do so. Our Revolution was fought in the twilight zone between loyalty to conscience and respect for the authority of King George III. Have our liberties become so secure now that we can abolish this twilight zone and still feel safe in the regimented silence of the night?

I have always been taught that loyalty is a thing which must work both ways. It must extend down from the top as well as up to the top. You don't get loyalty for nothing, you have to earn it; and one indispensable requirement for earning it is a decent regard for the honest opinions of your subordinates.

. . . .

The keystone of high morale in a military organization is confidence in leadership. Without such confidence no military organization is worth a damn, no matter how well equipped, well paid, and contented it may be.

You do not fall heir to that confidence simply by appointment to high office. You certainly do not earn it by the bull-in-a-china-shop approach of knocking heads together whenever competent professional men disagree with a new and desperately dangerous concept of defending the United States.

When the advocates of this new concept run out of answers to the Navy's plea for a realistic defense, they have one clincher which they always fall back on. They say, "Unification is the law of the land and the Navy had better learn to live with it."

That is really a tough one to answer, because through some magic process since the end of World War II, this word "unification" has become a fetish; anything with that label attached to it is assumed to be sacred. Nobody knows exactly what it means, but everybody is for it. It's one of those ideas like "Home and Mother" which no one dares to question, certainly not this writer.

I'm for unification, but if you ask me what it means all I can say is, "Read the law." Of course, this is a rather naïve answer because nearly everybody in Washington seems to subscribe to Humpty Dumpty's philosophy as expressed in his well-known remark to Alice: "When I use words, they mean what I want them to mean." Admiral Denfeld said he had no objection to the law; his grievance was with its administration and interpretation.

The law guarantees the continued existence of naval aviation and the Marine Corps. But there is not a word in the law against nibbling them down to a state of impotence. Congress passed a law telling the Navy to build a flush-deck carrier, but the law was not very well enforced.

"Duplication" is another fetish of the present era. It has got to be almost an obscene word, at the mere mention of which brass hats are supposed to blush and disgorge millions of the taxpayers' money which they have been hoarding. Some duplication, especially in matters of vital importance, is obviously necessary and desirable. But the cry is raised so indiscriminately these days that I wouldn't be surprised to see a ukase come out from the Pentagon saying, "We've got to eliminate all this duplication among the chaplains; let's unify the Chaplains Corps and make them all preach a common doctrine." That may sound a little extreme today, but as President Hoover remarked, "It takes time for an idea like unification to work."

The charge of "soreheads" has been leveled at the admirals. The columnists say, "The Army and Air Force are satisfied with unification . . . they abide by the 2 to 1 votes . . . why is it that only the Navy complains?"

That question is best answered by asking another one: "Who does the screaming when a rape is being committed?". . . .

Another fetish which calls forth a lot of sloppy thinking these days is that of "Civilian Control of the Armed Forces." This is, again, one of those "Home and Mother" concepts which everybody swallows without batting an eye. After all, Adolf Hitler was a civilian and so is Joe Stalin. Do we want their brand of control over the armed forces? In my humble opinion, what we need is democratic control through the elected representatives of the civil population, not control by police-state methods.

Many people wonder why Captain John Crommelin committed professional suicide as he did. They don't know John the way I do. He did it because of a fierce conviction that he is right and that the country is in danger. Had John Crommelin held his peace, the rest of the committee's agenda would have been swept under the rug after the deplorable fiasco of the anonymous letter; and the "nibbling to death" process would have been accelerated.

Call Captain Crommelin a troublemaker if you will. The Japs will agree with you on that score. Two of John's brothers were killed in the Navy making trouble for the Japs. If we ever have to fight again, I hope we have many men like the Crommelins in the Army, Air Force and

Navy. We owe the freedoms which we have enjoyed up to now to such men.

Admirals Radford, Blandy, Denfeld, Halsey and the others were actuated by motives similar to Crommelin's. It is absurd to brush off all these great officers as being simply "soreheads." This country should be grateful that we still have men in public service who place loyalty to country above personal advancement, and who have sufficient faith in their ideals to sacrifice themselves if necessary.

I suppose it is still all right for naval officers, under appropriate circumstances, to say such things as, "Don't give up the ship"—"I have not yet begun to fight"—and "Damn the torpedoes! Go ahead!" But if Lawrence, John Paul Jones and Farragut were alive and in Washington today, I doubt very much if you could make them confine their remarks to such simple noncontroversial statements.

Maybe we have progressed so far on the road to—wherever we are going—that we don't need men like these any more. If so, a lot of navy-blue uniforms will have to go into moth balls; but there will be many suits of Air Force and Marine blue, and Army khaki alongside them too.

In conclusion, the investigation conducted by the Armed Forces Committee has presented the American people with two grave issues. Our military security depends on one, and the future of our free institutions may depend on the other. I hope the common sense of the American people will solve them both correctly.

"If this be treason—make the most of it."

Admiral at Sea

AFTER HIS CONTROVERSIAL Pentagon tour, Gallery was sent to sea. In November of 1949 he suddenly found himself deputy commander of the Atlantic Fleet's Operational Development Force, "OpDevFor" being a seagoing research group based in Norfolk. Gallery wrote his brother Phil that "the job isn't much on paper but it's interesting work," [1] and he wrote another officer that he was certainly glad to be out of the Pentagon:

> I find it a welcome change after the past three years, to get out
> on the open sea where there are no dark alleys with unfriendly
> characters in them waiting to slug you if you get your guard down. [2]

For the ten months of this assignment, Gallery flew his flag in the USS *Adirondack* (E-AGC 15). Besides the technical and experimental side of the job, he oversaw the general operation of a variety of ships.

Again, he wasn't hesitant to voice his opinion. In July of 1950, for instance, he wrote an unofficial letter to the officer in charge of a couple of destroyer escorts he had visited personally, ships whose sonar work was excellent—but whose seamanship was "deplorable."

> Among other things they put me right back on my heels by
> blandly informing me that a DE cannot recover a torpedo.
> In my opinion any ship which can't recover a torpedo doesn't
> rate flying a commission pennant so I went over to the WILKE and

breathed down the back of their necks while they did recover one—
after a fashion, but without any damage. Their performance in
lowering a whale boat would have been uproariously funny if it
hadn't been so pathetic.

The ROBINSON wasn't even willing to *try* hoisting a torpedo,
unless I held the sack for them and assumed responsibility for any
damage which their lubberly handling might do.

I realize that these ships spend most of their time just going ping
ping ping, but I think they should spend a few minutes a day on
some of the fundamentals of deck seamanship.[3]

One recalls Gallery insisting that the *Guadalcanal* learn how to tow even
though an escort carrier wasn't expected to have to do so—and the
happy results of that insistence. Gallery always had great respect for the
basics of seamanship he had been taught at the academy, fundamentals
which he had practiced during his five early years as a blackshoe.

After this assignment, Gallery would spend six months as commander, Fleet Air Quonset, duty about which he would later have little
to say. But then he was given "a good job,"[4] reporting in March 1951 as
commander, Carrier Division Six in the Mediterranean. In this position
he was the embarked carrier commander in the Sixth Fleet.

Gallery would hold this position for ten months and fly his flag in the
Coral Sea, one of the attack carriers of the day. The ship of course never
saw combat in this theater; combat forces for the Korean Conflict that
continued to rage throughout the period that Gallery was in the Mediterranean were provided by Pacific ships. But the Sixth Fleet operated
at a high intensity nevertheless. Not only in its tactical and leadership
assignments but also in its social aspects this job provided ample latitude to Gallery's special talents.

Operationally, the fleet exercised at a variety of standard naval evo-
lutions: flight operations, war games, shiphandling, refueling, damage
control, and sea detail, to name a few. Gallery shows off much of the
operational savvy he employed in this tour in various short stories and
in his novels, some of the incidents of which are based on specific events
of Gallery's COMCARDIV SIX assignment. A few of Gallery's stories, in
fact, were written during this period, as were some essays and much
associated correspondence.[5] In a letter written several months after he
left the Mediterranean, Gallery itemizes his literary output: "I've got an

Admiral Gallery (commander, Carrier Division Six), *right,* and his boss Adm. Lynde D. McCormick (commander in chief, Atlantic) in the wardroom of USS *Tarawa,* sometime in 1951. *U.S. Navy*

article on ASW that will be in the Post soon, one on the Forrestal that Colliers may take, and 4 fiction stories (2 each in Colliers and Sat Eve Post) that should be out in a few months. . . ."[6] Most of the items mentioned above probably originated while Gallery was on the *Coral Sea.*

It may appear curious that Gallery would employ his yeomen in typing such extensive personal correspondence as appears in his files for this period, much of it dealing with his literary activity, but flag officers have always been allowed a good deal of latitude in using their yeomen. More to the point is whether it was unprofessional for Gallery to have spent underway, "operational" time on his stories and essays to begin with. Capt. Edward L. Beach, who authored *Run Silent, Run Deep* while naval aide to President Eisenhower in the early 1950s, heard complaints at the time about Gallery, to the effect that the admiral shouldn't be using "navy" time for writing fiction. So far as he knew, Gallery had never once failed on any job or commitment and, in fact, had carried out all his assignments to the credit of the navy and himself. Beach wondered if such invidious comments weren't, in part, aimed at him too. In his own case, Beach would argue that he wrote fiction while other officers played golf. Moreover, according to Beach, to say that every waking hour aboard ship was "navy" time was clearly absurd. Navy time and navy needs of course came first, but all services always had supported the concept that everyone had the inherent right to personal use of personal time.[7] However, from the days of sail until today, some naval authorities (often termed "martinets" and "sundowners") have been prone to puritanical positions about what constitutes "navy" time.

Other officials (arguably, more far-sighted ones) have seen public relations value in such writing activity, and even promoted it. As we have seen, William J. Lederer (then head of the Office of Information's "Magazine and Book" section) had been the person who sent Gallery's Iceland article to the *Saturday Evening Post* in the first place. Gallery's success with that article greatly encouraged the admiral to write more. Admittedly, "Our Hot War for Iceland" was an autobiographical piece, but fiction is only a step further on, and both can have public relations value. Probably many more Americans of the postwar period received their impression of wartime submarine experience from the novels of Beach (and others) than from official accounts and histories, and movies based on such novels have usually found official naval support. Admittedly, the fact that the navy could not directly control this literary output must have made many officials nervous, but the writings of both Gallery and Beach presented a very positive image of naval service.

Another connection Gallery made to the world of fiction during this period resulted in a great friendship. In 1951 Herman Wouk (a naval reservist during the war and after) published his famous novel, *The Caine Mutiny*. As this book's presentation of the navy was not entirely a positive one (particularly in its great neurotic character, Captain Queeg), the reaction of senior naval officials was guarded, even hostile. Indeed, when filmmakers began negotiations to get navy support for the movie, there were suggestions on the part of some officials that Queeg ought to be made a *reservist,* rather than a regular naval officer.[8]

However, when Gallery read the book, he immediately wrote Wouk, expressing his opinion in the most positive terms:

At Sea
Enroute Genoa–Istanbul
18 July 1951

Dear Mr. Wouk,

Just a line to tell you how much I enjoyed "The Caine Mutiny". Once I got into it I couldn't put it down—and sat up till 5 A.M. this morning to finish it.

It's a splendid yarn, and although I have never served in the "hooligan navy" [of destroyer minesweeps], it all rings pretty true. I hope people reading it won't get the idea that all brass hats are Queegs or de Vriesses, but if they do, it's their own fault, because I think you paint a pretty fair picture of the Navy as a whole.

It is by far the best book on the modern navy that I've ever read. If they make a movie of this book, and for your sake I hope they do, *please* keep an iron fist over the script writers and see that they keep the true flavor of the book—if such a thing is possible!

Congratulations on a fine job.

D. V. Gallery

Wouk wrote back that he had been deeply pleased with Gallery's commendation, and thus began a long correspondence between the two men. During the summer of the next year Gallery invited Wouk for a week at sea on the USS *Mindoro,* AVG-120 (Gallery was by that time in his next job, steaming in and out of Norfolk), and much later the Wouks visited the Gallerys in Puerto Rico. Mrs. Gallery remembers other occasions when the two men argued about each other's manuscripts and about religion in her Virginia farmhouse[9]—for of course one thing they had in common was heartfelt religious convictions, Wouk's Jewish and Gallery's Catholic and Christian. Wouk once wrote Gallery's publisher to praise the unusual religious feeling in one of Gallery's books. On his part, Gallery twice read *This Is My God,* Wouk's explanation of his Jewish faith.

They also helped each other with literary enterprises. Wouk read and critiqued several of Gallery's works, and a suggestion of his turned into Gallery's novel *The Brink.* At Wouk's request Gallery in turn commented at length on the naval aspects of Wouk's two epic accounts, *The Winds of War* and *War and Remembrance.* Besides correcting naval details, Gallery made suggestions for plot and characterization—particularly the characterization of some famous figures (like Halsey) whom Gallery knew.[10]

Overall, Wouk says Gallery was not an easy man to get to know, but that he came to love him; Gallery returned Wouk's friendship. According to Vee Gallery, only a few of Gallery's many friends made such an impression that they could get Gallery to change his mind (which surely tells us something about his personality). Among these were Ernest J. King, Arleigh Burke, and—Herman Wouk.[11]

Despite his feverish literary activity and wide correspondence, Gallery seems not to have shortchanged his operational or other leadership responsibilities while in his Mediterranean assignment. In one source we hear of him counselling Capt. James S. Russell of the *Coral Sea* on the loss of a pilot whose plane had crashed in the water with great impact and then been run over by the ship: "'Jim, don't give it a second thought. He was dead when he hit.'"[12] In another, we find him putting down his pen to see how a flight operation was proceeding: "Just took time out from this to go up to the bridge and watch the boys land— black night no moon. Last plane cleared all the barriers—4 strikes— nobody hurt!"[13] Gallery also played baseball with the ship's enlisted men, proud to be the only officer to do so. Finally, as always, he regularly set an example for the ship's pilots.

In his Mediterranean tour Gallery wanted to make a point of flying with the operating squadrons as he had in Iceland during the war, but now he was a very senior officer. Rather than serve as copilot of a transport plane flying to and from shore bases—a typical expedient for senior aviators to put in their flight time—Gallery decided to fly off the ship on an AD "Sky Raider," one of the single-seat, propeller-driven dive bombers aboard. Captain Russell was later to recall the first of Gallery's flights:

> One day, Admiral Gallery appeared on the navigating bridge, and he said, "Jim, I'd like your permission to fly a sky raider in the next launch." . . . Well, I knew that he'd been checking out in the cockpit. He was quite an aviator, very much interested in flying. He had a very thorough cockpit checkout and, sure enough, he got in a sky raider, and we launched him with the rest of the Air Group for that particular flight."[14]

Gallery later commented, "The Landing Signal Officer of the *Coral Sea* had never waved paddles before an officer senior to a commander. He was a bit skeptical the first couple of times he brought me aboard."[15] But Gallery landed successfully, and every so often after that he would fly off with the regular air group. According to Russell this gave him "tremendous standing with the groups."[16]

Russell also recalled a sequel to Gallery's first flight off and back:

> Well, he had a chief of staff, Eddy Renfro, who, seeing his boss cavort off the end of the deck and land back aboard, decided that he really shouldn't be outdone under the circumstances, and he appeared on the navigation bridge one time, and he said, "Jim, could you let me fly one of your SNJ's?" We had two training planes with hooks on them which we used as utility planes, to fly in to the beach, carry the mail, and all that sort of business. . . .
>
> I said, "Why, of course, Eddy." So he went down and took off with an SNJ in a regular launch. He was barely off the deck when Admiral Gallery appeared on the navigating bridge. And he had rather a sly smile on his face. . . . He said, "Jim you haven't had a fire drill recently, have you?" . . . When Captain Renfro came in the little training plane with the hook down and so forth, he landed nicely in the arresting gear and was ready to taxi up the deck, but the yellow shirt plane director jumped up and down, and gave him a frantic "Cut! Cut! Cut!" Cut your engine, you know. Whereupon the man with the asbestos suit came out along with men with fog nozzles, the foam, the fire hose, and Captain Renfro was lifted out of the cockpit by the fellow with the asbestos suit.[17]

Having endured this, Captain Renfro no doubt especially enjoyed the joke when, after twelve good landings without a wave-off, Gallery on his thirteenth try forgot to put his wheels down when landing, and had to be waved off. The admiral good-naturedly paid the landing signals officer and pilots of VA-15 the customary can of ice cream for this classic mistake, and then (never the one to miss a public relations opportunity) sent the photo of this presentation to *Naval Aviation News.*[18]

In his oral history, Russell recalled yet another prank of his former boss.

> I remember one time we were in a [war game] against the *Roosevelt,*
> and one of her sky raiders dived on us, but when he pulled up, he
> found he had a rough engine, so he requested a deferred forced
> landing and we took him aboard. Admiral Gallery was ready with
> a squad of Marines, and when he landed, he was made prisoner of
> war, and his head was shaved! So that's the way cruising with Dan
> Gallery was! [19]

Gallery was to use this shaving episode as the starting point of a short
story entitled "Monkey Business at Mers-el-Kebir," [20] a story set at the
military harbor of Oran, a port that the *Coral Sea* visited while Gallery
was aboard. No doubt sometimes Gallery carried his practical jokes and
good-natured ribbing a bit too far, which (according to Ned Beach)
made some officers take him less seriously than they would have otherwise.[21] Yet in looking back, one-time Vice Chief of Naval Operations
Russell had no condescending view of Gallery's style of leadership. And,
as we have seen, the most dour taskmaster of them all—wartime Chief
of Naval Operations Ernest J. King—was especially fond of Gallery.
Other officers found themselves imitating Gallery's lighthearted leadership style.

Naturally there was a social/political side of his Mediterranean command, which also evoked the vintage Gallery personality. For instance,
Gallery once had lunch and dinner aboard the Sixth Fleet flagship with
the king and queen of Greece.

> At the luncheon I informed the Queen that I had studied ancient
> Greek in high school and had picked up some modern Greek when
> I was in Istanbul back in 1922. Her Majesty asked me to say
> something for her in Greek. Our ambassador almost gagged on his
> artichoke when I said the only thing I could remember, "*Sagapo
> poly.*" This is the first thing a seafaring man learns ashore in any
> language, and means, "I love you very much." [22]

As for informal diplomatic occasions, Russell recollected that because
Gallery "was always out for a story, for an adventure," one had to be
careful going on the beach with him.

> I remember one time going ashore in Cannes. There was some sort
> of entertainment going on, and there was a beautiful lady sitting at a

table almost alone, and the good admiral went over and introduced himself and sat and talked with her, asked for a dance, and one thing and another. And it turned out to be the sister of the king of Egypt, who had been divorced from the Shah of Persia! And there were people with dark looks . . . haunting the grape arbor behind where this table was. And I wasn't sure about the wisdom of courting this beautiful lady in the presence of all the body guards that went along with her.[23]

Russell also remembers when he and Gallery chased around the boot of Italy from one party to another, at the second of which Gallery and the duke of Edinburgh (then on active duty in the Royal Navy, and commander of the small frigate *Magpie*) sat down and emptied a bottle of Scotch between them. In sum, Russell remembered it to be a "great treat" to be around Dan Gallery throughout this period,[24] and Gallery himself saw his Mediterranean command as something of a reprise of his experience on the *Pittsburgh* thirty years before.

After about a year in the Mediterranean, Gallery returned to the States and took command of forces in Norfolk building to deal with the growing Russian submarine threat, an assortment of jeep carriers, destroyers, VS squadrons, and shore support entitled "Hunter Killer Force, Atlantic Fleet." Gallery had been well prepared for this duty by his wartime antisubmarine service. Gallery wrote an article about HUKLANT in which he compared his force's search for its quarry to that of the New Bedford whaling fleet of a hundred years before, and opined that had Captain Ahab been able to transfer "his burning hatred of the great white whale to the black steel monsters of today," he'd soon be at home in the business.[25] He also pointed out that the craftiness of the American sub commanders posed subtle challenges to the attacking forces. The sub skippers liked nothing more than first to outwit the destroyers and then to smack the side of a HUKLANT ship with an exercise torpedo. A growing familiarity with the surface unit's tactics and radio frequencies often gave them an advantage. As Gallery reported,

On a recent HUK exercise three destroyers were just starting an expanding search of an area where a plane had driven a tame sub down. . . .

Gallery visited Pope Pius XII at the Vatican while commanding his carrier group in the Mediterranean. Here Gallery and Comdr. J. Kelly pose with members of the Vatican Swiss Guard. *U.S. Navy*

As the destroyers formed line at the point of last contact to start searching, the division commander announced to his boys over TBS (Talk Between Ships Radio): "Small boys, this is Papa—Commence Plan Charlie Clockwise."

All three small boys "Rogered" eagerly, and then a voice from the depths came in over the TBS: "Better guess again, Papa—you'll never find me going clockwise."

Gallery's discussion of the problems this announcement created (whether to believe that the speaker was telling the truth or was "trying to pull a shenanigan" instead[26]) and brief reflection on Dan's own highly mischievous nature combine to suggest that, very likely, Gallery himself was riding the sub (and speaking from its radio) this time around.

Overall, the forces in HUKLANT were relatively primitive compared to the august Sixth Fleet, and in his recollections Gallery has less to say about the later duty. He spent about ten months in this command, which he relinquished in November 1952. It was to be his last tour of sea duty.

REPORTEDLY, GALLERY was always seeking a story while COMCARDIV SIX—and during his tour in the Mediterranean, one story was almost literally handed to him. Two of the *Coral Sea*'s aviators strayed and then had to ditch because they were unable to find their ship. Gallery first initiated, directed, and oversaw the rescue operation to its successful completion, and then quickly wrote up the experience. The subsequent article—which contains a bit of fictionalized conversation on the part of the downed aviators but is otherwise pretty direct reporting on Gallery's part—yields an excellent picture of decision making from the flag bridge. It also offers a good self-portrait of Gallery in his most natural naval role—command at sea.

From "Mediterranean Rescue"

Shortly after noon on August 2, 1951, a Marine orderly hurried into the flag messroom on the aircraft carrier *Coral Sea,* where the admiral and his staff were at lunch, saluted briskly and said, "Sir, the ship reports two Banshee jets are 10 minutes overdue."

Lieutenant Commander Danny (D. H.) Deaver, of Evanston, Illinois, fighter director officer of Commander Carrier Division Six staff, excused himself hastily and disappeared in the direction of the Coral Sea's Combat Information Center. The flight operations then in progress were an individual ship exercise in which the division staff was not directly concerned, but the other members of the staff bolted their dessert and hurried up to the flag bridge where they were soon joined by the admiral. . . .

This job was a familiar one for the Combat Information Center. Planes do get lost every now and then, but they don't stay lost long after CIC goes to "Panic Stations" and fires up its search radars and direction finders. Operators huddled over a dozen oscilloscopes, while the various radar antennas in the masts and fire-control towers swept the horizon, sea and sky. Direction finder operators clamped on to every voice transmission—recording times, bearings and call signs. Fighter director officers called the missing planes continuously on every frequency which they might be guarding. No answers were forthcoming.

Soon Lieutenant J. M. Campbell (now lieutenant commander), of Laredo, Texas, circling the ship at 30,000 feet with 12 other Banshees from the lost planes' squadron and listening in on the traffic from CIC, called down and said: "*Coral Sea,* this is Banshee number five. I'm over ship at 30,000 waiting for landing instructions. I am in communication with Straychicks (the code name for the missing aircraft). Give me your message and I will relay it."

The fighter director replied, "Ask them where they think they are, what course they are steering, and tell them to keep talking so we can get a bearing on them."

"Roger," replied Campbell. But although the planes aloft could hear and talk to Straychicks intermittently, the *Coral Sea* could not. We talk to planes on a very high frequency (straight line) wave, and therefore our sending distance is limited by the curvature of the earth, as are television waves. Because the planes were high up, their transmitters could reach greater distances before the earth's curvature interfered. The *Coral Sea*'s direction finders were useless.

While the fighter directors sweated over the radarscopes, identifying and eliminating the blips from other planes in the air group, the hands of the clock raced toward the hour of 1310 (1 : 10 P.M.) when the errant jets would be out of fuel.

So would the other jets now circling over the ship. The carrier sent aloft a pair of long-endurance propeller planes with special radar equipment, swung into the wind and began landing her jets.

During the next 15 minutes while the jets were landing, uneasiness grew to grave concern, which soon gave way to the grim certainty that the Straychicks were not going to make it. Contact with them through the new relay planes was intermittent. An order to head for the nearest land when they had 10 minutes' fuel left did not get through. But the missing jets reported they had the carrier's homing beacon on their automatic direction finders, were following it in on an easterly course and the signal was getting stronger. CIC got this secondhand from the relay planes and could take no bearing.

At 1305 time ran out. The high relay plane reported, "Jets say they have only 300 pounds of fuel left and are starting down to ditch."

At 1310 the following operational priority message cracked out from the *Coral Sea*'s radio:

FROM: COMMANDER CARRIER DIVISION SIX
TO: COMMANDER SIXTH FLEET
        1310
CORAL SEA HAS TWO JETS IN WATER POSITION UNKNOWN X

Up to this time, August 2d had been an uneventful day for the U.S. Sixth Fleet in the eastern Mediterranean. Of course, operating in that area, the Sixth Fleet has to be always ready for anything up to and including the professional consideration that the outbreak of World War III is a possibility. But on this day, operations had been quite routine.

The fleet had just returned to Crete after a four-day visit to Istanbul, Turkey, where, anchored in the Bosporus—gateway to the Black Sea—our friends the Turks, and others not our friends, could see it and ponder over its significance. . . .

In Suda Bay, Crete, anchored near the beached and rusting World War II hulk of H.M.S. *York*, were the cruisers *Worcester* and *Columbus,* the aircraft carrier *Oriskany,* a squadron of destroyers, and numerous oilers and supply ships.

As the message to Admiral Gardner flashed out, a tense group of officers gathered around the chart table in Flag Plot of the *Coral Sea.* The admiral, his staff, Captain Russell and Lieutenant Campbell, the relay pilot, laid out and sifted the evidence.

"The first question," said the admiral, "is, can we handle this job ourselves or should we call out the whole fleet?"

"This ought to be a simple job," said one of the staff officers. "We should find them about 30 miles to the west. CIC says they tracked a radar blip in to a spot 30 miles west of us on course 115° [25° south of east]. It disappeared the same time the planes ditched. Our radar planes over the ship had an electronic distress signal 30 miles away at the same time. This distance checks, but there was no bearing. The pilots of the ditched planes had been briefed to operate to the west."

"The last transmission I got from Straychicks," said Lieutenant Campbell, "was, 'Look for us to the west.'"

"That makes it look pretty definite," said the admiral. "There can't be any doubt that they survived the ditching. With gas tanks almost empty and a 30-knot wind to ease the landing, the planes should float at least 15 minutes. We've got planes on the way to that area now and if they went down 30 miles west of us, we should have them in sight in a few minutes."

All hands around the chart table nodded agreement.

"Parker," said the admiral, turning to his operations officer, Commander O. M. Parker, of Austin, Texas, "you draw up all the messages necessary to sound the general alarm. Get a full-scale search operation going and have them ready to send if necessary."

The communications orderly handed the admiral the following, hot off the air from Admiral Gardner.

FROM: COMMANDER SIXTH FLEET
TO: COMMANDER CARRIER DIVISION SIX
        1325
YOU ARE DESIGNATED RESCUE COMMANDER X USE ANY SIXTH FLEET SHIPS REQUIRED X

In 10 more minutes it was obvious that the planes had not ditched exactly 30 miles to the west. A Banshee travels fast and glides far. Coming down from 30,000 feet to the surface, it can easily glide 75 miles. Draw a circle with a radius of 75 miles and you enclose an area of 17,000 square miles. The ditching point could not be considered pinpointed by any means.

The *Oriskany,* which had been exercising her CIC crew at anchor in Suda Bay by eavesdropping on *Coral Sea's* operations, now came through with this message:

WE HAD A RADAR PLOT WHICH DISAPPEARED AT EXACT TIME YOUR PLANE DITCHED IN POSITION FIFTY MILES NORTH OF YOU X

This was well within gliding range and tended to confirm the idea that the jets ditched not too far from home.

Meantime, the conferees in Flag Plot on the *Coral Sea* were piecing together some other fragments of evidence.

"They said their direction finder was reading 115°," said Lieutenant Campbell. "I couldn't swear to this, but I got the definite impression that they steered 115° until they went in."

"For how long?" asked Captain Russell.

"From 1230, when they were due over the ship, until they ditched at 1310—that's 40 minutes."

"Forty minutes at 400 knots would put them 270 miles east of the ship. It's almost inconceivable they would do that," said a staff officer.

"Yes, but if they figured everything right, they wouldn't have got lost," said another. "Maybe they missed us to the eastward in the first place. In which case they may be over 300 miles east of us now."

"Okay, Parker ," said the admiral. "Pull the plug. Call out the fleet, notify the British Air Sea Rescue outfits at Malta and Suez, and the Air Force at Tripoli. Broadcast the notice to all merchant ships."

The following message went out:

FROM: COMMANDER CARRIER DIVISION SIX
TO: COMMANDER SIXTH FLEET
          ORISKANY
          CORAL SEA
          DESTROYERS
          R.A.F. MALTA
          R.A.F. SUEZ
          USAF WHEELUS, TRIPOLI
          U.S. NAVY, PORT LYAUTEY, FRENCH MOROCCO
          1310

TWO JET AIRCRAFT DUE OVER CORAL SEA AT 1230 FAILED TO RETURN X OTHER PLANES IN VOICE COMMUNICATION WITH THEM UNTIL 1308 WHEN JETS DITCHED TOGETHER OUT OF GAS X CORAL SEA 1230 POSITION 40 MILES SOUTH-WEST OF WESTERN END OF CRETE X JETS WERE BRIEFED TO OPERATE WEST OF CORAL SEA X REQUEST AIR SEA RESCUE ASSISTANCE X

So began one of the biggest air-sea rescue operations ever conducted in the Mediterranean. It covered a stretch of salt water over 1,000 miles long, greater in area than the length of the combined states of Pennsylvania, Ohio, Indiana and Illinois. It involved two large aircraft carriers, a dozen destroyers, and shore-based planes of the U.S. Air Force, U.S. Navy, Royal Air Force, and Royal Greek Navy. It involved 1,100 hours of flying over more than a quarter of a million square miles. . . .

Shortly after the search got rolling, Commander Parker, operations officer of Commander Carrier Division Six, threw new light on the possibility that the planes might be far to the east. He pointed out that Jerusalem, over 600 miles to the east, had a homing station for commercial aircraft which was only one kilocycle removed from the frequency of the *Coral Sea's* homer. The identification sign of *Coral Sea's* homer was JV, that of Jerusalem JU. In Morse code V is • • • —, U is • • —. Could the missing jets have homed on Jerusalem instead of the *Coral Sea*? It seemed absurd—but, after all, they did get lost.

The following message went out:

FROM: COMMANDER CARRIER DIVISION SIX
TO: ALL SEARCH AGENCIES
            1430
EVIDENCE POINTS TO TWO EQUALLY LIKELY DITCHING POINTS ONE ABOUT THIRTY MILES WEST OF MY 1230 POSITION X THE OTHER OUT TO 200 MILES BEARING 115° TRUE X ORISKANY SEARCH AROUND FIRST POINT CORAL SEA AROUND SECOND X

By sunset, the carrier *Oriskany* was sitting on the first assumed ditching position and had thoroughly searched an area of 100-mile radius around it. The *Coral Sea* was combing the Mediterranean from Crete to the north coast of Africa, and working her way east toward the second point. Five destroyers in a 30-mile scouting line were sweeping down-course 115° from the 1230 position, and R.A.F. planes from Malta and Suez plus United States Air Force planes from Wheelus Field, Tripoli, were covering the sea west of Crete.

Up to sunset, nothing was sighted, but this didn't prove that the lost men were not in that area. In hazy weather, with the wind whipping the sea into a mass of whitecaps, it would be easy to fly over a tiny raft and not see it. That area would have to be combed several times before it could be declared empty.

During the night about 40 planes were in the air from the two carriers and the various shore bases. There were also 14 Navy ships and perhaps 20 merchantmen in the area.

As soon as the sun went down, business began picking up. It was a black, moonless night, so the gremlins got busy, and flashing lights and flares began sprouting all over the eastern Mediterranean.

FROM: COMMANDER DESTROYER SQUADRON TEN
TO: COMMANDER CARRIER DIVISION SIX
           2300
AT 2230 FLARES SIGHTED TO WEST X HAVE RUN DOWN THAT BEARING FOR 12 MILES WITHOUT RESULT X SUGGEST PLANES WITH FLARES SEARCH AHEAD OF ME X

FROM: COMMANDER DESTROYER TEN
TO: COMMANDER CARRIER DIVISION SIX
           0050
LOOKOUTS INCLUDING THREE OFFICERS INSIST TWO FLARES SIGHTED X UNLESS OTHERWISE DIRECTED WILL CONTINUE SEARCH THIS AREA TILL AFTER DAWN X

FROM: ORISKANY
TO: COMMANDER CARRIER DIVISION SIX
           0230
AT 0002 AIR FORCE 5580 REPORTED WEAK LIGHT ON WATER SENDING SOS AND STAYED WITH CONTACT X ORISKANY SENT TWO NIGHT SEARCH PLANES WITH FLARES X MERCHANT TANKER IN VICINITY CHANGED COURSE TOWARD FLARES USING SEARCHLIGHTS ON APPROACH X WAS SEEN TO LOWER BOAT AND PICK UP OBJECT RESEMBLING LIFE RAFT X COULD NOT DETERMINE IF PILOT WAS IN RAFT NOR IDENTITY OF TANKER X DESTROYER EN ROUTE TO SCENE X PLANES WILL STAY OVER TANKER TILL SHE ARRIVES X DO NOT EXPECT POSITIVE IDENTIFICATION TILL DAYLIGHT X

FROM: (UNIDENTIFIED SENDER)
TO: COMMANDER CARRIER DIVISION SIX
           0330
FOLLOWING INTERCEPTED ON INTERNATIONAL DISTRESS FREQUENCY FROM ESSO FAWLEY X HAVE FOUND NOTHING

YET X HAVE LOWERED BOAT BUT SEE NO TRACE OF
WRECKAGE X POSITION LATER X

The above messages, and others in similar vein, aroused strong
hopes that perhaps something definite would develop at sunrise.

Came the dawn and the gremlins vanished, leaving all concerned
gaping at an empty sea. The result of the night search was negative—
but as will appear later, the searchers hadn't heard the last of it yet. . . .

About an hour after sunup the following bombshell burst:

FROM: ORISKANY
TO: COMMANDER CARRIER DIVISION SIX
        0832
FOLLOWING RECEIVED FROM MALTA X TWO SURVIVORS ON
RAFT X AM CIRCLING AND WILL PICK UP X UNQUOTE HAVE
REQUESTED POSITION X

If words mean what the dictionary says they mean, this message
should have ended the search operations. There would seem no sense
in wasting fuel oil and gasoline on further operations when an airplane
was actually circling the missing pilots. But there was something about
this message that didn't quite ring true. Commander Carrier Division
Six got it thirdhand through Malta and *Oriskany,* no location was
given, the plane alleged to be in contact was not identified.

Commander Carrier Division Six decided to let the operation
continue for a while until confirmation of the good news came
through. . . .

Comes now another incident, not to be confused with the two
survivors on the raft:

FROM: MALTA
TO: COMMANDER CARRIER DIVISION SIX
        1245
FOLLOWING OVERHEARD FROM SUEZ ADDRESSED TO
ATHENS AT 1107 BY PLANE 60 MILES WEST OF CRETE QUOTE
SIGHTED RECTANGULAR LIFE RAFT, YELLOW COLOR, NO
SURVIVORS UNQUOTE REQUEST INSTRUCTIONS X

Oriskany was directed to pick up this alleged raft and check serial
numbers, if any. At the same time Commander Carrier Division Six
decided to kill the survivor rumor if possible.

FROM: COMMANDER CARRIER DIVISION SIX
TO: ALL SEARCH ENGINES
          1330
NO SURVIVORS HAVE YET BEEN SIGHTED X CONTINUE
SEARCH AS PREVIOUSLY PLANNED

Finally the mystery was cleared up:

FROM: WHEELUS
TO: COMMANDER CARRIER DIVISION SIX
          1345
LIFE RAFT WAS SIGHTED AT 2 : 30 A.M. X PLANE CIRCLED TILL
RAFT PICKED UP BY MERCHANT VESSEL X NO SURVIVORS X

It is now clear that the whole mix-up stemmed from the *Esso Fawley*
incident. A pilot from Wheelus, flying in the blackness, thought he saw
something on the surface and dropped a float light to mark the spot.

A light floating in the swells appears to blink because it disappears
periodically behind the swells.

An observer in the air with a good imagination can easily read SOS
into this blinking. So he keeps dropping more float lights to mark the
spot and calls the nearest merchant ship to the scene.

On arrival, the *Esso Fawley* lowered a two-man lifeboat which
naturally found the ocean littered with burned-out aircraft float lights.
While this boat was picking up the debris, our industrious friend in
the air popped off a parachute flare which was seen by every ship for
miles around and variously reported as a parachute flare, a Very-pistol
star, a skyrocket and a weak flashing light on the horizon.

By the light of this same flare our intrepid birdmen saw the *Esso
Fawley*'s lifeboat with two merchant seamen pulling the oars. So the
report flashed from one end of the Mediterranean to the other: "AM
CIRCLING LIFE RAFT WITH TWO SURVIVORS."

All this shows how an idle rumor, if it once gets started, can
snowball on a naval radio circuit just as fast as a rumor in a small
town—and get just as distorted. One careless transmission, overheard
and relayed a couple of times, can soon have everyone on the circuit
believing it to be gospel truth.

Fortunately, the search had gone on uninterrupted by the false
report. Deck crews and mechanics worked feverishly, servicing

airplanes, respotting carrier decks, and doing hurry-up up-air jobs
on planes which ordinarily would have gone into the hangar deck for a
leisurely overhaul. Pilots droned back and forth over the sea on search
plans which gave them corridors only a mile wide to scan. They wore
their eyes out eagerly searching every wave and ripple time and time
again. To insure thoroughness, the search area crept, rather than
swept, to the east as the afternoon wore on.

The scene of our story now shifts to a location which for the time
being can only be identified as somewhere in the Mediterranean. Two
Navy one-man life rafts are lashed together, drifting lazily in a northerly
breeze under the blazing afternoon sun.

The commander of this naval task group, whose flagship is the
port raft, is a lieutenant (junior grade) whom we will call Joe. The
commanding officer of the starboard raft, until 24 hours ago Joe's wing
man, is an ensign, hereafter referred to as Bill.

"Say, Joe," said Bill. "They've got *Kon-Tiki* in the library on the ship.
I'm going to draw it out and read it when we get back."

"Bill, I'm just as sorry as I can be about this," said Joe. "It was all my
fault."

"Aw, for gosh sakes, forget it, will you?" replied Bill.

"I never thought I could be so stupid," mused Joe. "We flew almost
a solid hour on course 115° at 400 knots. I don't know why I didn't
start an expanding square after 15 minutes like the book says to do.
We must be way the hell and gone southeast of Crete."

"Yeah," said Bill. "We went over all that about a dozen times before.
Remember? One thing they keep pounding into us all the time is that
you've got to believe your instruments, and our direction finders said
115° and the signal was getting stronger. You did what they're always
telling us to do."

"I know that," said Joe. "But I got hypnotized by just one
instrument. We also had a clock, an air-speed meter and a compass.
If I had paid some attention to them, we wouldn't be here now."

There followed a long pause during which Ensign Bill busied
himself tightening the moorings of the parachute sea anchor,
inspecting the lashings of the two rafts, squaring up the mast of
the kitchen screen radar reflector. "All secure and shipshape
in raft number two, sir," said Bill.

He continued: "So they don't find us for a week. This little solar still we've got is putting out more fresh water than we need. You can live for a month without food. They *will* find us eventually, you can bank on that. Now if we were Russians, it would be different. Uncle Joe would write us off 10 minutes after we were overdue and forget us. But this funny Navy of ours will keep on searching for at least a week after they are convinced that we crashed and went down with the planes. That's one of the reasons why they can get guys like us to fly off of carriers."

"I wonder what they'll do to us for losing a million dollars' worth of airplanes," mused Joe.

"Let's cross that bridge when we come to it," replied Bill.

"You know," Joe said, "I like this little mirror. It doesn't ever wear out. Now you take those eight smoke candles and the dye markers we've got, and after you use 'em, they're finished—we can't draw any more on this cruise. But as long as old Sol is shining up there, this little mirror will make flashes that can be seen a long way."

"You're absolutely right. Commander," said Bill facetiously. "Speaking of the sun reminds me, *we're* not the first aviators to wind up in the water around Crete."

"I guess not," said Joe. "Didn't old Belly Tank Bates off the *Midway* (Lieutenant Commander George B. Bates, of Philadelphia) go in around here somewhere last cruise?"

Bill suddenly shouted: "HEY . . . Don't look now, but I *think* I see a Banshee coming this way . . . I KNOW I see one—GIMME THAT MIRROR!"

As Bill almost goes overboard grabbing for the mirror, we now shift back to Flag Plot on the *Coral Sea*. For two hours, after the uproar over the two-survivors message subsided, Flag Plot was relatively quiet. At 1514, the staff officers were huddled around the chart table laying out tomorrow's search farther to the eastward when the squawkbox from Combat Information Center blared forth:

Combat to flag—Banshee No. 7 reports flashing light in sight on water

A dozen heads jammed around the squawkbox immediately. Then in quick succession:

1515

Combat to flag—Banshee No. 7 reports dye marker and smoke in sight . . .

1516

Combat to flag—Banshee No. 7 circling two rafts lashed together, wing tip tanks in vicinity, both survivors in good shape

From then on, the operation became a breeze as the rafts were only 84 miles from the *Coral Sea*. They were 350 miles east of the 1230 rendezvous for the previous day—just barely inside the search area laid out for the second day. Propeller planes relieved the jets to act as beacons over the raft and a destroyer took off at full speed for the spot, while *Coral Sea* recalled and landed the rest of her air group. Lieutenant (jg) G. R. Lewis, of Whittier, California, the jet pilot who sighted the rafts, had his hand shaken so much it was sore for a week.

Just before sunset, the destroyer *Stribling* picked up the two lost sheep and transferred them later by high line to the *Coral Sea*. Two destroyers remained at the spot for an hour or so picking up debris and tidying up the ocean before proceeding to Suda Bay.

As soon as the glad tidings were relayed to Commander Sixth Fleet, he followed the time-honored naval tradition for situations of this kind, by coming through with "a pat on the back and a kick in the pants":

FROM: COMMANDER SIXTH FLEET

TO: COMMANDER CARRIER DIVISION SIX

CONGRATULATIONS TO YOU AND YOUR STAFF ON THE PROMPTNESS OF INITIATING SEARCH OPERATIONS, THE VIGOR WITH WHICH CONDUCTED AND THE SOUND ASSUMPTIONS ON WHICH BASED X SUCCESS WAS WELL MERITED X

REQUEST FULL INVESTIGATION AND REPORT OF THE UNDERLYING CAUSES AND CIRCUMSTANCES OF THE DITCHING WHICH NECESSITATED THIS EXTENSIVE OPERATION NOT TO MENTION LOSS OF VALUABLE AIRCRAFT X

Before the downed pilots had been aboard five minutes, it was verified that they had indeed been on a pilgrimage to Jerusalem. So Commander Carrier Division Six replied:

FROM: COMMANDER CARRIER DIVISION SIX

TO: COMMANDER SIXTH FLEET

APPRECIATE VERY MUCH YOUR MESSAGE X DOWNED PILOTS MADE IT DIFFICULT FOR US BY VIOLATING THE OLD NAVY

RULE, WHEN IN DANGER OR IN DOUBT RUN IN CIRCLES
SCREAM AND SHOUT X THEY FLEW IN A STRAIGHT LINE AND
DIDN'T SAY MUCH X

Admiral Robert B. Carney, in Naples, Commander in Chief, North
East Atlantic and Mediterranean, wrote finis to the story with:

FROM: CINCNELM
TO: COMMANDER SIXTH FLEET
THAT WAS A GRAND RESCUE JOB X WELL DONE X

THE END

Admiral Ashore

Naval OFFICERS OFTEN discount the significance of their shore tours, and Gallery was no exception. Outside of his Pentagon assignment, he has comparatively little to say about the official duties he performed ashore as a senior officer. For instance, in his autobiography Gallery remarks that when assigned as commander, Naval Air Reserve Training Command in Glenview, Illinois, in late 1952, he typically flew from base to base throughout the country, inspected multitudes of reservists, and spoke to the press—but that's about all he has to say concerning this duty.[1] Gallery is somewhat more loquacious about his official activities in Puerto Rico, where in December of 1956 he was assigned as commander, Caribbean Sea Frontier.[2] This job did have some political and minor strategic importance. Still, his discussion of the "operational" activities he was involved in is very wry and dismissive.

He tells, for example, of the "lighting-bolt" rescue he planned for Richard Nixon when the vice president was mobbed in Venezuela in May of 1958—but then laments that the evolution never took place, as Nixon escaped his predicament through diplomacy.[3] Similarly with most of the other operational plans the "ComCarib" command meticulously put together. According to Gallery, these operations were either reasonable and forceful responses to real threats but were never enacted because the State Department was too timid to order them, or they were frantic scrambles ginned up to encounter threats that never really existed. An example of the latter involved the CIA's warning of a projected invasion of the Dominican Republic supposedly being mounted by Cuba. According to the message Gallery received, several good-sized fishing boats had been loaded with troops and equipment near northeast Cuba, and had begun sailing southward. The CIA believed the boats would land guerillas to destabilize Trujillo's regime. Obeying orders, Gallery sent his planes to monitor the boats' progress toward likely landing beaches in the Dominican Republic, and kept tabs on the boats' progress overnight. The next morning the boats kept coming, so (listening to Pentagon anxiety) Gallery also cancelled a nearby amphibious exercise and sent the marines on the way. When the fishing boats unaccountably bypassed the best beaches and kept moving, Gallery suddenly called the Coast Guard on a hunch, and found that both the CIA and Pentagon had misinterpreted the movements of a shrimp boat fleet from Tampa, Florida, that had just happened to pass near both Cuba and the Dominican Republic on its way to fertile shrimping grounds further south. For Gallery, this ludicrous episode typified the operational uses his Caribbean forces were customarily put to by Washington.[4]

But if little of official or operational significance took place, that doesn't mean that these two long tours, which ended Gallery's active service, were uninteresting or unimportant. For one thing, the Gallery family had a most engaging social life during this period. Dan was a major public figure in his hometown of Chicago, to begin with. Vee, Danny, and Connie all took parts in some of the official entertaining and many of Dan's visits throughout the city. Also, at about this time the naval connections of Dan's children grew to be of special interest to him. Jimmie had enlisted in the navy after high school, and Dan wanted him to go to the Naval Academy. Consequently Jimmie spent a period at the Naval Academy Preparatory School. However, he did not succeed in getting a Naval Academy appointment, and letters in the Gallery collection suggest that Dan got on his son's case about this. Indeed, Dan seems to have written Jimmie in the same blistering way his own father (Dan Senior) appears occasionally to have written to him. In any case, Jimmie finished his tour in the navy as a seabee, then left the service and married. A bit later Connie got married, too—to a naval supply officer.

Gallery demonstrates one of his wrestling holds to boxer Jack Dempsey.
According to Vee, Gallery loved Dempsey and Gene Tunney "because they were
fighters." This photo was probably taken on the occasion of a re-creation of the
famous Dempsey-Tunney "long-count" fight, an event staged at Soldier's Field
in Chicago in the 1950s. *U.S. Navy*

In 1954, while the family was still in Chicago, Danny also decided to
enlist. However, not only did he have no interest in the Naval Academy,
but he did not even want to attend boot camp at Great Lakes—for by
this time, his famous father was in charge there. So Danny told the
admiral he wanted to become a marine. Dan replied that he could go
into the marine corps *after* a tour in the navy. The upshot was that
Danny entered navy boot camp at San Diego instead of Great Lakes,
became a navy airman, and was sent to the fleet carrier *Intrepid*. During
this tour, incidentally, while the *Intrepid* was in the Med, Danny fell
down the forward elevator shaft from the flight deck to the hangar deck,

badly injuring his legs. Although hospitalized for several months and offered a discharge with disability pay, Danny declined, and he completed his four-year enlistment in VR-22, a heavy transport squadron. The family in the meantime had moved to San Juan, and Danny was pleased to be able to visit his father and mother in "Quarters A" when his squadron visited Puerto Rico. After Danny left the service in 1958 and married, the young couple spent their honeymoon in San Juan, too.[5]

Although not burdened professionally, both in Chicago and San Juan Dan engaged wholeheartedly in extensive collateral duties. Simply put, Gallery was a public affairs genius, and in both of his long shore tours as an admiral, Gallery used his position to forward unusual projects that were to have striking P.R. effects.

Gallery poses with his sons, Seaman Apprentice James J. Gallery and Daniel V. Gallery III, early 1950s. Each boy spent a tour in the navy as an enlisted man. *U.S. Navy*

Of course, even the short pieces Gallery had been writing aboard his carrier in the Mediterranean often had public relations implications, if only by helping to place a naval viewpoint squarely in the public eye. One of his stories had interesting ramifications when Gallery came to Chicago. In 1951 Gallery had published a short piece of fiction about a football game in *Sports Illustrated,* a story in which Navy defeats the national champion Army team by the aid of technology. In the story, the Navy quarterback wears a helmet fitted with a tiny receiver, and is coached to victory over the radio from the sidelines through a walkie-talkie.[6] Although the story sounded plausible enough—some people called for Navy to forfeit the Army-Navy trophy![7]—"The Secret of the Great Upset" was basically no more than a science fiction sports story dashed with some good old-fashioned Navy propaganda.

But George Halas, the fabled owner of the Chicago Bears and a friend of Gallery's, took it seriously. When Gallery came to Glenview to head the air reserves, Halas called him up to ask whether the technical concept was feasible. Gallery told him it was, and together they visited the Motorola Company to get the Chicago quarterback and defensive captain wired for sound. Somehow a couple of other teams in the league got wind of the idea, came up with helmet receivers of their own, and beat Chicago to the punch. Halas did run his team by electronics a couple of games that year. However, soon the NFL stepped in and outlawed the practice.[8] In the 1990s, of course, the NFL has reversed itself, and quarterbacks from Brett Favre to John Elway get signals through their helmets regularly. When people discuss the roots of this invention, George Halas is usually given credit. But Halas himself gave credit to Dan Gallery.

While in Chicago, Gallery continued to publish both short fiction and some prose, building an enthusiastic readership. But at this point writing was still a secondary activity for him. In particular, immediately upon arriving in Chicago and for a couple of years after, Gallery poured himself into a different kind of project, which had long been on his mind.

In 1945, after the surrender of Germany but before the end of the Pacific war, an American crew had sailed the *U-505* to East Coast and Gulf Coast ports as part of a war bond drive. (Son Danny remembers that you had to buy a war bond to get on the boat.[9]) When the war ended the navy moored it in Portsmouth, New Hampshire, and allowed it to rust. A year or two after the war, the navy set about scuttling the German submarines that had fallen into its hands (through surrender at sea or in port) and which by treaty with the Russians and British had to be destroyed. The navy made plans to sink the *U-505* along with the others. Gallery objected, pointing out that this submarine had been captured, not surrendered to the Allies, and hence was not bound by treaty to be destroyed. He won a temporary stay.[10] In succeeding years the navy tried again and again to "sell her as scrap"[11] or otherwise destroy the *U-505,* but Gallery kept an eye on the issue and always managed to block the process. He had conceived other plans for this particular vessel.

As early as 1947 Gallery determined to try to have the submarine brought to Chicago and parked alongside the great Museum of Science and Industry there. At that time his brother John personally broached the idea of making a permanent exhibition of the *U-505* to the museum's head, Maj. Lenox Lohr. Hearing this suggestion, "the Major lit up like a Christmas tree, pushed a button, and told his secretary to bring in the Museum's 'submarine file.' In this file there were letters going back twenty-four years asking the Navy Department to give them an obsolete submarine for display at the Museum." As it turns out, when endowing the museum in 1926, Julius Rosenwald had specified that he wanted it patterned after the Deutsche Museum in Munich—which, as an example of modern technology, had an actual submarine alongside.[12] Despite the museum's interest, the navy had never responded.

Even now, despite the museum's enthusiasm, the navy didn't see much virtue in Gallery's idea. In his oral history, Adm. Roy Benson recalls Gallery coming to see him, not too long after the war. At the time Benson was the staff captain in the Navy Department responsible for submarines.

> Well . . . he wanted to have that submarine brought to Chicago and there it would be a museum. I told him that I didn't think this was very feasible.
>
> I said, "Why don't you do as we did with the SQUALUS. The conning tower of the SQUALUS is sitting on top of a large block of concrete, but not the submarine itself. This is something they

can look at, and why don't you—or if you insist on having this submarine, why don't you take it down to Pensacola? It could be down there. . . .

Well, he wasn't very happy with me when he left and I hadn't given him any encouragement. I said, "It's impossible." [13]

Benson's response seems to have been typical of navy reaction, a stance which perplexed Gallery. In his opinion there was "an amazing lack of appreciation on the Navy's part of a golden opportunity in the field of public relations." [14] Actually, probably few navy people opposed Gallery's idea directly. In 1950, Gallery wrote to the navy's chief of information, Rear Adm. R. F. Hickey, to introduce him to the project. Gallery argued to the chief that "from a Navy Public Relations point of view this is hitting the jack pot—because it would give us a *permanent* exhibit in a part of the country where we need support, and in one of the biggest museums in the country ($1\frac{1}{2}$ million visitors per year)." But in the same letter he voiced this complaint:

Everybody in the Navy Department whom I have talked to about this in the past 4 years tells *me* that they think it is a swell idea. But I'm beginning to think that the minute I get out of their office they say "That SOB Gallery is trying to blow his own horn again", because up to date the Navy Department has thrown cold water on the project every time it has come up. [15]

Gallery's intuition was correct. Some navy officials thought that Gallery's desire for notoriety was getting out of line. Edward L. Beach indignantly remembers the projected move of the *U-505* to Chicago being labelled the "Dan Gallery aggrandizement project." [16] Had he heard that, Gallery would probably have been unfazed. In that same letter to Rear Admiral Hickey Gallery went on to say,

It seems to me that Navy Public Relations and CNO's attitude in this thing so far has been very short sighted. You just can't buy the sort of permanent favorable public relations that the Navy would get out of this thing, for any amount of money. [17]

Although Hickey apparently didn't help much, either, Gallery was undeterred. With the help of friends and officials in Chicago, he kept the idea alive, until in 1952 he found himself stationed in Glenview (near Chicago), now in a position personally to galvanize the Chicago community.

Again Gallery met official naval indifference, but in person and in writing he forcefully argued his case. One of the big issues, of course, was how to pay for this venture, with the navy's position being that it could not put forth a dime of its own. Gallery had successfully pressed for private donations, but he still wanted something from his own service. At one point Gallery went out of channels to try to get Senator Dirksen to influence the navy to tow the ship to Chicago and assume some minor repair expenses. For this he won an official reprimand.[18]

But under Gallery's championship, and with the enormous aid of individuals and groups throughout Chicago, the momentum behind the project eventually became irresistible. After an Act of Congress was passed that authorized the navy to give the submarine to Chicago (itself two years in the process), plans were formalized to tow the U-505 down the St. Lawrence, clean her up a bit, lift her out of the water and put her on the beach, move her across Lake Shore Drive, and park her beside Chicago's Museum of Science and Industry. It was a daunting project, but because of the enthusiastic support of all of Chicago's newspapers, many of its corporations, and countless individuals, Gallery succeeded spectacularly. As an example of the support received from the community, Gallery tells a story of his attempt to get the services of the only floating dry dock in the Great Lakes big enough to lift the U-505 out of the water and put it on the beach.

The owner of the dry dock was Mr. William P. Feeley. Although some of Feeley's own staff thought the dry dock wasn't big enough for the job, Gallery thought he knew better. One day the admiral and his chief engineer, Seth Gooder—who had volunteered a year of his own time to the project, having retired shortly before—called on Mr. Feeley to try to talk him into participating.

> He was a poker-faced gentleman who sat back and listened for a long time saying nothing and indicating nothing. I gave him an earnest pitch about the civic aspects of the project, benefits to the school kids, etc., and then Gooder went through all the engineering angles proving mathematically that his drydock could handle this

job. When we got through I felt it had all been a waste of time and we had made no impression, Mr. Feeley sat in silence at the head of the table for a few minutes and then fixed a cold eye on us and said, "Just what sort of proposition did you want to make to us for the use of our drydock?"

I figured we had lost the battle and there was no use wasting time beating around the bush. I said, "Mr. Feeley, we would like to borrow your drydock for six weeks." Mr. Feeley didn't bat an eye, "Okay," he said, "you can have it."[19]

Though "poker-faced Feeley" may have had more on his mind than mere generosity—his advertising literature for years afterward featured photos of his dry dock supporting the *U-505*—still, his loan was typical of the support Gallery received in Chicago.

The submarine was towed up the St. Lawrence River (by tugs whose companies had donated their services) and across the Great Lakes in the summer of 1954, under the supervision of former *Guadalcanal* chief engineer (and original *U-505* salvage party leader) Earl Trosino, and with Gallery personally riding the tugs part-way. Preparations made to get the submarine alongside the museum included building a steel cradle to fit around the vessel for its overland transport, dredging a five-hundred-foot channel out into the lake, and building a pier capable of carrying a thousand tons to receive the submarine. The dry dock lifted the submarine up to the pier on August 13. At 7:00 P.M. on September 3, Lake Shore Drive was blocked off, and the cradle with submarine was dragged on rail ties across the road at a rate of some eight inches per minute, an operation reportedly witnessed by some fifteen thousand Chicagoans. The submarine had crossed the drive by 4:15 the next morning, in time for rush hour, and then it was moved three hundred feet further to be installed on a concrete foundation alongside the museum.

After that, the submarine was cleaned more thoroughly, holes (for access) were cut into the pressure hull, covered passageways were rigged, connecting the submarine to the museum, and overall the process of readying the boat for the public began. This too was a major effort, as the navy had afforded the vessel virtually no maintenance for the nine years since the war, and souvenir hunters had stripped the boat of anything movable. As a gambit to provide at least some of the missing equipment, gauges, and name plates, Major Lohr of the museum had written the German firms that had originally helped build the submarine, asking for replacements. Astonishingly, they all responded with the equipment requested. Typically the firms replied that, as long as the Americans had the vessel, they wanted it to be a credit to German technology.[20] They did stipulate that in displays they wanted the ship to be termed a "German," not a "Nazi," submarine. The museum changed its signs and literature accordingly.[21]

The *U-505* was dedicated on September 25, 1964, as a memorial to the 55,000 Americans who had lost their lives at sea in World War II. Gallery got his friend Arthur Godfrey (a radioman during the war, and now a naval reserve pilot) to be master of ceremonies, and Fleet Adm. Bull Halsey as the principal speaker, while Bishop Chris Weldon (former chaplain of the *Guadalcanal*) said the prayers. Nine members of the *Pillsbury*'s boarding party sat on the speaker's stand during the ceremony. Despite the navy's official disinterest up to this point, Secretary of the Navy Charles Thomas also was a member of the audience. But, then, Thomas's son Hayward had served as an engineering officer on the *Guadalcanal*.

The submarine immediately became the museum's most popular exhibit, and has maintained its popularity since. In fact, the *U-505* display has more than justified Gallery's faith in its unique public relations value. As of 1998, about twenty-four million visitors had gone through the *U-505*.[22]

This was Gallery's great project in Chicago, and of course it stemmed from his wartime success years earlier. In contrast, one of his major innovations while stationed in San Juan from late 1956 to 1960 was invented on the spot. In 1957 Gallery was in Trinidad during the carnival, and dozens of steel drum bands studded the carnival parade. He was enormously taken by them.

What are steel drums? Gallery briefly described them:

> Steel drums originated right after the war in Trinidad, where
> the natives have rhythm and harmony in their souls but can't afford
> to buy musical instruments. The waterfront musicians down there

The *U-505* rides its cradle on the beach of Lake Michigan, awaiting its trip
across the outer drive and its final placement in front of the Museum of Science
and Industry. *U.S. Navy*

discovered that by taking a fifty-gallon oil drum and grooving,
"punging," tempering, and tuning the top, one can produce an array
of musical notes. The "ping-pong," or melody, drums have a range
of an octave and a half. In the very low registers a drum can be used
for only two or three notes, but with an array of five drums, the bass
player can cover the range of the bass viol. Between the base at one
end of the scale and the ping pong at the other are the "tune booms,"
"seconds," and "guitar pans," in an array of twenty-one drums for a
good steel band.[23]

Gallery decided to buy a set of drums, and have his navy band learn to play them. So he sent for his bandmaster:

> He didn't know what a steel drum was. So I explained to him. He looked at me as if I were nuts. But, being a good Navy Chief he just said, "Aye, aye sir." He told me later that he had just become eligible for retirement and he figured, "What the hell. I'll have a look at this deal, and if I don't like it, I'll retire."[24]

When the drums were ready a few weeks later, Gallery sent the band to Trinidad for a week to learn how to play. Wandering about the waterfront, the navy people began to pick things up, but the local musicians scoffed. No one could learn to play steel drums in so short a time—it would take three months, at a minimum. Some local band members argued that only natives could really figure it out.

The navy's "Steel Band," organized by Gallery, performs at Carnival time in Antigua in 1957. Each circle as identified on the drum represents a different note—the sailors read the notes as identified on the inside surfaces. *U.S. Navy*

At the end of the week, the bandmaster invited some of those experts to the sea plane hangar where the navy band was playing its last rehearsal.

> When the boys blasted off on "Happy Wanderer" with a real Trinidad beat the jaws of all the local musicians dropped. At the end of the piece one of the locals happened to look up at the wall of the hangar. There the Chief had written on a blackboard the parts for the various drums. The local pointed to it and said, "Aw hell— you guys can read music."
> Unfair competition![25]

According to Gallery, his boys ended up wanting to abandon all their regular instruments and only play steel drums from then on. Perhaps this was an exaggeration, but it is true that his band came to excel on pieces ranging from "Steam Pipe Rhumba" to Gounod's "Ave Maria." Within a year or so they had made a record for Decca ("Pandemonia") and played for thousands at the World's Fair at Brussels (the band was the only U.S. exhibit held over for a second week there[26]). They would have played for the Pope, too, but Vatican approval came only after the band had returned to the States.

The show was in demand for state fairs and navy parties throughout the country. Gallery used it locally to entertain visitors to San Juan, including the vice chief of Naval Operations, the heir apparent to the Spanish throne, Winston Churchill and his wife, and many governors and senators who happened to come through, or who were official guests. (As the senior federal official in San Juan, Gallery had many diplomatic obligations, especially in the winter; he offered his guest house to visitors ranging from the secretary of the navy and members of the White House staff to celebrities like Herman Wouk, C. S. Forester, and Joe E. Brown.[27]) On one occasion, "Admiral Dan's Steel Band" briefly captivated President Eisenhower when he visited the local air base.[28]

Gallery also corresponded widely about his band. He wrote his friend Rudy Onsrud, president of a Chicago machine works, suggesting Rudy put the drums in production.[29] He also wrote the musician Pete Seeger, because he had heard Seeger was playing and even manufacturing the instrument. Seeger responded that while his family and neighbors played together occasionally and his students at UCLA put on a short

Gallery shows off his steel band to President Eisenhower on the president's overnight stop in Puerto Rico. *U.S. Navy*

performance, these informal bands were very small, knew only two or three songs, and were short-lived. Seeger also said he was trying to make some steel pans personally, as no one in the country was making them—but he had not yet succeeded at it.[30]

Like Seeger, Gallery personally attempted to manufacture a steel drum. He wanted to encourage his own musicians not only to play but also to make and tune their instruments. So he read all the literature he could find on converting empty oil drums into musical instruments. On a weekend, with a drum emptied of oil, cut in half, and shipped to his quarters by his Supply Department, Gallery tried his hand at it:

> The first step in making a drum is to dish in the barrel head and make it concave. I tapped around the barrel head lightly with a small hammer as per instructions but this had no noticeable effect. So I tapped harder and this did no good either. So I sent out for a

bigger hammer, and then a bigger one. One sledge led to another with no apparent result, finally the machine shop had no bigger sledges so they got the weekend duty section to saw about 16″ off the end of a telegraph pole, stuck a 5 foot handle into it and sent that out.

When I clouted that goddam barrel head with that one we began to get somewhere.

But after six hours, a bloody thumb, and blisters on both hands, all he could get was "clunks" on the drum he had prepared according to the instructions.

Later, when in Trinidad on other business, Gallery stopped in to talk to drummakers. He found there were *different kinds* of steel drums, from very light ones to extra heavy ones meant to be dropped out of aircraft supplying the DEW line in northern Canada. He realized what had happened.

When the boys in the Supply Department heard that I wanted an empty oil drum they figured "nothing but the best is good enough for the Admiral." So they finally sent me out one of those sons of bitches made out of special steel designed to be dropped full of oil from a jet airplane at 5000 feet without busting open.

I might just as well have spent that weekend trying to make a ping pong drum out of a piece of case hardened steel plate![31]

It's clear that when Gallery got interested in a project, he put his whole soul into it.

Gallery's band was a great success, not only in the three years Gallery remained in Puerto Rico, but ever since. Right after Gallery left, the band made a highly successful goodwill tour of South America. In 1971 the band's very full schedule included Busch Gardens and Disney World, among other locations in this country and abroad.[32] Inquiries in 1997 (the band's fortieth year) indicated that the U.S. Navy Steel Band had moved its headquarters to New Orleans but continues to play all over the country (and occasionally overseas) and at all kinds of festivities, including state fairs, ethnic festivals, schools, clinics, and arts and heritage activities. Still a unique organization, it continues in its own way to promote what all navy bands promote—navy awareness and navy recruiting.[33]

The other special naval project Gallery set to work on in San Juan was not an activity inspired only by the admiral's Caribbean experience; instead, it had roots in a lifelong interest of Gallery's—the sport of base-ball (including softball). It is worth recounting his lifelong experience with this pastime.

As a child Dan had sold scorecards at Comiskey Park,[34] and he had played for the St. Ignatius High School team. He had to settle for wrestling at Annapolis, at which sport (paradoxically) he excelled. But he did play intramural baseball there, and continued to play ball when commissioned. While aboard the *Stevens* he reported to his dad that he was pitching on the ship's team,[35] and a bit later said that he had broken a small bone in his left foot sliding into base.[36] Later, while on the *Pittsburgh,* Dan captained the baseball team that played at Cairo in early 1923 and that also played in Chatham, England, in Baltic ports, and in Amsterdam. Dan's father's log reports that his son's team won the "championship of Constantinople" (probably a competition among military teams) when the ship was there.[37]

Dan also played while stationed aboard the *Idaho* in the mid-1920s. In the *Idaho Yarn* we find this curious entry about his pitching—probably penned by Dan himself:

Gallery twirled in masterly style for the ward room, holding the J.O.'s to sixty scattered hits, and being invincible in all except the 1st, 2nd, 4th, 6th, and 7th innings.[38]

Later, he played ball while in flight training.[39] In 1937, while commanding Scouting Squadron 4 on the *Saratoga,* Dan reports that he has dislocated his shoulder in a game. He then comments on his reasons for continuing to participate in the sport:

I have been playing regularly for the last two years for two reasons: (1) because I like the game, and (2) because I think it is good for the squadron morale to have the skipper get out and play on the team—especially when he is able to say to the crew "any of you guys that can do a better job at third base can have my suit."[40]

Even during wartime in the 1940s we find him on the diamond. In Iceland, for instance,

I played third base on the officers' team; and the sailor and marine umpires took great delight in calling all the close ones against me, just to hear me squawk, and to be able to say, very, very respectfully, of course, "Cap'n, sir, if you don't shut up, I'll have to heave you out of the game, sir." [41]

Sometime during the war he also organized baseball back on his own farm. His son Danny remembers his father erecting a net for the catcher, a number of jeeps pulling up, and their occupants piling out onto the grass to play ball. [42] Dan may also have played some in port with the *Guadalcanal* crew, but when he took over the *Hancock,* he found a way to make baseball a part of the ship's life, *underway.* He staged a game on the carrier's flight deck right in Tokyo Bay, and forced his tired crew to play even though they didn't feel much like it. (His men came to appreciate it later.) Then, when *Hancock* was assigned to bring service members home from the Pacific, Gallery ordered that baseball be a part of the daily routine, with passengers using the "field" during working

Gallery frequently played baseball with his men, and he loved to argue with the umpire—especially when the umpire was from his own unit. Here the ump is a third-class petty officer. *Gallery Papers, U.S. Naval Academy, Nimitz Library*

hours, and the ship's company taking over after "secure." A press release that Gallery sent off—complete with diagram and photographs— describes the physical circumstances, beginning with the "grey monster" found in right field.

> Right field is blocked by the island structure, about 90 feet from home plate. . . . A line drive off the island structure is in play, and usually worth only a single; a ball which lodges in the island goes for two bases.
>
> Centerfield is the target for long distance swingers. A low netting around the gun mounts is the only obstruction there, and a hard-hit fly to that area will go for four bases. Left field is a different matter —it's over 400 feet to the end of the flight deck; teams at field usually concentrate their outfielders in this area.
>
> A special backstop cage has been built to minimize the loss of foul balls overboard. . . . If a pitcher is wild enough to deliver a pitch over the backstop, the batter gets a homerun and the pitcher is automatically out of the game.[43]

The release claimed that when passengers were aboard, most games drew a thousand spectators. Once, a game between a team of nurse passengers and ship's company officers—who batted left-handed to even up the contest—drew a crowd estimated at two thousand. The ship's officers (who no doubt included the ship's captain) lost the game 10–9, in extra innings.[44]

Even when Gallery made admiral, he continued playing. He was keeping careful track of his batting averages on both the OpDevFor team in late 1950 and then in early 1951 while he was ComCarDivSix in the Mediterranean. We find that he was hitting as high as .475 in Norfolk (second highest on the team at the top of an eight-team league), but in the Med he had slipped to .350.[45] Incidentally, it is not by happenstance that through all Gallery's forty-some years of playing ball, we most often find him playing *third base*. Rather than attracting athletes with great finesse, the "hot corner" typically draws a pugnacious guy who loves to be in the middle of the action, someone always looking for a challenge, and maybe looking for the spotlight, too. It was Gallery's natural position.

After his last operational tour, Gallery mainly became a fan. When he came to Chicago, the White Sox once took Gallery into the Yankee dugout and introduced him to Casey Stengel. That same day they stole Yankee signs with a Japanese spyglass Gallery had loaned them (they signalled curves and fast balls to their batters by altering electric numbers on the scoreboard).[46] About the same time Dan also wrote another article for *Sports Illustrated*,[47] this one about loopholes in the baseball rules, a subject in which he had long been interested; he had written Commissioner Landis about problems with the rules even while on wartime duty in Iceland![48] In the article Gallery suggested (among other things) that a runner could field an easy doubleplay ball hit to a fielder, and toss it to the umpire. Gallery claimed that, under the rules, though the runner would be out, the hitter would be safe at first, and the runner would have broken up a double play. (As the admiral pointed out, Jackie Robinson had already craftily allowed himself to be *hit* by a batted ball to break up a double play; for a runner to actually *field* the ball was taking things one step further.)

Gallery's essay provoked a sharp response. In an article in *Sporting News,* both the head of baseball's rules committee and the supervisor of American League umpires (Cal Hubbard) were quoted defending the rules book, and the publisher of the magazine also argued against Gallery's case. These authorities claimed either that such an incident would never happen, or if it did the umpires would probably rule it a double play anyway.

However, in a subsequent Cincinnati-Milwaukee game on April 21, 1957, Cincinnati third baseman Don Hoak grabbed a batted ball and in effect retired himself, breaking up a double play in the process. The umpire ruled that only Hoak was out. Heads of both major leagues felt impelled immediately to meet and telegraph all league umpires that, in the future, both runners would be called out for interference. In reporting this whole episode, *Sports Illustrated* commented by headline, "The Admiral Laughs Last."[49]

Also while stationed in his home town, Gallery got interested in the aerodynamic forces governing pitched fast balls and curves, and he wrote another article for *Sports Illustrated* on this matter.[50] The idea was basically that the density of the air affected a curve ball's break in the same way that it affected the "lift" on the wings of an airplane. If the same plane with the same load would take 3,900 feet to get off the runway on a cold dry day with high barometer in Boston, but would take 6,900 feet on a hot humid day with low barometer in Kansas City, it stood to reason that a curve ball would also vary greatly in its effectiveness, depending on the density of the air. Gallery half-seriously suggested that there ought to be assistant coaches for aerodynamics in baseball, experts who would help the manager select the pitcher whose "junk" was best suited to prevailing weather conditions. Later, he even proposed getting White Sox pitchers into the wind tunnels of the National Advisory Commission on Aeronautics in Cleveland, to have them run their catalogues of sliders, curves, knucklers, and fast balls through varying densities of air.[51] However, he was transferred to San Juan (Gallery suspected by Yankee manipulation) before he could get the experiment conducted.

Although most of Gallery's baseball interest in Chicago was not formally connected to his navy work, he did sponsor a local navy club. This club played for recreational and benevolent purposes—but it inevitably engaged Gallery's emotions. In May of 1956 Gallery wrote a letter to Rear Adm. J. P. Womble, Jr., commander of the Service Force, Atlantic Fleet:

> Here in Chicago, my ball team at the NAS Glenview plays an annual series with the Chicago Police, the proceeds of which go to the Police Benevolent Fund which takes care of the widows and children of policemen killed in line of duty. We make about $150,000 a year for them out of this and without this the fund would go broke in six months. As a result, the Navy stands ace high with the Chicago cops. . . .
>
> The only trouble with this series is the goddamn cops have beaten us 5 years in a row and I'm sick and tired of it.

Gallery knew that Johnny Podres, who the year before had pitched the last game of the World Series for the victorious Brooklyn Dodgers (and who was voted MVP of the series), would be assigned to Womble's Norfolk staff in June. Indeed, Podres spent a whole year in the navy despite his professional contract, and thus was completely out of pro ball for the 1956 season. (Podres was at the very height of his abilities at this time, incidentally; his 1957 ERA was the lowest of his career). Gallery wanted to borrow Podres to pitch one game for the navy team against the police—he'd furnish air transportation both ways, and would be "forever grateful" to Womble for helping him out.[52]

In his response, Womble seems reluctant, and refers Gallery up the chain. Gallery apparently received one or more negative answers to further inquiries. But as usual, he pressed the issue—and eventually got his man. In a later letter to another correspondent, Gallery adds this note:

> P.S.   The Cops beat us again. Podres pitched five innings, allowed one scratch hit, walked none, struck out 9. We went into the 9th with a 4 to 0 lead and then the roof fell in on us. Final Cops 12 – Navy 7.[53]

The cops, of course, had been delighted to take their bats against a great professional, and Gallery—always alert to public relations potential— had advertised the episode widely. This was vintage Gallery as he grew in seniority: always keeping an eye out for ways to further the navy's presence and image (and perhaps his own into the bargain), and to have a great time doing it.

ONCE HE GOT to San Juan in late 1956, Gallery put his naval staff into the baseball business in a big way. Although baseball had long been a passion in Puerto Rico (as throughout much of Latin America), there were no Little Leagues on the island, and at the same time there were many areas infested with poverty. Seeing both a need and opportunity, and drawing on his friendship with the "lady mayor" of San Juan, Doña Felicia Rincon De Gautier (who consistently helped him keep his sailors out of trouble), Gallery quickly went to work.

Little League in San Juan

I have been in baseball all my life, and in San Juan, I was Commissioner of Little League Baseball for Latin America.

There were no Little Leagues in Puerto Rico when I got there. But it seemed an ideal place to start some because the Puerto Ricans are rabid *beisbol fanaticos,* you can play all year round there, and the population explosion supplies plenty of little ballplayers.

With the help of Donna Felicia, the Rotary and Lions clubs, and many generous citizens we organized twenty Little Leagues. By the time I left we had eighty teams with 1,200 kids in uniform playing in official leagues. In 1959, Puerto Rico nosed out Venezuela for the Latin-American championship and played at Williamsport, Pennsylvania, in the tourney for the world's championship.

Most of our leagues were in the slum areas and in housing projects, which are the next step above the slums. We concentrated on them because obviously this was where we could do the most good. Many of the kids in those areas had nothing to do in their spare time except learn how to steal.

I financed the leagues by putting the bite on well-heeled citizens. Donna Felicia dug up managers and league officials for me, the Naval Station laid out six Little League fields and we were in business. I asked fifteen individuals for $1,600 each, the amount needed to finance one league. Although many of them didn't know me from Abner Doubleday not one turned me down.

The day we issued the first sets of uniforms to the slum kids, I had expected a mob of tough ragamuffins to show up. But Donna Felicia didn't want the kids to be embarrassed, so she fitted them out with new T-shirts and clean dungaree pants. They were all overawed at being allowed on the Naval Station and behaved like a bunch of choirboys. Their eyes nearly popped out of their heads when they received uniforms that were duplicates of those of the Yankees, Braves, Pirates, and the rest. And when they got brand-new gloves it made them believe in Santa Claus again. After a week I had to issue strict orders that uniforms could be worn only when playing ball. The kids had been strutting around their neighborhoods wearing uniforms all day long every day.

I can't produce statistics to show just how much good the Little League program did. But cops and parish priests told me it did "*mucho* plenty." Obviously it gave 1,200 potential juvenile delinquents something to do which kept them too busy, at least while the games were in progress, to commit any major felonies—except on the ball

Gallery roots from the dugout alongside his Puerto Rican Little Leaguers.
U.S. Navy

field. I think in addition we taught the kids something about law, order, and respect for authority.

Anyone associated with the Little League program in the U.S. knows that it has its problems, disgruntled parents being one of the biggest. We had all the usual ones in Puerto Rico, plus some special ones. I soon found out that each Puerto Rican kid had three birth certificates: his correct one which he hardly ever used for anything; a second one, which made him a couple of years older so he could get a job; and a third, which shaved a couple of years off his age so he could play in Little League.

I had to "confiscate" twenty games and deprive a team of the championship before we finally corrected this practice and got everybody to use the correct birth certificate.

Puerto Ricans are extremely competitive, and at first, our games had a tendency to break up in riots with the losing team trying to lynch the winners and the umpires. By constant patient preaching, confiscating a few games, and suspending wild-eyed managers, I finally got things to the point where riots were the exception rather than the rule. By the time I left Puerto Rico there was still an attitude of smoldering hatred and contempt for the opposition and umpires. But it was an undercurrent rather than an open, raging storm. At the end of a game the opposing teams would give each other a reluctant cheer and go home muttering curses more or less quietly.

I found out that although managers and league officials were inclined to go berserk on the field when something displeased them, they were reasonable when I got them into my office after they simmered down. When I confiscated games or suspended offenders they took it with good grace, because they knew I was the same kind of son-of-a-bitch with everybody.

I had to suspend one whole league for "unsportsmanlike conduct," which is a mealy-mouthed way of saying assault, battery, and attempted murder. When I left Puerto Rico, this league, which was located in a housing project where mostly woodworkers lived, presented me with a set of hand-carved rum goblets.

Little League was a lot of work, although just between you and me I "let" my staff do most of it. But it was also a lot of fun. I used to get a great bang when I drove around town in my official car and shoeshine boys would stop work, wave, and yell *"Almirante GOLAREE!"*

Autobiographer

GALLERY WAS SHOCKED when the Soviet Union launched Sputnik in late 1957. Still serving as commander, Caribbean Sea Frontier, he wrote Arleigh Burke and offered the CNO help with guided missiles— if there were a relevant billet. Burke searched, but found none.[1] This negative was to be prophetic of 1960, when Gallery's tour in Puerto Rico drew to a close. According to Gallery, as Burke had unsuccessfully nominated him for several three-star jobs before, so the CNO first attempted to get him a billet as chief of the Military Assistance Group in Germany.[2] It may be so. But in January of 1960 Burke wrote Gallery a relatively long letter explaining that because the new chief would have to have a great deal of tact, the odds were not in Gallery's favor. As Burke put it, in obvious understatement, "You are a little bit tempestuous and that is known to the other services."[3] After an army general got the job, Admiral Burke called Gallery in.

> [He] sent for me and gave me a pep talk about requesting retirement to make room for some up-and-coming captain. The CNO was not completely successful in selling me this bill of goods. After all, when I was an up-and-coming captain, no old poops had retired early just to make room for me.[4]

With three years to go before mandatory retirement age, Gallery decided to play a "poker game" with the Bureau of Personnel, hoping a good billet might eventually be offered him. But then he failed his annual physical examination. In September of 1960 Gallery unceremoniously retired, after over forty years of commissioned service.

Retirement took Gallery a bit by surprise. He moved back with Vee to his Virginia farmhouse, and didn't immediately strike off in another direction. He was almost sixty, to be sure, and there was no reason he shouldn't take it easy. But he was still full of energy, and was confident he yet had much to contribute. Soon he got himself a consultant job with the New York firm of Kollman Instruments (a position he kept for two or three years), and he continued to maintain an active correspondence. But just as he had apparently done relatively little writing while in Puerto Rico, so apparently he didn't immediately turn to writing now.

Dan and Vee at their Virginia farmhouse near Fairfax, Virginia, after Dan's retirement. *Courtesy of Mrs. Daniel V. Gallery*

There is at least one good reason for this. The disorientation that naturally might occur upon an abrupt halt to a very active and public career was exacerbated in Gallery's case. A manageable but undeniable problem that he had pretty much controlled throughout his naval service had ample opportunity to develop now—an addiction to alcohol.

If Dan had not learned to drink heavily as a midshipman or in his first two blackshoe tours (we have little evidence about this), he had ample opportunity to swim in the stuff when on his *Pittsburgh* cruise. Any time Gallery and his pals went to parties or bars on the beach—which seems to have been almost every day when not on watch or underway—they found liquor at every hand, and they seem almost always to have heavily indulged.[5] While "peer pressure" was no doubt involved, Gallery seems to have had few inhibitions to overcome. Rather than a sinful vice that was fascinating despite one's better judgment, liquor seemed to have presented itself to Dan simply as a new and rather a wonderful aspect of experience. He just liked alcohol (of all kinds) a bit too much.

While an aviator in Pensacola and after, Gallery resumed (or continued) the habit. As Vee Gallery commented, "when we were young, my goodness—the parties. . . . They drank the hard stuff, and you carried them home." You certainly *drove* them home. According to his wife, Dan was similarly addicted to smoking, and never paid much attention to the speed limits either, for that matter.[6]

Gallery really had known all along that this periodic heavy indulgence in drinking was problematic. In his 1923 diary he reports more than once during his European cruise that he has put himself on the "water wagon"—but we also find there that he never stayed on the wagon for long. After he married, he occasionally backed off again. For instance, he successively writes his dad: "I'm on the wagon, for the duration of Lent at least" (February 15, 1929); "I'm still on the wagon" (March 11, 1929); and "I'm still up the pole" (December 17, 1930). Apparently he kept his problem pretty much in hand after that, for there is little mention of this kind of problem in the letters from the late 1930s, nor in his Iceland diary of early 1942. Although between seagoing assignments he had occasional problems, he once wrote his nephew Phil that he had never mixed alcohol and flying.[7]

As Dan took over admiral's billets, with substantial social responsibilities, he became more susceptible. We've already cited Dan's downing a bottle of Scotch with Prince Philip during his Mediterranean tour, and the habit continued during subsequent shore tours. Especially in Puerto Rico, where the job itself required extensive entertainment of visiting and vacationing dignitaries, the booze flowed freely. Dan later explained to his brother Bill that for the last five years of his career, "I was drinking too much (for *me*) and I knew it."[8]

So it is quite natural that the habit would eventually overtake Dan at the conclusion of his naval career. In January of 1964, Gallery had to write a letter of explanation to an official at Kollman Instruments (the return address is an alcoholic treatment center). He speaks in his characteristically forthright, upfront way:

> The reason for the snafu on the meeting . . . was that I got plastered and failed to get the word on a change in arrangements. . . .
>
> . . . I'm one of those guys who if he takes one drink feels he has to finish the bottle. My pattern has been, bone dry for 4 to 6 weeks at a crack, then a bender lasting 3 or 4 days and then up the pole again.
>
> After kidding myself for much too long that I was getting away with this and it was getting better I have finally faced facts and taken the big step that all alcoholics must take sooner or later or else go down the drain—admit you are licked and give the stuff up permanently and completely.[9]

Overall, this drinking problem seems a characteristic outgrowth of Dan's extremely active life. He drank hard, drove fast, smoked hard, played (baseball) hard, and was addicted to the daring and thrills of flying, too. He also loved a party and a good time with his friends. Given his early and rather substantial introduction to social drinking in Europe, it would have been somewhat remarkable for him *not* eventually to have run into difficulties of this kind. Once he fully faced his problem (with the help of Alcoholics Anonymous), he pretty much solved it. In a letter to his brother Bill written in 1967, Gallery says that "I've been bone dry for a little over 2 years now, haven't missed the stuff a damn bit, and have done a bit better without it."[10] Gallery even wrote a brief article about conquering his drinking problem, but never got it published.

While fighting and winning this battle, too, sometime in the early to mid-1960s Gallery decided again to try his hand at that subcareer of writing he had first embarked upon some fifteen years before. As a writer, Gallery would now be in a somewhat different situation than before. In his various naval incarnations—as an expert seaman and flier, a combat leader, a senior executive, and a prominent navy spokesman—people had listened to him partly because of his official navy position. On retirement he would not carry so much automatic sway. Still, he had already became a nationally-known author in three major genres, and he would soon follow up on his earlier efforts in each of these fields. In the next three chapters we'll consider Gallery's efforts in autobiographical writing, in fiction, and in controversy. In each case we'll first look at works he wrote while on active duty, then consider what he wrote after retirement, seeing his writing career in perspective. We'll begin with autobiography.

It is not surprising that a senior officer would turn to autobiography soon after his career was over, but for Gallery this field had already become a kind of subspecialty. He had first become widely known with his *Saturday Evening Post* article about the capture of the *U-505,* and his description of his Iceland experiences (one of the next pieces he wrote) added to his reputation. Gallery's success with these articles encouraged him to more fully explore this genre, which he would find a natural medium for his writing talent. Near the end of his tour at the Pentagon, even as he was concurrently arguing against the Air Force Association in short essays and beginning to write some short fiction, too, Gallery began to draft a book-length autobiographical work to be named *Clear the Decks!,* which was published in 1951.

This book is an expansion of his earlier two articles into a full-length work on his wartime experience in the Atlantic. As in most of his autobiographical writing, Gallery incorporated his existing pieces pretty much directly into this book, and to that extent his stories lose some freshness in the retelling (at least to readers familiar with them). But while scanning events from his arrival at Iceland in 1942 to his capture of the *U-505* in 1944, Gallery related many stories he hadn't yet told in print. Some of these were experiences Gallery had heard others recount. There was, for example, the story of a tiny harbor tug, the USS *Redwing*:

> She showed up in Reykjavik, Iceland in December, 1941, twenty-three days out from Argentia, Newfoundland, having clawed her way through the North Atlantic blizzard to get there. Whoever ordered her up to Iceland should have been court-martialed. She had no business outside the inner harbor of Boston in the wintertime, and she nearly foundered several times in the howling gales and mountainous seas she encountered. Her crew actually kept her afloat by bailing with buckets. I sat in the officers' club in Iceland and listened to her skipper's story of that voyage in popeyed amazement. When he finished, I asked, "Wasn't your crew scared stiff when they had to bail?"
>
> "No," he said. "They were all pretty green, so I told them that bailing ship was a routine maneuver in the Navy!" [11]

Gallery drew the lesson that young sailors can sometimes do more than old salts, precisely because they don't have long-ingrained expectations.

At other points in *Clear the Decks!* Gallery narrates new stories of wartime events in which he personally played a role. For instance, on the *Guadalcanal* there was a dispute about the proper rigging of safety wires on depth charges, the explosives carried aboard the carrier's aircraft.

> I refereed the final argument about this and decided in favor of the way our ship's gunner wanted to rig them. As the conference broke up, the gunner said to me, "Cap'n, I'll bet my life on that rig." I felt the same way about it.
>
> Next day the gunner went out in one of our torpedo planes to make a test drop. Just after take-off the engine quit, but the plane made a successful water landing only a few hundred yards from the ship. As we headed over to pick up the boys we saw all three climb out of the cockpit and stand on the wings. Before we got there the depth charges exploded.
>
> There were no survivors. [12]

Episodes like this one add a counterpoise to Gallery's account of his many wartime successes.

To fill out his narrative, Gallery also discussed common naval customs and explained many technical facts about navy ships. His detailed description of the origin, transformation, and work of a single puff of steam in a modern boiler reminds one just a bit of Richard McKenna's *The Sand Pebbles.* As for the human side of shipboard life, Gallery tried to be evenhanded in his treatment of the continuing squabbles between naval aviators and the blackshoe navy. For instance, he mentions in *Clear the Decks!* an argument he had once overheard aboard that same ship:

> For some obscure reason the sailors in the air group are referred to by the ship's company as "airedales." They get fifty percent extra pay for flying duty. One day I heard one of the ship's company arguing with an airedale about which one had the toughest job, and the argument broke up with this classic summation of the case: "Well, I can see how you airedales earn your fifty per cent flight pay, but what the hell do you do to earn the base pay?" [13]

In *Clear the Decks!* some passages dealing with politics cause the tale to slow a bit and the wit briefly to disappear. But popularly speaking, this was a successful book, solidly in the convention of the "I was there" narrative.

Not only did Gallery get a wide range of public responses, but many naval veterans wrote to express their appreciation. One particular veteran's note of thanks for the copy of the book that Gallery had sent him is especially worth remarking:

"Streamliner"
Enroute: Berkeley, California
13 Sept 1953

Dear Gallery:

As we speed westward in this luxury train thru this beautiful country of ours, Mrs. Nimitz and I get vast enjoyment from my reading aloud of "Clear the Decks." Visitors to our compartment share our merriment and pleasure in hearing your salty narrative and humorous anecdotes. . . . May you live long and continue to wield your pen for the benefit of your country and for the entertainment of your readers. . . .

Sincerely,
C. W. Nimitz

Overall, the book successfully builds on Gallery's earlier articles, and more fully portrays Gallery's engaging leadership style and confident philosophy—indeed, one might say it is almost a handbook on how to be a successful (and colorful) commanding officer.

Within a year of publishing *Clear the Decks!*, Gallery was transferred to Chicago to head the Naval Air Reserve. While travelling throughout the country to inspect reserve bases and also using his local authority and prestige to push through the move of the *U-505* to his hometown, he began to write yet another book on the sub's capture—a book from a different angle, and only partially autobiographical. *Twenty Million Tons Under the Sea*[14] would sketch the whole history of the *U-505*, discuss the boat's place within the German submarine war generally, describe French resistance in occupied submarine ports, and—especially—offer a detailed account of the capture from the perspective of both Allied and German commanders.

Of course Gallery could easily sketch the U.S. side of the conflict by drawing on library research, official records, his own notes, personal recollections, an extensive photographic collection, even a nineteen-minute film documentary, *Away Boarders!,* that he had gotten the navy to put together on the capture.[15] (For years, this film anchored Gallery's innumerable speeches to civic clubs and other organizations.) For the German side, he looked into war diaries, logs, charts, and records of prisoner interrogations. He queried various official sources in England, Germany, the United States, and elsewhere about various details of the submarine's career, and also read some of the books on U-boat operations that by the mid-fifties were beginning to appear. Most important, over nearly a year, he corresponded with Germans who had served on the *U-505* at one time or another. These included the *U-505*'s first skipper, Axel Loewe; the boat's first officer at the time of the capture, Paul Meyer; and Gallery's chief adversary, Capt. Herbert Lange.

Gallery had been in contact with Lange since 1949, when Lange had read Gallery's Iceland article in the *Saturday Evening Post* and had written the admiral. Injured in the engagement, Lange had lost his leg despite the efforts of doctors in Bermuda, and after further internment in Fort Meade, Maryland, and Ruston, Louisiana, he had returned to Germany with his crew in late 1945 (to the astonishment and happiness of family members who—because the sub's capture had been kept secret—had received no notice of their loved ones' survival). After further hospitalization for tuberculosis, Lange got a job managing the fruit docks in Hamburg. He wrote Gallery that he didn't mind the work (particularly since he had two good assistants, both, like himself, former captains in the merchant marine!), and he asked Gallery for a copy of the admiral's earlier (*U-505*) article.[16]

So began a correspondence between the two men. Building on letters like these and all other available sources, Gallery traced the eventful history of the *U-505*—not only in its ultimate capture while under Lange's command, but also its highly successful patrols under captain Axel Loewe in the heyday of the U-boats, and the stunning episode of the suicide of its next captain Cszhech in the very midst of an Allied depth-charge attack (see the narrative at the conclusion of this chapter).

Gallery performed the documentary part of his work very well. As just one example, from reading the war diaries he was able to inform the British Admiralty of the events surrounding the loss of one of its antisubmarine aircraft that for twelve years had been listed only as "missing, fate unknown." On November 10, 1942, this aircraft had surprised the *U-505* on the surface. In attacking, the plane had let loose four depth charges that wrecked the superstructure of the U-boat, punctured some fuel tanks, damaged the port engine, and for a while inhibited the boat's ability to dive. Frantic damage repair enabled the sub to submerge and limp home. However, the aircraft had come so low that it had been hit by the explosion of one of its own depth charges, crashed into the water, and sunk just aft of the submarine.[17]

Besides the *U-505*'s history, Gallery also expanded on related issues, such as the submarine *U-515*'s encounter with the S.S. *Ceramic,* a history that explained why its captain (Henke) had been so leery of being transferred to British captivity, and perhaps why he eventually committed suicide. In other ways, too, Gallery described the human side of the U-boat story, relying on some long descriptive letters from Axel Loewe for his general portrait of life on the boats, but drawing partly on his own knowledge and imagination to picture such subjects as shakedown cruises, nights on the town, attitudes toward new skippers, and so on. For the American side, Gallery incorporated in this book a few stories he had told before, from the shenanigans in Iceland to his leadership methods aboard the *Guadalcanal,* and then the actual capture of the *U-*

505. Finally, Gallery made a spirited argument against the "barefaced hypocrisy" of the Nuremberg trial that convicted Admiral Dönitz on the charge of violating the laws of war at sea—despite the fact that American submarines had operated in the same way as Dönitz's forces had. (As Clay Blair points out, Gallery was one of the first and most outspoken critics of the Allied decision to put Dönitz on trial.)[18]

Overall, Gallery's willingness to portray the emotional context of the U-boat's history is refreshing. Also among the book's successes is the portrait of the thinking and actions resulting in the capture itself. Gallery's dual-perspective approach portrays especially well the particularly dense "fog of war" that can characterize a surface-to-submarine engagement. In such an encounter, not only is neither commander sure of the enemy's intentions, but each remains throughout much in the dark as to the enemy's exact identity, specific location, direction of movement, and overall capabilities. For instance, as we have seen, the approach of the American warships was almost a complete surprise to the *U-505,* which had just piped down for lunch when it detected the attacking task group; the German submariners had no idea that the American force was near. Less than thirteen minutes later the sub had been blown to the surface.[19] On the other hand, as Gallery was perplexed to learn when he explored the charts and logs of all combatants involved, "The U-505 was never where I thought she was until the moment she popped up almost under foot. I was searching the wrong areas all the time, except that last night when my planes must have missed her by inches once, and by seconds another time." Gallery meditated on this anomaly:

> This whole operation is an example of the fact that a military commander controls events only up to a certain point. . . . He can anticipate certain things, perhaps even set the stage for them to happen, and can be ready to cash in on them if they do happen. But whether they will happen or not depends on many things over which he has no control.

In the end, rather than one's own preparation, "nebulous things which occur inside men's brains decide the issue."[20] Because of this, Gallery concluded there ultimately is no alternative but to trust to Providence.

On publication of *Twenty Million Tons,* Gallery sent copies of the book to several people, including Samuel Eliot Morison, himself in the midst of preparing the eleventh volume of his comprehensive naval history. Morison wrote back this summary comment: "You have in my opinion written the best account so far of submarine vs antisubmarine warfare in the Atlantic—how it was conducted on both sides, the hazards and difficulties, and the personal aspects."[21] Morison went on to praise Gallery for manifesting the humanity of the U-boat crews. Adm. Friedrich Ruge of the new (and old) German navy also appreciated the book's balance: "I think your book is the right mixture of positive and negative, of black and white, just like life."[22] Lotte Meyer wrote "without knowledge of my husband" Paul to thank Gallery for the fairness of his account of the Cszhech episode and the U-boat's capture,[23] while Admiral Dönitz himself—having recently been released from prison—wrote Gallery with special thanks for his copy of the book, and particularly "for the spirited and righteous words which you, in the interest of truth, found for me in the Epilogue chapter of your book. . . . I am of the opinion that there exists a comradeship of the Navy blue cloth which transcends even national boundaries."[24]

Sometime after his retirement Gallery began one more project in which he would tell of Iceland, the *Guadalcanal,* the *U-515,* and the *U-505.* This project was a general autobiography.

As we've pointed out, Gallery found autobiography a very natural genre. His life was filled with events, and as *Eight Bells, and All's Well* also crackles with his characteristic humor, for the most part it makes for a very good read. We've quoted from the autobiography often enough in this book to get across an idea of the vitality of Gallery's recollections. Although occasionally slapstick (and sometimes in error as to dates and other facts), his anecdotes are nevertheless typically brisk and humorous. In other words, to the extent that Gallery focuses here on the highlights of his own interesting career, the book succeeds. But he did not always so limit his focus, and in other ways, too, the book is not an unqualified success. Partly this is because he was lazy. He had now told many of his great stories dozens of times orally and several times each in print. To be sure, many episodes occur in print only here. But Gallery has not related his life's history with a fresh eye or the insight born of new perspective. The book's other, more important fault is the presence of an overlay of unthought-out political opinion that surfaces at many places in the narrative and dominates the final chapter, which he entitled "Epilogue to My Relief." His editor, Eric Swenson, argued strongly and repeatedly that the book should end with his retirement, and not include the last chapter or so of Gallery's political commentary. In the editor's view, that material was

> intemperately expressed, undocumented, and incompletely thought out in a way which would be obvious to any but the most dedicated fanatic. . . .
>
> It is almost as though Richard Haliburton were to write one of his marvellous books about his adventures, and then tack on to the end of it a dissertation on the law of thermodynamics. I urge you with complete conviction, and with a sense of horror if you refuse, to drop this political material.[25]

Swenson was politically more liberal than Gallery, so eventually he had a more conservative editor look at it, too, and that man also said the last chapter would spoil the book; Gallery's opinions were not well expressed. But Gallery was adamant about keeping the material. As he wrote Herman Wouk, he wanted to leave a record behind him, and he felt that without the last chapter, the record would be incomplete.[26]

In the end, Gallery insisted on having his way, and the publisher eventually backed off. Hence Gallery's last chapter rambles through the sins of political parties, Congress, the Supreme Court, labor unions, the Defense Department, and the United Nations, and his description of everything wrong with the nation (but without incisive recipes for change) is quite uninspired. As a result, reviews of the book were mixed, and as Swenson had predicted, many reviewers primarily focused on—and spoke unfavorably of—Gallery's political commentary. As one of them commented, "His life is interesting, but his opinions are second-hand ones, at least as expressed here."[27] This is a pretty fair assessment.

We'll conclude this chapter by citing some of Gallery's advice on how to write about one's own experience, as this advice shows something of how Gallery himself learned the narrative part of the craft. Shortly after *Clear the Decks!* was published in 1951, Gallery's editor, Marty Somers, wrote the admiral, asking him to correspond with a fellow naval aviator, a Lt. Comdr. Frank Metzner, who had sent an unpolished piece called "I Fly the Night Skies Over Korea" to the *Saturday Evening Post*. Somers thought the article had promise but that Metzner's writing needed work, and the editor thought Gallery might be the person to help the flier out—perhaps partly because Metzner had flown his missions from the USS *Princeton* while it was commanded by Gallery's brother Bill.[28]

Gallery reviewed several drafts of Metzner's article, and passed on to the junior officer some words of advice that Bill Lederer had taught him only a few years before. For example, he dwelt on the need for brevity, telling Metzner he should work on replacing short words for long ones, and that he should cut his story to five thousand words: "I found when I started writing that cutting was the hardest job of all. But that's where you really learn to write. . . . Almost invariably you express it better in fewer words than in many."[29] Gallery also advised the aviator to salt the narrative with typical sailor or aviator expressions: "Conversation always livens up a piece and can be quite colorful."[30]

Above all, Gallery urged Metzner to make sure he got across the *context* of his autobiographical narrative—what the reader wouldn't necessarily know about the circumstances, but needed to:

> As one example, you speak several times of flying below mountain top level at night. I know why that is an important item to you but the average reader won't. Explain to him that when you are above that level you know damned well that none of the clouds have centers of solid rock—when you get below, then you never know. . . .[31]

After several revisions, the *Post* accepted the article; it was published in the December 27, 1952, issue.[32]

However, about a year after their correspondence ended, Gallery had to write Somers again.

> I'm sure you will be saddened to learn that our friend Metzner (I Fly the Night Skies in Korea) was killed recently at Corpus Christi. A wing came off the SNJ he was flying and neither he nor his student got out.
>
> It makes you wonder what sense or purpose there is in life on this earth when a guy goes through what he did in Korea and then gets it on a "routine flight."[33]

Gallery had himself endured many events that made him question the meaning of life. But except for his intriguing musings on the impact of standing night watches at sea (as we've seen, the admiral thought it "good for the soul"), Gallery's best vein when he wrote autobiography was seldom philosophical reflection, and not often political or social commentary, either. He was at his autobiographical best when he stuck with his lively anecdotal narrative—a narrative regularly salted with an irreverent comment or two.

TWENTY MILLION TONS was really a reconstructed historical narration, though of a special sort, one that requires its author to take a new point of view about the battle he had just fought. The part in Twenty Million Tons that tells the U-505's story would correspond, in analogy, to Santa Anna penning an account of the fall of the Alamo, through the eyes of the Alamo's defenders, a decade after the event.

One of the points of special interest to Gallery in his letters to the German submariners was the psychology of the U-505's second captain, between Loewe and Lange: Kapitän Leutnant Cszhech. Suffering under the pressure of repeatedly failed missions, Cszhech had become rattled and shot himself in the height of a depth-charge attack. Gallery recognized that after such an event a crew would hardly be at its steadiest. Indeed, he believed Cszhech's suicide was "the factor that did most to bring about the capture." Lange had taken over a crew, said Gallery, "completely demoralized by a long run of very bad luck climaxed by the outrageous suicide of their skipper under fire. It would have taken a John Paul Jones to straighten out that crew."[34]

In the prologue to Twenty Million Tons Gallery alludes to his practice of enlivening his narration with interpolated details and bits of dialogue, stressing, however, that "the main facts of the story are historically correct and are documented. . . . The minor incidents are based on interrogation of prisoners, and on letters I have had from the U-505's crew. . . ."[35] This apparent candor actually belies one of Gallery's strengths as an author.

In 1958–59, Germany's most popular magazine, Der Stern, ran a thirty-piece series on the U-boat war. A substantial part of it had to do with three boats Gallery had defeated: U-68, U-515, and U-505. It seemed clear to Gallery that much of the material had been taken directly from his writings. When, at his urging, his publisher complained to Der Stern about it, the reply was that the series had been composed completely from public sources and independent interviews. Not so at all, replied Gallery, "It is quite obvious that the author had Twenty Million Tons in front of him." Citing a particular episode, he says, "This incident is obviously lifted from page 206 of our book. The amusing thing about it, and the thing that really nails down the plagiarism, is that I made this incident up out of whole cloth!"[36]

In the piece of "whole cloth" printed below, Gallery shows us Cszhech being led to his fatal last decision. While Cszhech's final act was a matter of record, as were many of the relevant operational details, Gallery had to imagine the doomed skipper's thoughts and words. He also completely invented such episodes as the one purloined by *Der Stern* wherein Cszhech sits drinking in a waterside café in Lorient. The writing here is some of Gallery's best.

From "The Suicide of Cszhech"

By the end of June, 1943, when the *U-505* was declared ready for sea again, only one-third of her original crew was left on board, the rest having been transferred to other boats while she was being repaired. Of these, about half had been killed in the terrible retribution which the Allies were then exacting out in the Atlantic. Still on board were the four leading chief petty officers and a dozen plank owners who had put her in commission. All the original officers were gone.

The *U-505* was scheduled to sail on July 1, and on the night of June 30, the crew made a final round of the bars and bistros in Lorient to bid adieu to their friends. U-boats always sailed in the late afternoon and everyone could get good and drunk the night before sailing knowing they would have all the next day to sober up.

The *U-505*'s crew put on the customary binge on June 30. Theirs was even more frenzied than most departure parties because anyone who had spent the last six months in Lorient knew better than the usual transients how heavily the dice were loaded against them. Since January they had said *auf wiedersehen* to several dozen crews that didn't come back. Now it was their turn to go out and act as decoys to keep RAF bombers away from Germany. It was late that night before the last of them got to bed. At noon the next day all hands mustered on board the *U-505*, bleary eyed but ready to go to sea for ninety days.

Cszhech, with a bad hangover himself, took his boat down the river that evening and headed out into Biscay. He started this cruise with mingled emotions. A lot of his friends had disappeared forever into Biscay during the past six months. In a way, he was lucky to still be alive. But meantime, others of his contemporaries had come back with good scores, been decorated, promoted, and assigned to shore duty. He had fallen behind them and now he must try to catch up after the tide of battle had definitely turned. But there was no use brooding over his bad luck. This was his fate and he just had to make the best of it. He was bound for the Azores where the opposition would not be too heavy and there were still some targets for a skillful skipper to sink. He took a last look over his shoulder as the French coast dropped out of sight and thought, "If I'm lucky, I'll be assigned to shore duty next time I step off onto the dock."

He was back on the dock within twenty-four hours with a long list of minor discrepancies in the shipyard repairs and one major one which couldn't be fixed at sea but wouldn't take long at the dock. U-boat headquarters had a crew of experts on the dock to meet him. They made short work of his discrepancy list, freed the jammed valve on one of his ballast tanks and had him ready to sail again by the next evening.

Some of his boys got in another last fling ashore that night, repeating the same ritual as the night before. Like the U-boats at sea, the madams, gals, pimps, and bartenders of Lorient were on a Yesterday, Today and Tomorrow routine too. One night was the same as another to them. They had already forgotten they had said goodbye to these same men the night before. They said it all over again with equal fervor.

Next evening, July 3rd, the *U-505* sailed again, this time in company with four other outbound U-boats, and an escort of seven motor torpedo boats to furnish antiaircraft protection until they reached water deep enough for them to submerge.

The change in the tide of battle that had occurred in the past six months is graphically shown by the *U-505's* war diary for the first five days out of Lorient. While trying to get across Biscay to Cape Finnestere, she spent only about twenty per cent of the time on the surface. She averaged twenty hours out of each twenty-four submerged. Her distance run on the surface was only twice that submerged—quite a change from Loewe's first cruise when the surface distance was forty times the submerged run!

After four days of this Cszhech got impatient and decided to make a break for the open sea. It was a clear day with excellent visibility so he should be able to sight any aircraft in time for a crash dive. He surfaced at noon on July 8 and boiled along at eighteen knots until one P.M.

when he submerged again feeling that he had stolen a march on the enemy.

It would have taken him at least twelve hours to run eighteen miles submerged. This sprint on the surface in broad daylight put him half a day's run closer to the comparative safety of the broad Atlantic. Fifteen minutes after submerging, all hands in his crew were still grinning at each other like a bunch of small boys who had just raided a candy store when hell broke loose around them.

Six stunning blows slammed into the hull in rapid succession, knocking men off their feet, smashing lights, and jarring great flakes of paint off the bulkheads.

The watch officer and Cszhech had been flung against opposite sides of the conning tower. They remained braced there staring at each other silently, waiting for the battering to stop. Some seconds after the sixth explosion had died away, the watch officer inquired incredulously, "Destroyers?"

"*Nein,*" said Cszhech, "There were no destroyers in sight fifteen minutes ago. It's an airplane."

"But how could he see us down at forty meters?"

"These new listening buoys that they drop into the water . . . they have a microphone and a radio that broadcasts our propeller noises and. . . ." There were four more crashing explosions much too close for comfort but not quite as close as the first ones.

Cszhech dropped down into the control room. The grins were gone from the crew's faces now and all eyes stared at him questioningly—big with fright. "All stations report damage," he ordered.

The reports showed no serious structural damage had been done and the engines were still OK. But the Metox and listening gear were completely out of commission. Loss of the listening gear was a very serious matter indeed. A submerged U-boat without listening gear knows nothing about what goes on in the ocean around it except, of course, when the explosion of depth charges serves emphatic notice that bad things have been going on.

"You hear nothing whatever?" demanded Cszhech of the sound operator.

"Nothing Kapitän . . . the whole set is dead."

"Silent speed," said Cszhech to the man on the engine-room telegraph, and then to the depth control man, "Hold her at forty meters." For the rest of the afternoon the crew tiptoed through the boat as she crept along 240 feet below the surface at one knot, gradually putting distance between herself and the scene of the previous attack.

There is little that a skipper can do in a situation like this to influence events. Unable to hear or see, he just has to trust to his luck. When the situation gets that tough, a show of nonchalance by the skipper does a lot of good. After a couple of hours of creeping, Cszhech said [to] the first watch officer, "I don't think any more planes are coming out. Just hold everything as it is now. I'm going to take a nap. . . . Call me at 6:00 P.M."

For the next few hours Cszhech lay in his bunk wide awake braced for the next series of explosions, but with the curtain drawn so no one could see. Reassured by the knowledge that the skipper had turned in, many of the crew grabbed off a nap they would have missed otherwise.

Meantime, Cszhech kept turning over in his mind the chain of events leading up to the attack, and always came to the same conclusion—he must be leaving an oil trail on the surface. That attack had been too accurate to explain by sonobuoys alone. . . . A sonobuoy only tells the plane there is a sub within a mile or so of the buoy. But a sonobuoy, plus a telltale oil slick would pinpoint the submerged sub. If he was leaving an oil slick he was in a desperate situation—blind and deaf himself, but plainly advertising his own location, at least in daylight, to aircraft and surface vessels alike. He decided to surface after dark, check for oil leaks and then make up his mind whether to keep going or head back to Lorient.

At 8:00 P.M., before it was dark enough to surface, he got sudden and emphatic confirmation that, despite his forty meter depth and creeping speed, something was indeed revealing his location. A salvo of nine depth charges made the ocean quake like a bowl of jelly. As the thunder subsided and he realized that he still wasn't hurt Cszhech barked, "Full speed on electric motors. . . . Fire decoys!"

He now had fifteen minutes when reverberations of the sea would make it impossible for destroyers to use their sonar gear, and if luck was still with him the enemy might concentrate on the decoys instead

of the *U-505* when the rumblings died down. Fifteen minutes later
six more depth charges exploded, but further away than the others.
Apparently the decoys had worked. This gave him another fifteen
minutes to run at high speed, and when this reprieve expired there
were nine more explosions plainly audible to all in the boat but
obviously aimed at the chemical bubble which the decoys had made
a couple of miles astern.

Cszhech settled down to creeping noiseless speed again for an hour
during which time all was quiet. Evidently the destroyers, or aircraft,
or whatever they were that had beaten that chemical bubble to pieces
were satisfied that they had destroyed a submarine. With his sound
gear inoperative, the only way Cszhech could find out what was going
on was to come up to shallow depth and stick his periscope up. An
hour and a half after the attack he poked up his scope cautiously and
took a look.

There were three destroyers sniffing around the ocean a mile to
the north of him. The sea was glassy calm, and a quick swing of the
periscope astern confirmed that the boat was indeed leaving a
conspicuous oil trail behind her. But it was nearly dark now, and if
those destroyers were convinced they had destroyed him, they might
not pay too much attention to a little stray oil on the surface in the area
of the "kill." This would just add weight to their claims for a kill and a
medal for their skippers. Cszhech went back down to forty meters and
crept toward the coast of Spain.

A few hours later he entered Spanish territorial waters where he
surfaced and ran east the rest of the night under the lee of the coast,
taking stock of his situation. It would be humiliating to limp into
Lorient again and his pride made him want to go on, but common
sense told him not to. That oil leak was a conspicuous one and could
not be fixed at sea. Without radar or sound gear he couldn't accomplish
much anyway even if he went on. And finally, Doenitz had stressed the
need for caution and preserving his trained crews until the new types
of U-boats were ready. Cszhech decided to go back.

He hugged the Spanish and French coasts close into the beach, lying
on the bottom during daylight and surfacing for a few hours sprint
each night. Oil came up when he sat on the bottom, but a stationary
oil puddle in these waters, where there were lots of fishing boats wasn't

as conspicuous as a moving streak out in the middle of Biscay. On July 14, he tied up again in Lorient.

The dockyard found, in addition to the troubles Cszhech reported, that all the gaskets on the vent valves had been eaten away by some corrosive substance and there was a hole the size of a lead pencil drilled into one of the underwater oil tanks. It was two weeks before they got these things fixed, repaired the radar and listening gear, and pronounced the boat ready for sea again.

During July, thirty-seven U-boats failed to return from the operating areas. Fourteen of these had been killed in the Bay of Biscay, and every one of the skippers was a personal friend of Cszhech.

On the first of August, *U-505* sallied forth again but was back in again the next day. There were ominous noises when they dove deeper than fifty meters, sounds as if the joints in the hull were coming apart or a ballast tank were being crushed. There were also noises of water coming in somewhere. They could find no leaks but every time they went down to fifty meters the noises began again, indicating at least that something was being strained close to the breaking point.

For two weeks the shipyard checked the hull rivet by rivet and joint by joint. They could find nothing wrong but Cszhech and all his men swore they had not imagined these noises. The shipyard sent them out again on August 15, and exactly the same noises were repeated. This time Cszhech took her a little deeper and when he surfaced, found the main air injection had been crushed in and was full of water. At least this would prove to the dockyard skeptics he hadn't been dreaming about the noises. They were back in the dockyard again on August 16th, for another week to repair the injection.

They went out again on August 22nd, and came back in again as usual the next day. This time they found the vent gaskets eaten away the same as they had been on their first cruise. The gaskets had been OK when they sailed the day before. The dockyard inspectors smelled a rat and half a dozen French laborers who had renewed these gaskets were arrested on suspicion of sabotage and shot.

On September 18th, the *U-505* took her fifth departure from Lorient in the two and a half months since her overhaul had been "finished." [This fifth foray was also a failure, for after five days out the main ballast pump was overloaded in a crash dive. Loss of that pump's armature meant the boat could not go deep. Cszhech spent a whole night trying to figure how to repair the pump at sea, but then decided the repair was impossible and that continuing the cruise without the pump would be futile. So once more he returned to port.—eds.]

The most damning charge you can bring against a military man is that he is unlucky. As he was bringing the *U-505* back to Lorient again, Cszhech, in the silence of the conning tower could sense this charge being preferred against him by all the men in his crew, who no longer looked him in the eye when they spoke to him.

As the sub came in to tie up to her usual dock in the shipyard, the French underground got in a shrewd blow at the Captain's morale. Painted in large white letters which could not be seen by anyone standing on the dock, but which couldn't be missed by anyone on the deck of a U-boat coming alongside the dock, was the legend, "U-505's Hunting Ground."

Fixing the motor was a major job that took ten days even in the shipyard. Cszhech spent most of this time brooding over his series of failures. He had been fully justified every time he turned back and no one could have done any different. But his contemporaries now were beginning to treat him rather patronizingly, almost as if he were a cripple who wasn't to be blamed for his infirmities, but who was not the same as other men. When he joined a circle of them at the club there was an embarrassed lull in the conversation. He took to solitary drinking and avoided the company of his friends.

The night before he was to sail on his seventh attempt to get out, he was seated in a booth at a waterfront café with a gal of the evening getting drunk. In the next booth, separated from them only by a thin partition, was a noisy group of U-boat sailors hashing over recent events. Cszhech was listening in absent-mindedly.

At this stage of the war there were no successes to brag about and most of the talk was about recent losses and boats reported missing.

"*U-68* and *U-515* sail tomorrow," said a voice on the other side of the screen, "And the way things are going now at least one of them won't come back."

Another voice challenged this statement, "Both have good captains —Henke and Lauzemis—they will be back."

"Many just as good as they are haven't come back . . . the odds are two to one against *anybody* now."

There was a lull in the conversation while that ominous statement sank in. Then a joker trying to relieve the tension said, "At least we've still got one ace who will always come back."

"Who?" demanded several voices.

"Cszhech."

The blood drained from Cszhech's face, he clamped his jaws together and tightened the grip on his glass. As a roar of derisive laughter from the other side of the screen greeted this quip, Cszhech sat staring at his glass and squeezing his grip tighter until his knuckles were white and the sinews of his wrist stood out like steel wires. The glass shattered in his hand, cut into the flesh, and for several seconds more he squeezed the broken pieces. Then he flung the fragments against the wall, threw some money on the bloody table, and reeled out into the night.

Back at the dockyard a hospital corpsman picked pieces of glass out of his hand, bandaged it up and told him it would heal in about a week. The wound to his soul was a mortal one. When he sailed the next day nothing in this world could have induced Cszhech to return from that cruise prematurely.

He literally crept out of Biscay. To insure against being spotted from the air he stayed submerged twenty-two hours out of every twenty-four. He had to surface for a minimum of two hours each day to recharge his battery and during these two hours he ran wide open putting about thirty-five miles behind him. But at creeping speed submerged for the other twenty-two hours he only covered about the same distance, so his daily run averaged about seventy miles. He crossed Biscay so slowly, keeping radio silence, that U-boat Headquarters sent him a message when he was ten days out, asking if he hadn't forgotten to report reaching the Atlantic. He replied that he had not—and continued at creeping speed.

In the early evening of their fourteenth day out, the *U-505* was cruising slowly at forty meters when the sound room reported, "Screw noises at medium distance." Meyer, the first watch officer, notified the Captain and got ready to come up to periscope depth and have a look.

As Cszhech climbed up the ladder to the conning tower, favoring his injured right hand, he inquired nervously, "What is it Meyer? What is it?"

"Sound room can't tell yet," replied Meyer. Then nodding at the periscope he asked, "Shall I bring her up to shallow depth so you can see, Captain?" This was the natural reaction of any U-boat man in these circumstances. A submarine's sensitive listening gear would nearly always pick up propeller noises much farther away than a surface vessel could hear the echo of a ping from her sonar gear. The sub therefore, always had the big advantage of surprise on her first attack, and to a normal skipper any screw noises were a challenge to a battle, with the opening odds heavily in his favor. But Cszhech was not normal now.

"No," he said, "Hold her at forty meters. This must be a destroyer."

Meyer thought it strange his captain made up his mind so quickly that this was a destroyer rather than a merchant ship and that he had no intention of attacking. But Meyer obediently passed the word below "Hold her at forty meters."

"What do you hear now?" demanded Cszhech on the voice tube to the sound room.

"Twin screws making 180 RPM . . . diesel engines . . . approaching rapidly," came the answer from below.

"Another submarine?" asked Meyer.

"No," said Cszhech. "There are no other submarines near us. This is a Britisher, just as I thought."

"Maybe he won't find us Captain," said Meyer. "We can't even hear his sonar pings yet."

"He will find us," said Cszhech, a hunted look coming over his face. "I *know* he will find us."

Soon a report came up from the sound room, "Bearing holds steady—he is heading right at us."

Cszhech cast a furtive look, like a cornered animal, at his first watch officer.

"Shall I change course ninety degrees, Captain?" suggested Meyer.

For some seconds Cszhech made no reply. Finally he said, "Very well, Meyer. . . . But it won't do any good—we *can't* escape."

"Left full rudder," said Meyer to the helmsman, wondering what had come over the Captain, "Steady on course 180."

Cszhech stared at the dial on the bearing indicator from the sound room as if he were looking at a ghost. "The bearing remains steady," he said in a hollow voice, "He knows where I am."

"Not yet, Captain," said Meyer. "We don't hear any pings yet."

Almost immediately the sound room called up, "Hear pings now on same bearing as screw noises—approaching fast."

Cszhech shot an accusing glance at his first watch officer as if to say, "I told you so," but took no other action.

"Shall I go deep, Captain?" asked Meyer.

"It's no use, Meyer," said Cszhech despairingly. "We can't get away . . . they have caught us again . . . my luck is bad."

By now everyone in the boat could hear the propeller noises without benefit of listening gear. "Shall I sound the alarm, Captain?" asked Meyer with his hand on the button.

For perhaps half a minute Cszhech made no reply. He stood there in the conning tower as if in a trance, clenching his fists so tightly that he split the scabs on his right hand. "No," he said, "Everyone knows now anyway. . . ."

A minute later all hands heard the tempo of the screw noises change, indicating that the destroyer was slowing so she could hear better in the final stage of a carefully calculated attack. There was no doubt whatever now that the destroyer had them pinpointed. As the destroyer neared the firing point, Cszhech seemed to shrivel within himself as if he knew the battle was hopeless. Screw noises were very loud now and all hands braced themselves knowing that the climax was close at hand.

"Destroyer is firing-depth charges," said the sound room.

Cszhech stared at the gauges like a man who was already in another world and said nothing.

"Right full rudder," said Meyer on his own initiative.

For fifteen seconds everyone in the *U-505* held his breath and prayed silently as the depth charges were sinking. They all knew now from experience that a depth charge attack was a terrifying experience but that unless the charges were set to explode at exactly the right depth, they might come out of this with just another bad shaking up.

The charges were set *almost* exactly right, and the rippling salvo of explosions gave the *U-505* the worst jarring she had ever received, even including that direct hit by the aerial bomb.

Oberleutnant Meyer says that the first depth charge smashed the lights, and a few seconds later, while the other depth charges were exploding all around him, he heard an explosion which seemed to be from an extra close depth charge and saw a flash of flame in the conning tower. He thought the flame came from an electric switch. He smelled pungent smoke which might have been from burning insulation. In the darkness his Captain slumped against him and fell to the deck.

There was no time to investigate what had happened now. The skipper had apparently been knocked out by being slammed against the periscope. But the boat was in a desperate situation and until Cszhech came to again and could resume command, it was up to Meyer to take over.

"One hundred meters," barked Meyer, "Full speed—fire decoys." Then he yelled down the hatch to the control room, "Come up here and get the Captain. He is knocked out." He concentrated on the gauges again while they lugged the Captain below. "Left full rudder," he said to the helmsman.

As the boat circled to the left, Meyer noted that they were still at forty meters and at creeping speed. He stuck his head down the hatch and yelled, "Achtung! Full speed! One hundred meters! What the hell's the matter down there?"

The men were all huddled like sheep around the Captain, who was stretched out on the floor plates. One of the chief petty officers looked up at Meyer with despair in his eyes, pointed his forefinger at his temple and moved his thumb like the hammer of a revolver. At this same moment Meyer saw the pool of blood on the deck of the conning tower with the Captain's Luger lying alongside it. Cszhech had shot himself!

Meyer leaped down into the control room, saw at a glance that Cszhech was done for, and then faced what were now *his* crew. This was a change of command ceremony to put the new skipper's soul to the acid test. Cszhech had quit—deserted under fire. The destroyer was circling to make another attack.

Discipline, based on regulations, went overboard when the Commanding Officer pulled the trigger of that Luger. Meyer's gold stripes meant nothing now. Why should these men obey a junior with less experience than the man who had just deserted them? What happened now would depend on Meyer the man, not Oberleutnant Meyer. The whole Officer Corps of the Kriegsmarine was discredited in the minds of those terrified men standing on the brink of eternity.

"I am in command now," said Meyer to his dazed men, "Go back to your battle stations."

No one moved. Meyer reached up into the conning tower, got the Captain's gun, cocked it, toyed with it for a moment looking around the circle of faces and then tossed it onto the chart table.

"Anyone who wants to die—help yourself," he said. "The rest of you do as I say and I'll get you out of this. . . . One hundred meters—full speed—fire decoys."

No one was ready to die. The gun lay there untouched.

Some men went slowly back to their stations and began executing his orders. Others hesitated, motionless. Panic was very near.

Willi Bunger (the "Ostrich") broke into uncontrolled sobbing. Meyer slapped him across the face, shoved him toward his battle station, and said, "Get going son, you're not old enough to die yet." Willi pulled himself together, took his battle station, and all the others did likewise. "The worst is over—we will escape," said Meyer coolly.

"Steady as you go," he called to the helmsman. "Fire two more decoys."

"What shall we do with *him,* Captain?" asked one of the chiefs, nodding at Cszhech's body, as the men resumed their duties.

For the leading chief to call him "Captain" at this moment meant more to Meyer than a direct commission from *der Führer* himself.

"Lash him up in a hammock, put a weight at his feet, and I'll put him overboard when we have time," replied Meyer.

In the face of mortal danger some men come apart if responsibility is suddenly thrust upon them. Others exceed anything they have ever done before. Meyer carried out his promise to his men and got them out of the jam. The destroyer was fooled by the decoys and for the next few hours the *U-505* heard depth charge explosions receding farther and farther astern as the destroyer blasted away at phony echoes from chemical bubbles.

At six bells of the mid watch, Meyer surfaced. They carried Cszhech's body up on deck and committed it to the deep beneath the eternal stars.

This whole eight hour period is tersely recorded in the war diary of the *U-505* as follows:

1952 Propellor noises in medium distance.
1954 Piston engine noises.
1956 Sonar noises.
1958 *Wabos*—very close. (Note: *Wabos,* depth charges)
1958 *Kommandant ausgefallen.* (Literally, "Captain fell out of ranks")
2100 *Kommandant tot.* (*tot,* dead)
      First Watch Officer Meyer assumes command.
0406 Captain's body overboard.

Above is the whole story so far as the official log of the U-505 goes. "*Kommandant ausgefallen.*" "The king is dead—long live the king." Note that although Meyer took over at 1958 and saved the boat, he doesn't officially record assuming command until an hour later when Cszhech dies!

So, after putting Cszhech overboard the *U-505* headed back to Lorient again, Oberleutnant Paul Meyer, Commanding.

They got back in on November 7th. Meyer made his report to Doenitz and was "absolved of all blame."

That's all he ever got out of this operation—absolved of all blame! He had saved a U-boat from certain destruction under almost impossible circumstances, after the regular captain had quit under fire and blown his brains out. He had preserved a trained crew for Doenitz and had restored respect for authority in a group of men who had just seen the highest authority there is at sea fail them shamefully. The first watch officer's reward was, to be "absolved from blame."

The only way I can explain this is that Doenitz considered the incident had to be hushed up to avoid dishonoring the Officers' Corps and damaging the morale of the surviving U-boat crews. Meyer's outstanding conduct could not be recognized without publicizing Cszhech's cowardice, so Meyer stayed on as first watch officer of the *U-505* and got nothing to show for what he had done—except his own life, and the lasting respect of some fifty men, who had felt the long finger of death tap them on the shoulder, hesitate and be snatched away by Meyer.

Fiction Writer

IN THE EARLY 1950s Gallery began writing fiction, mostly humorous stories about the navy. By late 1955, he had written seventeen short stories and published eleven of them, seven in the *Saturday Evening Post* alone.[1] Comparatively speaking, that's pretty good work, especially for someone who waited until age forty-eight and rear admiral's rank to attempt it.

What accounted for this success? For one thing, Gallery had been writing voluminously since childhood. As we've seen, as a midshipman he wrote separate letters home weekly to his mother and father, and he continued writing to several family members at least every other week into the late 1930s. He maintained diaries for most of his early overseas tours. He wrote for his school paper and then for ship and station papers throughout his career, and composed cartoons, poems, and other witticisms at his many stations. Naturally he did his share of official report writing, too, and he maintained increasingly extensive naval correspondence as his responsibilities grew. Finally, his late development in autobiographical and essay writing taught him a bit about what civilian journals would expect of a fictional piece.

Second, in his short navy stories Gallery both stuck to and built on his naval experience, and he worked hard at describing that experience well. Many of his stories, for instance, open with a description of some time-honored naval evolution, and proceed from there. For instance, a short story originally titled "Bomb's Away" opens this way:

> As the *Okinawa* approached her anchorage in Naples, Dopey Dugan leaned over the side from the leadman's platform on the foc'sle swinging his lead like a pendulum in gradually increasing arcs. When he got up enough momentum he wound it around in a complete circle up over his head and down behind him. As it started the ascending arc forward again he let the lead fly, paying out the carefully coiled line from his left hand. As the lead plunked to the bottom he hauled in the slack briskly with both hands while his striker faked it down on the deck, keeping the line taut as the ship ran ahead. As he passed over the lead with the line vertical, Dopey cocked a careful eye at the red marker rag just at the water's edge and sang out, "By the ma-a-ark seven, Sir," thus informing the bridge they were in seven fathoms of water.[2]

The story's subsequent description of the anchor being let go bristles with details about the cable and hawsepipe and wildcat and even about the burners and tubes in the boilers (for in anchoring the engine has to be stopped along the way). And so the story has begun.

But of course description is only one aspect of fiction, and editors often had to tell Gallery to cut back on the technical detail, or to discipline himself so as to drop in technical descriptions only while he was also getting on with the story, which Gallery soon learned to do. Typically, he quickly moved from portraying a technical evolution to describing a character of two.

Gallery's favorite enlisted fictional character is Fatso Gioninni, a highly decorated World War II veteran and expert boatswain's mate who believes he has performed his share of labor and now deserves a pampered life. He knows every professional prerogative in the book, and is highly inventive in hoodwinking authorities to obtain perks he doesn't yet rate. In Gallery's Fatso (as in his main aviator counterpart, Lieutenant "Curly Cue"—another excellent naval professional and trickster of the first rank), we have an effective comic characterization, quite plausible to current or former military men. Just as Herman Wouk received letters from individuals throughout the military services professing to know the model for his Captain Queeg,[3] so, too, many servicemen and veterans confidently described to Gallery the "original" Fatso on whom they thought he had built. As one retired commander wrote, "I *know* all the guys you talked about. Especially that operator 'Fatso.' Tell the truth, isn't his real name Angelo and didn't he transfer off the Okinawa to VR-24 because he didn't want to leave the Med? No box lunches for the crew when he was aboard our Med flights. 'Steak Angelo'—I can still smell the garlic." [4]

Besides general characterization, Dan did especially well at depicting the "hot buttons" common to naval characters of particular billets and ranks. Of course, from recent experience Gallery could describe what was likely to upset an admiral commanding a fleet. But he could also portray well the sweat typically induced by an instant summons for a chief engineer to report to the bridge; the effect of a soiled collar on a Pentagon staffer; or the mutual suspicion of a wayward petty officer and a member of the master-at-arms' force. Gallery broadly sprinkled such details into his text.

> "Holy smokes," said Fatso, "I didn't think Admirals bothered [about enlisted assignments]."
> "They don't," said the Commander, "I doubt if the Admiral knows anything about this memo. It's from that little twerp of a Personnel Officer," he added bitterly. (Commanders don't usually refer to two-and-a-half-stripers as twerps when speaking to enlisted men, but in this case the Exec was burned up by the officious meddling in the internal administration of his ship.) [5]

Beyond characterization, Gallery worked hard on his plots. For instance, he learned to end his stories with reversals that are solidly based on the story's particulars but also wrap everything up, quickly and convincingly. He was not always successful at snapping his stories about; sometimes the endings are artificial or predictable. However, the best of his conclusions are both surprising and natural; often they are hilarious.

Let's illustrate these elements by recounting one of Gallery's first stories, appropriately titled "Un-holy Smoke." [6] The story begins with Gallery's description of flaghoist signals from a carrier, signals by which the admiral directs the tactical maneuvers of a formation of thirty ships. Both the signalmen's handling of flags and the ships' subsequent geo-

Gallery was familiar with this admiral's frustration. *Gallery Papers, U.S. Naval Academy, Nimitz Library*

metrical turns are vividly drawn. Also pictured is the admiral's touchi-ness about a cloud of smoke emitted out on the edge of the formation from a single destroyer's stack—"a serious breach of naval decorum," according to the narrator.

The story then introduces Gallery's favorite character, Fatso, who is forever inventing scams aboard the USS *Okinawa*. He is aided in this by his relationship with the exec and the ship's captain, with both of whom he served (with distinction) in World War II. Rather than require of Fatso any regular boatswain's mate work, they assign him the ridicu-lously light duty of managing the ship's incinerator. As the story gets going, we get a good picture of Fatso and his cronies in the incinerator spaces, especially in the evening when they dine on steak and down a few forbidden drinks while Fatso graciously holds court. (Gallery omits most four-letter words, but he gets across the salty tone of their conver-sations anyway.)

However, when a member of the admiral's staff is tipped off that some older men are doing jobs that could be done by new recruits, Fatso suddenly finds himself assigned a tough billet on the flight deck, and a seaman is assigned his cushy incinerator job. Fatso quickly invents a scheme to retrieve the situation. With the aid of his buddies he installs an oil pump in the uptakes outside the incinerator compartment, and rigs the pump in such a way that black smoke will billow from one of the stacks whenever the seaman lights off the incinerator. Fatso counts on the natural aversion of the flag officer to smoke over the formation to put him to rights—especially smoke billowing embarrassingly from his own flagship. By Fatso's arrangement, soon a great cloud darkens the sky.

There follows a succession of ridiculous but somehow also quite believable events. The officer of the deck, the ship's captain, and the admiral all flurry about to stop the smoke but without effect, and the ship (the formation's guide!) swings several degrees off course during the confusion. Eventually the smoke stops and the ship veers back to course, but the captain has been so embarrassed that he blames the engineering officer (whom he has summoned "on the double" up to the bridge); the chief engineer in turn claims all his water tenders had reported clear stacks. When black smoke comes again and continues to billow without impediment, the captain restricts the liberty of the engineers' force. Then he takes the extraordinary measure of stationing a lieutenant in the ship's superstructure to locate which flue from the carrier's stack is the source of the problem.

Upon another disconcerting billow, the lookout announces at the top of his voice that the smoke is coming not from the boilers but from the ship's *incinerator,* but since the incinerator is not on the ship's emergency battle circuits, the captain must have the junior officer of the deck scurry down to have the smoke cut off. Meanwhile the executive officer thinks up an instant solution: kill the power to the incinerator's blower. Bad idea. To be sure, no more smoke fouls the air above the fleet, but since the effects of combustion have to go somewhere, perforce the smoke blows the incinerator door open instead and begins to fill the furnace room and the starboard side of the hangar deck. Soon someone sounds the fire alarm, the whole ship goes to fire stations, the sprinklers automatically activate below decks, and the fire team arrives and thoroughly drowns the whole area. An embarrassing, landlubberly, even hilarious sequence—but given the situation and the propensities of each of the characters, not entirely an unlikely one. Moreover, to make sure it won't happen again, the admiral insists that a highly experienced petty officer take over the incinerator again—and so Fatso gets his old job back.

All is humor of situation and event, humor that turns on the characterization in the sense that *any* admiral, captain, engineer, OOD, and sailor would have done about the same in the circumstances, and of course, *any* slightly non-reg petty officer like Fatso might have attempted in such a way to work the situation back to his advantage, to begin with.

Where did Gallery draw his inspiration for his tales? One reviewer speculated that they came from Gallery's decades of listening to the narratives that sailors recited at captain's mast.[7] Actually, Gallery often based them on specific incidents. For instance, we've quoted Adm. James S. Russell's recollection that while Gallery flew his flag aboard the *Coral Sea,* an "enemy" aircraft from another carrier division had to land on the ship because of an aircraft emergency, and that Gallery actually ordered a squad of marines to "capture" that pilot and shave his head. Similarly, in Gallery's first humorous story, "Monkey Business at Mers El Kebir" (published in *Collier's* in September of 1951[8]—some six months after Gallery became commander of COMCARDIV SIX)—Lieutenant "Curly Cue" lands on the fictional USS *Wilson* because of an emergency, only (as just one event in an ongoing competition between the two American admirals) to have his flaming red head of hair completely shaved off.

To this point the episode in the short story has clearly been based on Gallery's own high jinks, but as the shorn redheaded lieutenant is furiously calculating ways by which he might revenge himself on the admiral, the story has just begun. The conclusion involves an associate and Lieutenant Curly Cue debouching from a limousine as the *Wilson* approaches the Moroccan pier. The two are disguised respectively as an Arab admiral and his boss: an Islamic sheik. The American admiral is so flustered about the unexpected appearance of "nobility" and the immediate need for protocol that he orders a brow lowered even while the ship is still being maneuvered by tugs, with the result that the brow is splintered between the mole and ship's side, a highly undiplomatic (but to Curly, a hugely satisfying) event. After this the sheik bows, doffs his turban and beard, and reveals his newly cropped red head. Then the hired limousine speeds off.

A humorous but somewhat unlikely episode, one might conclude . . . except that the following anonymous letter was received by the editors of *Collier's* immediately after the story's publication:

> 23 September 1951
>
> EDITOR: Your short story "Monkey Business at Mers el Kebir", (Sept. 22nd) was the most hilarious piece of "imaginative" sealore I have ever had the opportunity to read. Being a seafaring man myself (of a sort) I enjoyed the story immensely and followed each move and counter-move that the Admirals made in their game of stratagem with ludicrous concern. After a while it became apparent that the events were falling into a pattern which I was only too well aware of.
>
> However, I will have to agree with the writer "that the incidents described are wholly imaginary". I ought to know, too. I was
>
> > The SHEIK of ISLAM
> > Boston, Massachusetts

In a P.S. prefaced "PLEASE DO NOT REPRINT!" the author reported, "Because of my position I am unable to disclose my name. However, you can imagine my surprise on reading such a story concerning myself and my shipmates." He went on to say that he had some photographs of the "Welcoming Committee" at the pier, and that all the Norfolk newspapers had run a small article and photo about the events not long before.[9]

Apparently, then, Gallery had seen this piece, put his own experience together with it, and produced his first humorous work of fiction. Many other stories of less certain inspiration were to follow soon after.

Although Gallery seems to have stopped writing fiction for a while in the late 1950s, when he retired he eventually resurrected an idea of putting a book together involving his favorite character Fatso, and queried publishers about it. The response of one editor is interesting, in illustrating what kind of writer Gallery was—and what kind he was not.

Merrill Pollack (of Simon and Schuster) responded to Gallery's inquiry, in an apparent dissuasion:

> Let's think about Fatso for a minute. In these stories . . . we know
> he's an old hand, Italian, a sometimes friend of the top brass. But
> he's not a real, dimensional character as he'd have to be in a book.
> Where does he come from, who are his family, what was his
> background? What does he eat, drink, like, hate? How about
> dames? What are his fears, his anxieties, his shattered dreams? Et
> cetera. You know, I'm sure, what I'm getting at. I want dimension,
> I want weight, size and smell, nobility and venality, fun and
> passion . . . the whole kaboodle that makes a person real.[10]

Pollack is of course describing the protagonist of a work of "serious"
fiction, and certainly Fatso is nothing like it. But Pollack is mistaken in
asking from Gallery anything of the sort. The admiral's writing talent
was of a wholly different kind.

For Gallery is not a failed novelist—nor does all successful book-
length fiction have to be of the kind Pollack suggests. Gallery is writing
a particular kind of comic humor, perfectly appropriate for short fiction
of his sort, or even for collections of it. His humor is not one of the more
sour forms—parody, for instance, or satire. Instead, he is by nature
what one would properly define as a "caricaturist." His art is like the
cartoons that he was so fond of drawing—he's something like a Mort
Walker in print.

This comparison is not entirely accurate. Walker's characters are usually "travesties" of a kind, so that the joke is usually on them, whereas
Fatso and his comrades typically succeed in their schemes. Still, the
parallel is instructive. Just as no one ever asked where Beetle Bailey was
born, or about his nobility or venality, let alone his passion or shattered
dreams, for heaven's sakes, so no one ought to ask for "dimension" in
Gallery's comic heroes. Gallery's characterization is shallow, to be sure.
But that is appropriate to the kind of comedy he was writing. One
should judge his art *on its own terms.* As C. S. Forester wrote Gallery
when in receipt of the manuscript for *Now, Hear This!* "Of course it's low
comedy, but that's a phrase that gives a wrong impression; there are
clowns in Shakespeare as well as Hamlets and Macbeths."[11]

Pollack's pronouncement notwithstanding, the book Gallery eventually put together based on his Fatso material (with non-Fatso stories
modified to fit, all loosely linked together) was a success. *Now, Hear*

Gallery's interest in caricature was evident as early as the Fourth of July, 1926, when he drew this cartoon (with commentary) for the *Idaho Yarn*. *Idaho Yarn*

This! (1965) was reviewed positively in the *New York Times*,[12] and also made that newspaper's bestseller list. Other reviews were quite favorable, too, even if they did say the humor was "wild" or "puckish" or "light." One reader appreciated Gallery's "fine eye for actual detail" aboard a warship, and went on to comment, "A message or two about honor and courage are so well coated with humor that they may be absorbed without notice."[13] In contrast to his autobiographical texts, there was comparatively little "propaganda" in this collection.

Navy people especially liked the book, copies of which Gallery sent out to many friends. These included the CNO of the day, David L. McDonald, who reported his wife was worried about his sanity while he was reading it because of the tears she saw rolling down his cheeks.[14]

Arleigh Burke in his return letter commented particularly on Gallery's story about the "sea bat" (a naval version of the proverbial "snipe hunt"):

> I can personally attest to the sea bat, or at least I could have in the MICHIGAN in 1920 on a cool summer evening in the North Atlantic. That's supposed to be the very best place and very best time to see these rare little beasts, I was told. As a matter of fact I was so told by some of your esteemed classmates who had had a very unsuccessful year in their endeavors to reduce the stern sheets of a big plebe whose ancestors were all big amidships. They wanted one more crack at me, and the sea bat fortunately was captured by them at a most propitious time. My seagoing education was greatly enhanced just as I was about to see the shy little beast—and since then I have never believed anything that any of your class ever said.[15]

Gallery followed up his success in *Now, Hear This!* with a book primarily about aviators; *Stand By-y-y to Start Engines* (Norton) came out in 1966. This book was also a loose collection of stories clustered around wayward navy characters working on an aircraft carrier. Although Lieutenant Curly Cue is now the central figure, fellow aviator Willy Wigglesworth is equally exuberant. One of Willy's reported activities is typical. Because he was owed money by a railroad that refused to pay him (and that used his out-of-country assignment to stonewall him), Willy sent letters to the railroad's president. But the letters got no response. So on his return to the States, Wigglesworth took off in an aircraft and imitated a runaway engine by screaming down the railroad tracks at night with his big landing light on, just ten feet above the tracks. He lifted off just before he hit an oncoming train. The engineer of that train believed another train was rushing at him on the same tracks and (scared to death) put on the emergency brakes. The train's wheels were all flattened out, costing the railroad thousands of dollars. And so Wigglesworth got his revenge.

This book's fresh focus on the irrepressible antics of high-spirited aviators (who in their own way are just as outrageous as Fatso) helped it succeed. If we can believe George Kenney, who in the 1940s had commanded the Fifth Air Force for General MacArthur in the Pacific, there is more than a little verisimilitude to Gallery's portrait of the aviator type.

Dear Dan:

I haven't enjoy a book in years as much as I did your *"Stand By-y-y to Start Engines."*

"Curly" Cue and "Willy" Wigglesworth are the type of loveable, exuberant rascals who win wars for you but drive you almost nuts at times keeping them out of trouble. You find yourself bawling hell out of them and then decorating them. I had a lot of them working for me in the Pacific and you must have had some of them working for you to be able to write the stories of their wonderful but screwball escapades.

I remember once, some of MacArthur's staff complained that my kids should grow up. The General's reply was, "No. You had better leave General Kenney's kids alone. I want to be sure that they keep on shooting down Jap airplanes and sinking Jap ships." [16]

Kenney's comment notwithstanding, Gallery of course didn't have to learn about madcap aviators from outward observation. One will recall our earlier discussion of Vice Admiral Stroop's recollection of his wonderful service in VT-9. He fondly remembered Gallery as the leader, always "thinking up screwy things to do that you could get courtmartialed for nowadays, if you got caught." [17]

A year or so after writing this second collection, Gallery departed from humor and tried his hand at a serious action novel. Briefly, the plot of his novel *The Brink* (Doubleday, 1968) involves a Soviet breakthrough in detection of American nuclear submarines (the Soviets have learned to trace a heretofore unknown leak from U.S. reactors), and their consequent attempt to sink several American subs. The reader first follows the USS *Nemo* as she unsuccessfully attempts to lose a Russian destroyer that has inexplicably detected her, but breathes a sigh that of relief as the American sub turns under the Arctic ice cap, which maneuver of course stymies the Russian ship. While this is happening, the narrative also depicts the scene in the Department of Defense in Washington, as senior American officials attempt to cope with the situation.

Although the action scenes are riveting, the novel was not a success, and not just because of some unconvincing dialogue and wooden and somewhat predictable characters (for instance, Gallery's secretary of defense was correctly called a "dead ringer" for McNamara).[18] More important than these faults, Gallery's imagination failed him in what was usually his strength, in his creation of the story's events.

For example, usually Gallery recommended great assertiveness for his commanders, but that's not what happens in one of this book's key passages. When the *Nemo's* captain comes back to the edge of the ice— the place of danger where the Russian destroyer may attempt to attack—he essentially does nothing. He doesn't shoot a torpedo at the Russian, deploy countermeasures, or effectively evade. The Russian destroyer, instead, shoots at him—and the torpedo is a faulty, circular shot, which paradoxically and fortunately blows up the Russian ship. Very convenient, but hardly convincing or illuminating—just happenstance.

Equally problematic is the import of an episode involving the CNO's offer to the president surreptitiously to blow up a Soviet sub. Up to a point, this suggestion would seem vintage Gallery thinking. The Soviets have taken out the USS *Lincoln,* shot at the *Nemo,* and no doubt plan additional attacks, yet the Americans have done nothing in response. We are not surprised that the McNamara clone is off in left field and that the CNO is the only official to dare taking action. Admiral Baker tells the president that—in response to the Soviets' aggression and to prove U.S. resolve—if the president doesn't object, he will have one of the diesel Soviet subs off the East Coast (which an American destroyer has detected and is holding down) casually disappear. CNO will have the attack carried out in such a way that the president can deny he has had anything to do with it. The president does not *dis*approve, and shortly after, the commanding officer of that destroyer (on receiving private orders) sends all the sonarmen out of the ship's sonar room, dons the sonar earphones, and presses the button to shoot a homing torpedo. He waits long enough to hear an explosion, and then walks out past the waiting sonarmen, who (realizing what has just happened) are appropriately flabbergasted.

In relation to this episode, it is interesting to note that Gallery had asked for Arleigh Burke's critique when writing the novel. Burke (then retired) liked it, and read it at one sitting well into the night. The former CNO had criticisms about such things as where the SecDef would sit at the table in Washington, whether the *Nemo* should go home under the pole for protection or not—but as for the "deniable" blowing up of a Soviet sub, Burke said nary a word.[19] One might reasonably conclude that Burke's Pentagon experience had made him quite familiar with unofficial "signals" of this sort.

At any rate, just as the novel's CNO regards destruction of the Soviet sub as a kind of measure for measure, so normally one might think such a tactic would be Gallery's solution. The novel's Admiral Baker believes such an action will contrast with America's weak response to events like the *Pueblo* incident by showing the Soviets the strong resolve of the enemy they are dealing with. But in fact it is not clear that such is the novelist's intent. Although the Soviets do come to the negotiating table as a partial result of this American action, the U.S. president regrets sinking the sub, and doubts that such toe-to-toe confrontations are as appropriate now as they might have been in the past. Instead of solving anything, they might bring the world to the brink of nuclear war. What *will* work is not clear; the final crisis is again resolved primarily by chance.

Overall, it is certainly to Gallery's credit that he took the nuclear threat seriously and recognized that nuclear capabilities required some changes in military thinking. But the "solutions" found in this novel are not convincing.

A year or so later, Gallery turned back to Fatso, with a humorous book of a new type. What would happen if Fatso were his own ship's captain, Gallery wondered. He worked out the details convincingly and uproariously. In *Cap'n Fatso* (Norton, 1969) Fatso has charge of LCU 1124, a 70-foot amphibious craft meant for carrying vehicles and heavy equipment, which itself is usually carried in the belly of a landing ship dock. While this small craft is en route to Malta to fetch some supplies, its mother ship, USS *Alamo,* is suddenly diverted to Vietnam, and when the *Alamo*'s helicopter happens to go down at sea, all orders and papers for the LCU are lost.

Fatso is astonished to learn on returning to Crete that he and his crew of seven have been completely abandoned. In response, Fatso does as required in such a case—he steams to Piraeus and reports to the "senior officer present afloat." Soon a lieutenant commander on a destroyer escort (named the *Pillsbury,* by the way) is unkindly routed out of bed by the OOD when a commodore's gig heads for his gangway, only to find a mere Boatswain's Mate First Class (and a portly one at that) climbing the gangway in dress whites to salute him. The officer curses, chews out the OOD, turns on his heel, and goes back to his bunk.

With that reception, Fatso regards himself as officially released from duty. The LCU has no orders—but it does happen to have several interesting items in its hold: the commodore's car, a curious geodesic frame that has interesting possibilities for camouflage, the commodore's fancy motor boat, assorted electronic gear, even a light tank (which had been destined for the *Alamo's* embarked marines).

And so at the same time the 1967 Israeli-Egyptian war begins raging and the USS *Liberty* is attacked, Fatso changes his craft's designation to the USS *Turtle,* bamboozles several Russian ships and individuals, blows up an Egyptian patrol boat, visits the ports of Athens and Haifa, and generally causes consternation for everybody in the whole Eastern Mediterranean, U.S. authorities included. As one reviewer commented, Fatso "manages to confound and confront the Russian navy, the Israelis, the Arabs, and the Joint Chiefs of Staff." [20]

Of particular importance is the book's theme of ingenious toughness with willful enemies, which is successfully employed here, as it was not in *The Brink.* As was often true during the Cold War, in this short novel Russian ships tend to play "chicken" games with American naval vessels, and so we are not surprised when a Russian destroyer zigzags across the LCU's bow several times and then bullies up to it a few feet alongside. In response, Fatso invents a "tin can opener," so that the next time the Russian ship cozies up, Fatso's LCU veers right and puts on the brakes, simultaneously cutting a long gash in the Russian vessel's side. After that, the Soviet ship keeps its distance.

A bit later, in mock penitence at this event, Fatso fakes ceremoniously arraigning, condemning, and hanging a sailor at the yardarm, to the Russians' amazement and credulity. In these humorous events, as in Fatso's false messages to a nonexistent American submarine near Russian anchorages, and in his blowing up a Russian boat sniffing about an odd buoy Fatso has thrown in its way, this enlisted ship's captain uses the Soviets' nefarious curiosity to confuse and thwart their intentions—while his own craft manages to escape scot-free.

Not surprisingly, through Fatso Gallery will once again have his say. As a reviewer commented, the narrator and Gallery's characters "decimate the Whiz Kids, the way the Navy is run, typical military and civilian brass reaction, the UN, the poverty program, the Arab-Israeli fracas, our policy toward the Russians, the 'sorry about that' sinking [*sic*] of our noncombatant ship by the Israelis and suchlike. . . ."[21] Such "propaganda" tainted Gallery's autobiography, but because much of this excoriation occurs naturally in the course of the enlisted men's conversation (and, is scattergunned so widely), it doesn't really detract. In fact, it adds to the verisimilitude of the text.

Overall, by refocusing on Fatso, Gallery had returned to his best comic vein. As one reviewer perceptively remarked, for this admiral of the offbeat imagination Fatso was a "vicarious second self."[22] A sequel to *Cap'n Fatso* that Gallery published in 1971 (*Away Boarders!*) was less humorous, and less successful.

FAMILIAR TO ANYONE in the older seagoing navy is the phenomenon of "water hours"—in which limits have to be placed on sailors' use of fresh water simply because the ship's engineering plant can't meet the demand. The frustration of ships' engineers and the anger of ships' captains—to say nothing of the irritation caused to ordinary bluejackets who need the water the worst because they do the dirtiest work—can be imagined. But on the fictional carrier *Okinawa*, as usual, Fatso and his cronies find ways to work a problem to their advantage.

This story appears in Gallery's 1965 collection, *Now, Hear This!*

"Water Shortage"

In the captain's cabin of the *Okinawa*, several senior officers had met to discuss the alarming expenditure rate of fresh water on the ship. The whole Eastern Mediterranean area was currently suffering from a severe drought and the situation was becoming critical on certain islands such as Crete. But this had nothing to do with the *Okinawa's* troubles. Naval ships make their own fresh water. The Chief Engineer was summing up after telling a long sad story.

"Captain, these post-war sailors just don't understand the value of fresh water and this crew of ours is wasting water a lot faster than I can make it. The supply in the ship's tanks has been going down steadily for the past two weeks even though I've had the evaporators going full blast all the time. We've just got to start rationing fresh water, and that's all there is to it."

"I guess you're right, Chief," said the Captain reluctantly, "I hate to do this. But we've tried everything else and it hasn't done any good. OK—put water hours into effect tomorrow."

All around the table heads nodded grave agreement with this unpleasant command decision, and the meeting adjourned.

Next morning long lines of sailors formed outside each one of the crew's wash rooms. Fresh water, instead of being available twenty-four hours a day, was now turned on in the wash bowls and showers for only one hour in the morning and evening. This was a grievous hardship to all on board because it meant you had to stand in line for half an hour just to wash your face and hands. You could have all the salt water you wanted without waiting, but washing in salt water leaves you feeling as if you had scrubbed down in glue. It's like trying to make love wearing a winter flying suit and heavy leather mittens. It's unsatisfactory.

"Where do they get this stuff, rationing water," growled a Marine near the end of the line. "We got a right to have water. Don't we?"

"Well, you see," said the sailor behind him, "this here Mediterranean Sea is salt water and we gotta distill the sea water to get the salt out of it. The Black Gang claims that we been using 150,000 gallons a day, and they can't distill it that fast."

"I don't believe it," said the Marine. "That's 50 gallons per man, a whole gasoline drum full of water. You know darned well nobody uses that much."

"Yabbut that includes everything," said the sailor. "Water for the boilers, the galley, the laundry, the scuttlebutts, the washrooms, and the officers' country too. I'll bet them officers use half of it. Some of these new ensigns we got on board probably think the ocean is fresh water."

"I don't know about that," muttered the Leatherneck. "But I think it stinks in more ways than one when they won't give you enough water to take a bath on a ship as big as this."

"I suppose in Korea the top sergeant drew a warm bath in a tub for you every morning?"

"Korea was different, but I'm going to beat this game," said the Marine craftily. "I got a bucket, and I'm going to fill it up every time they turn the water on and keep it in my locker so I'll have it when I want it."

"They thought of that too, soldier," observed his friend, "There's an eagle-eyed master-at-arms at the head of this line and you can either use a wash bowl or shower, or else take about a cupful of water out in a bucket, but not both. There's nothin' you can do about it but ship over in the Army next time."

While this conversation was going on down on the berth deck, Fatso was tinkering around in his incinerator compartment on the starboard side of the hangar deck.

At this moment he was in a corner behind the big furnace, screwing a length of one-inch pipe with a spigot on the end of it into a larger pipe running through the compartment. The larger pipe supplied fresh water to the Captain's and Admiral's cabins on the *Okinawa,* and naturally water rationing was not going to affect the supply of fresh water in *that* pipe. Neither was it going to affect Fatso's supply, after he got this plumbing job completed.

You might say that in some way Fatso drew almost as much water on the *Okinawa* as the Skipper. When he got this spigot installed this would be true literally as well as figuratively.

It is fundamental in the Navy that long years of faithful service earn certain privileges. As Fatso saw it, this water rationing order certainly had nothing to do with old seafaring men like the Admiral, the Captain—or himself.

That night just before taps Fatso's cronies began drifting into the inner sanctum in accordance with their regular custom. Half a dozen of them were seated around the inner sanctum when the door opened and admitted Scuttlebutt, covered with grease and sweat.

"This is a hell of a way to run a Navy," remarked Scuttlebutt to the assembled crowd. "Here I come off a 4-hour watch below and the water is shut off all over the ship. I'm the 'Fresh Water King' of this bucket and *I* can't even get a bath. What I want to know, Fatso, is how long can you go without a bath?"

"That all depends on how dirty you don't mind being," answered Fatso philosophically. "But, since you're a friend of mine, just get yourself a bucket, hang it under the spigot behind the furnace and you can have all the fresh water you want."

Fatso's revelation of this new convenience of the "club" was greeted enthusiastically by all hands. Each new arrival that evening was proudly informed of it and added his approval.

About a half hour after taps Fatso remarked, "I wonder what's holding up old Bellyache—I'm getting hungry." Bellyache was the head man in the crew's galley. It was his duty each evening to bring up a basket full of steaks, eggs, bread, butter, and various trimmings to be cooked and eaten in the incinerator compartment. This was a custom of long standing in Fatso's inner sanctum, just as much a matter of routine on the *Okinawa* as hoisting the colors each morning at eight bells.

"I think I hear him coming now," said Beer Bottle.

It was indeed Bellyache that Beer Bottle heard coming, but he entered with a long face and with no basket. There was a shocked silence for a moment and then Fatso said, "What-ho, Bellyache, where's the grub? We're all gettin' hungry."

"There ain't gonna be no more grub," said Bellyache as if he were announcing that the end of the world would occur at 7 bells of the current watch.

This statement was greeted with outraged and unbelieving protests from all hands almost as incredulous as if he had made such a prediction. It took Bellyache some time to quiet them down so he could explain.

"It's this new Paymaster we got the other day. He's always popping into the galley at odd times and he won't stand for no monkey business. I mean for sure. He put a mess cook on the report today for swiping a couple of apples out of a whole barrel full."

"But there was no monkey business about what we were doing," said Fatso indignantly. "We weren't *swiping* that stuff."

"That's right, certainly not. Of course we weren't swiping it," agreed Bellyache emphatically, "It was . . . it was . . . just stuff that happened to be left over when I got through feeding the crew. You can't make things come out exactly even when you cook for 3,000 men. Can you?"

"Of course not," agreed Fatso. "And this left-over stuff would of been thrun out and wasted if you hadn't brought it up here. Wouldn't it?" he demanded righteously.

"Well—not *exactly*, maybe," said Bellyache thinking of the dozen sirloin steaks that always happened to be left over even when the crew had beans for dinner.

"What are we gonna do about this?" asked Fatso addressing the gathering. "We certainly gotta eat!"

"Couldn't we get the, er—left-overs, out of the butcher shop before they go up to the galley, so the Paymaster wouldn't know about it?" asked Satchelaft. "Then there wouldn't be no left-overs in the galley for the Paymaster to squawk about. Things would come out exactly even—no waste at all."

"You can't get nothing from nowhere without this long-nosed guy knowing it," said Bellyache sadly. "He's snooping around checking up all the time. He weighs everything down to the ounce, and I'll bet he'd find out if even a cracker got adrift."

In the next fifteen minutes many schemes for obtaining food were proposed, examined, and rejected. The situation looked grim. All this time "Judge" Jenks, the Executive Officer's yeoman was in deep thought, taking no part in the discussion. Judge was one of the legal experts of the crowd, being the courts-martial yeoman for the ship and a recognized authority of the U.S. Navy Regulations.

"There is one way we could do this," remarked the Judge, clearing his throat—"We could buy the stuff."

Indignant snorts greeted this announcement. It was almost unthinkable to *buy* the stuff. The only thing worse than that would be to go without. Finally Fatso demanded scornfully, "What do you mean, buy the stuff?"

"I mean buy it like the other messes on the ship do," replied the Judge. "The Admiral, the Captain, the Wardroom and the Chiefs, they all buy their food from the Paymaster's stores and it's perfectly legal and regulation."

"Yabbut this guy won't sell it to no unauthorized mess like this one," said Bellyache. "You gotta think of something better than that."

"We can wangle it through the Captain's mess," said the Judge. "Fatso,—wasn't the Captain's steward one of the guys you saved when the *Franklin* got hit and they had that big fire down on the hangar deck?"

"Yeah, that's right," said Fatso. "Old Garcia Mendez. I got scorched kinda bad myself dragging him out of the cabin pantry."

Well," said the Judge, "Suppose we have Garcia draw whatever stuff we need with the Captain's stores. We get it from him and pay him cash for it. At the end of the month, when he settles the Captain's bill, he just adds our money to what the Captain gives him. The government gets paid for every bit of the stuff we use, the Captain only pays for his own stuff, and nobody gets gypped or ever knows the difference. It don't cost the taxpayers nothing. We *give away* millions for foreign aid and for farmers. This thing would be a sound economic program."

The idea was examined from all angles and nobody could find any flaws in it.

"The next question is," said the Judge, "where do we get the money from? I guess we'll have to start charging dues for Fatso's old sailors' home here. How much a day will it cost us, Bellyache, to live in the style to which we are entitled?"

Bellyache did some figuring and said, "I would think about a dollar and a half per man per day."

"Hmm," said Beer Bottle, "Forty-five bucks a month! We don't all of us have that kind of money." All the heads nodded sad agreement.

After a long pause, Fatso said thoughtfully, "Maybe I've got an idea about how to do it. That food has already been bought for us once by the government. I don't see why we should dig down in our own jeans for money to buy it again and maybe we don't have to."

Although nobody knew what Fatso had in mind, all indicated emphatic agreement with whatever it was.

"How much do you think," asked Fatso, "a bucket of fresh water is worth nowadays on this ship?"

"Depends on how bad you need a bath and how the guys who've gotta live with you feel about it," said Beer Bottle. "Maybe two bits, if you smell bad enough. What's that got to do with it?"

"Well," said Fatso, "I've got a water supply here all day long now. We'll need about twenty dollars a day to pay for our chow. If I could sell eighty buckets of water a day at two bits a throw . . ."

All hands indicated jubilant agreement with this stroke of genius.

Finally Satchelaft said, "I dunno. It sounds kind of illegal to me. Wouldn't that be selling government property?"

The Judge considered the legal aspects of this question and handed down an opinion. "Naw. To make a conviction stick under that charge the property has to be of some value. The government gives this water away for nothing, doesn't it? So, we're not doing anything illegal by selling it to guys silly enough to pay for it."

"As a matter of fact," said Fatso, "we'll be doing the taxpayers a big favor selling it. That's the best way in the world to teach this crew of drugstore cowboys the value of fresh water. The officers can preach to them about it till they're blue in the face and it won't do no good. But let 'em pay hard cash for it and they'll soon learn."

All hands concurred with this theory, so they got busy and mapped out a program for handling the sale and distribution of water.

The next day was a busy one for Fatso. It doesn't take long for the "word" to spread all over the ship when some new and slightly shady enterprise is afloat. Each of Fatso's cronies dropped a word here and there during the morning watch, and by noon everyone who wanted fresh water bad enough knew where they could get it.

Soon Fatso was doing a land-office business. It involved practically no risk of being caught, because water rationing was about as popular with the crew as prohibition had been with the country some years before. No sailor would report this thing to the officers any more than a citizen would turn in his bootlegger during the prohibition era. Fatso's regular occupation was a perfect front for the new racket. Traffic around the incinerator increased considerably but this didn't arouse the curiosity of any officer because sailors are carrying buckets of trash up to the incinerator all day long. They are always lugging buckets of salt water around the ship too, and you can't tell from looking at a bucket of water whether it is fresh or salt.

That night the club met in a jubilant mood. There had been no difficulty arranging the deal with Garcia, the Captain's steward. Garcia was a simple straightforward soul who felt that he was under obligation to anyone who had saved his life. He delivered a basketful of steaks, eggs, and bread to the incinerator just after taps and threw in some olives, celery, potatoes, and onions, that weren't on Fatso's grocery order, but which were left over from the Captain's table.

While the steaks were sizzling, Fatso reported on the day's operations to the board of directors. "Two hundred buckets of water at two bits a bucket—that makes fifty smackers. This stuff we're eating tonight only cost us eighteen bucks, so we make a clear profit of thirty-two dollars. This thing is like a gold mine, or striking oil."

"You know," said Beer Bottle stuffing a big hunk of steak in his mouth, "this water rationing is going to be the best thing ever happened to this ship."

"That's right," agreed the Judge. "Make that steak of mine medium rare, Bellyache."

"Matter of fact," said Fatso between mouthfuls, "it will improve the battle efficiency of the ship too. When these kids learn the value of fresh water, we'll burn a lot less fuel oil and we'll save the taxpayers thousands of dollars."

"Not if you keep on selling it hand over fish," observed Satchelaft. "Water consumption will go *up*—instead of down."

"Aw, eighty buckets is nothing," said Fatso. "Why, even if I sold five hundred buckets that's only 1,500 gallons. We've been using 150,000 gallons a day up till now, so that would only be 1 per cent of the total. It ain't even hardly—well—a drop in the bucket."

"The water consumption has dropped way down already," said Scuttlebutt whose job it was as "Fresh Water King" to sound the tanks every day, keep track of the figures, and run the pumps. "These guys are learning fast."

"It's like anything else," said Fatso. "You don't know how good a thing is till they take it away from you and in this modern Navy with washbowls all over the ship, they take too much for granted. Now, you take me for instance, I *lived* out of a bucket my first two cruises in this Navy. I'll bet even some of you guys never had to do that."

Several paused in their steak eating long enough to admit this accusation.

"Why," said Fatso, "they used to give us a half a bucket of water a day and that's all you got. You'd brush your teeth first, then shave, then take a salt-water shower and rinse off with fresh water in your bucket, saving every drop of the fresh water so you could scrub your skivvies in it later."

A bunch of well-fed sailors at peace with the world fall into a reminiscent mood very easily. "I can remember," said the Judge, "on the old *Tuscarora,* when Billygoat Jones was skipper back in 1935. We was surveying the equator and boy, it was hot. But half of a bucket every *other* day was all *we* got. So we used to keep the awnings spread and we had rain barrels all over the ship wherever the awnings drained. That way we got all the water we needed—it rains a lot down there on the equator and I remember . . ."

When the clambake broke up that evening, the general feeling was that everything was squared away and all was well. For a few days things continued that way, getting even better, in fact. By the fourth day water sales were up to 380 buckets. That night Fatso's treasury showed a surplus of $135.00 for the four days' operations, even after deducting for the chow.

"Boy, ain't this something," said Fatso. "Instead of retiring at the end of this cruise I think I'll ship over again, if I can get on this ship."

But at this point a small cloud appeared on the horizon. "You talk as if this was going to last forever," observed Scuttlebutt, the "Fresh Water King." "But we've been saving so much water we're almost caught up now, and water hours will probably be abolished in another couple of days."

This was a rude jolt to all hands, one that nobody had foreseen. The world over, whenever people start getting something for nothing they think it's going to last forever. Nobody expects their oil well to run dry.

"Wait a minute now," said Fatso, "that's going to be bad. This Paymaster will still keep charging us for our grub. If you stop rationing water it will cut our food off. We can't let that happen."

"Well, it's going to happen, and pretty soon," predicted Scuttlebutt. "Water consumption is way the hell-and-gone down. This rationing has made everybody water-conscious and the galley and laundry are only using about half as much as they used to. That's where the big saving comes in, not from the washrooms."

"Why don't you cut down on the evaporators and just not make so much," asked Satchelaft. "That would keep up the shortage."

"I don't have nothing to say about the evaps," said Scuttlebutt. "The assistant Engineer Officer tells them what to do and he's got 'em going full blast twenty-four hours a day and checks up on them like a hawk. I just take the water that they make, pump it around into the various storage tanks, and keep the records on it."

"Can't you fudge a little bit on the records," asked Satchelaft. "You could keep on reporting high consumption every day and nobody would know the difference."

"Yeah. That's what I *been* doing. But my tanks have got 100,000 more gallons in them than I'm reporting right now. They're getting filled up. I won't have room for no more water pretty soon."

The board of strategy immediately went to work on this new problem. All sorts of bookkeeping dodges were proposed, but Scuttlebutt kept insisting that the bookkeeping was the least of his worries. There were dozens of ways to make the figures look right on paper, but his problem was where the hell to put all that water that the evaps were making.

Finally Fatso hit on a solution. "Look," he said, "this ship has got hundreds of double-bottom compartments with nothing in them. They've all got connections for flooding and pumping them to take care of battle damage. Why don't you just put the excess water in one of them for a while? 100,000 gallons is only about 300 tons. Compared to the tonnage of this ship, that's just a fart in a whirlwind."

This was regarded by all hands, except Scuttlebutt, as another stroke of genius on Fatso's part. In this way it seemed that water rationing could be prolonged almost indefinitely. Scuttlebutt knew he would be hung at the yardarm if he were caught at this business, but the others finally talked him into it, although he instinctively knew there was a "bug" in it.

So, the evaporators boiled merrily away, making water galore; rationing continued making the crew more and more water-conscious; and actual daily consumption dropped to only 50,000 gallons, about one-third what it used to be. But Scuttlebutt kept reporting the consumption figure at about 100,000 gallons, so that meant he had 50,000 gallons a day that he had to hide in the double bottoms. Meantime, the money rolled in up in Fatso's sanctum and by the end of two more weeks the surplus was $1,003.50. Disposal of the excess profits was also becoming a problem, so the club began to lay plans for a whale of a binge ashore in Lisbon with the accumulated surplus.

"This is better," remarked Fatso, "than running a gin mill on the dock in Panama during fleet maneuvers."

But all good things must come to an end and finally the balloon blew up. One night the Judge came hurrying into the inner sanctum and announced to the steak-eaters, "Boys, we got trouble."

"How come," demanded Scuttlebutt between mouthfuls.

"You ought to know," said the Judge, "because you're the guy who's got the most of it. How much extra water have you got hid in the double bottoms now?"

"Oh, I dunno," said Scuttlebutt. "I guess about 400,000 gallons, but there's plenty more room down there. This is the biggest ship in the Navy."

"Yeah," said the Judge, "but you can sink any ship in the whole world if you put enough water in it. 400,000 gallons of water is pretty near 1,200 tons. Did you ever think of that?"

"No," said Scuttlebutt, "but shucks, this ship displaces pretty near 60,000 . . ."

"Yeah, but look. I was just talking to a quartermaster who takes the draft figures every day. While you been stowing water in the bottoms, we've been burning oil, and so the draft of the ship has been coming up slowly like it should between fuelings. But pretty soon we will fill up with oil again and then we'll be caught with our pants down. It will show up in the draft figures right away. 1,200 tons of water will make this ship draw 8 inches more than she should. What are you gonna do about that?"

This was a shocking development to all hands, especially to Scuttlebutt, who would be holding the sack, or perhaps more accurately, the bucket.

"Well—can't we get the quartermaster to fudge a little on the draft figures?" asked Scuttlebutt.

"Not a chance," said the Judge. "In the first place, everybody would notice right away that the gangway platforms were closer to the water than they should be after the next refueling, and you couldn't miss seeing it on the waterline of the ship. Besides that, we draw so much water anyway that we gotta come in to some of these Mediterranean harbors on high tide to get over the bar. Eight inches extra draft could run us aground. You just gotta get rid of that water before we refuel again."

"Couldn't you just pump it overboard?" asked the Marine Top Sergeant.

Scuttlebutt looked at the Leatherneck as if he had just spit tobacco juice on the quarterdeck. A sailor man of Scuttlebutt's type would no more think of pumping fresh water overboard than he would of treason. He'd go to jail first. "What kind of a left-handed rubber swab handle do you think I am?" demanded Scuttlebutt.

Scuttlebutt was thinking fast and hoping for some suggestion, but none was forthcoming. Finally, he said desperately, "I'll just tell the Chief Engineer my tanks are all full. Then he'll shut down his evaps and I'll use it up out of the bottoms."

"Boy, what a sharp operator you are," said the Judge. "I don't suppose the Chief will give it a second thought when you keep on reporting 100,000 gallons used every day and the tanks stay full with the evaps shut down. This Chief Engineer ain't very smart, but I doubt if he's that dumb."

"I guess you're right," said Scuttlebutt miserably. "If I can't figure out something before we refuel, I guess I'll just have to take the rap." And, on that depressing note the meeting adjourned.

At this same moment another grave conference was in progress in the Captain's cabin between the Old Man, the Exec and the Chief Engineer. They were studying the following dispatch from the CinC to the *Okinawa*.

ISLAND OF CRETE IS SUFFERING FROM PROLONGED DROUGHT. TOWN OF IRAKLION MUST HAVE 300,000 GALLONS FRESH WATER IMMEDIATELY. GREEK GOVERNMENT URGENTLY REQUESTS ASSISTANCE. CAN YOU SUPPLY WATER.

This put the *Okinawa* over a barrel. If she gave that much water away she would be left high and dry herself because of her own extravagance and wasteful methods. But the one thing no Navy Captain wants to do is to reply to an inquiry from the Commander in Chief saying, "No can do."

"Well, how about it, Chief?" asked the Skipper dubiously.

"It's impossible, Captain," said the Chief glumly. "We're just barely holding our own now with the evaps going full blast and making 100,000 gallons a day. I hate to let you down this way, Cap'n, but we're just up against cold facts. Even if our tanks were full, we couldn't give them 300,000 gallons."

"It's going to make us look awful bad," said the Captain, "if I have to answer that message and explain we can't do it because we waste so much water ourselves."

The Exec and Chief ruefully agreed that this was indeed true. But could offer no suggestions.

"Let me sleep on this," said the Captain, wishing to postpone the inevitable as long as possible. On that pessimistic note the conference adjourned.

When word of this dispatch and the proposed answer got down to Fatso's inner sanctum—as word of every important decision on the *Okinawa* always did very quickly—Fatso's face lit up.

"Well, I'll be dipped in gook," he said, "I guess we just live right."

A few minutes later the Marine orderly informed the Captain rather dubiously that one Gioninni, bosun's mate first class, requested an audience with him. If any other sailor on the ship had made such a request late in the evening, the Captain would probably have told the Marine to take him down to sick bay and have his head examined. But Fatso was a special case. Paddling around after the Lexington got sunk and holding the Skipper's head out of water had established a camaraderie between them not usually found between four-stripe Captains and bosuns' mates first class.

"Send him in," said the Captain to the surprised Marine.

"Hello, Fatso," said the Captain sociably. "And what kind of a jam are you in now?"

"I ain't in no jam, Cap'n," said Fatso, "I just wanted to make a suggestion sir, that I think would be of benefit to the ship."

"Oh?" said the Captain, on his guard immediately. "You're sure it's the *ship* that will benefit from this?"

"Yes *Sir*," said Fatso. "But, Cap'n, if you don't mind my saying so, it would have to be handled very carefully."

This statement confirmed the Captain's suspicions, and doubly on guard he said, "And just what is this proposition of yours, Gioninni?"

"Well Sir, Cap'n," said Fatso, "I would like to respectively suggest that we give them Greeks that there water they want."

The Captain shot a shrewd look at Fatso to see if he was drunk. Satisfied on that score he said, "Well now, Gioninni, that's very nice indeed of you to come all the way up here to tell me that—"

"Yessir, I know Sir," Fatso interrupted, "it's none of my business, Cap'n and maybe some people think we can't afford it, but we *can* do it, Sir."

"That's ridiculous, you know what the water situation is on the ship. HOW could we do it?"

"That there is the one question I'm hoping you won't make me answer, Sir," said Fatso. "But I *know* we CAN do it."

Knowing Fatso as he did, the Skipper knew that such a statement from Fatso, no matter how wildly improbable it sounded, was credible. His eyes narrowed and, after a minute's thought, they began to bulge and he said, "Well I'll be . . . do you mean to stand there and tell me that you've got pretty near half a million gallons of water stashed away somewhere on this ship?"

"Nossir, Cap'n," said Fatso piously. "That ain't what I *said,* Sir—but now that you've brung the subject up, there is a certain amount of truth in it. You can give them Greeks 300,000 gallons and never miss it, Sir."

The Captain eyed Fatso with mingled emotions of righteous wrath and grudging admiration. "Where the hell is it?" he demanded, "In the double bottoms?"

Fatso smirked coyly and said, "Yessir. You shore guessed it, Cap'n."

"I ought to keelhaul you and fling you in the brig for the rest of this cruise," said the Captain, trying his best to assume a baleful scowl.

"Yessir," said Fatso. "But them Greeks will be very grateful to the Admiral for that there water, Cap'n."

"Get the hell out of here, you blackmailer," snorted the Captain. "I should have gone down with the *Lexington* instead of letting you save me."

"Aye aye, Sir," said Fatso, cracking up with a snappy salute, executing about face, and retiring from the cabin.

As Fatso disappeared with a satisfied grin on his face, the Captain reached for a dispatch blank and wrote his answer to the Commander in Chief's message, "Can Do."

Both the Commander and Chief Engineer protested against sending this message and thought the Captain must have gone off his rocker.

"Why Cap'n," said the Commander, "it will take all the water we've got on board plus all we can make in two days."

"Yes I know," said the Captain with a look of bold determination on his face. "But I have a great confidence in you and Chief Engineer. I'm sure you both know *all* the angles of this water business, and I'm sure you won't let me down on this."

"But CAPTAIN," they both said in alarm.

"But me no buts," said the Captain. "My mind is made up."

The two officers left the cabin muttering to themselves, and as soon as they got outside, the Commander shook his head sadly and made circular motions with his finger around his temple.

Next day, the *Okinawa* anchored in Suda Bay, Crete, and pumped nearly half a million gallons of fresh water into barges. After a couple of hours' pumping the Chief, who as Fatso said, was a little slow in the uptakes, began to smell a rat and when he found his regular water tanks were still full, he popped down below and checked the valves of Scuttlebutt's headquarters. That let the cat out of the bag—or at least left the Chief now holding the mouth of the bag, so he could let the cat out *if* he wanted to.

A short time later he appeared in the Exec's cabin and said rather sheepishly, "Commander, we've been taken for a sleigh ride—" and explained the whole deal.

"Looks to me like that 'Fresh Water King' of yours and maybe some other people in your department are due for courts-martial," observed the Commander.

"They certainly are," said the Chief, "but there's one angle to this we've got to consider. The Captain must have found out about this before we did, otherwise he never would have agreed to give all that water away."

"By golly, you're right," said the Commander. "Makes *us* look kind of foolish, as if we didn't know what goes on on this ship, doesn't it? Remember how he said 'I'm sure you both know ALL the angles' last night? I guess the thing for us to do is just wait for the Old Man to say something. Maybe he won't be too anxious to air this deal either—after all, we're making a lot of character with the CinC by being able to supply the Greeks. He probably wouldn't want the Admiral to find out how we actually did it."

That evening there was a meeting in the Captain's cabin to discuss the water situation. The Chief Engineer opened the discussion. "Cap'n, due to rather—uh—er—unexpected improvement in the water consumption, I think we can now dispense with water rationing."

The Damage Control Officer cut in with, "It's just like I said three weeks ago, Captain. All we needed was getting tough for a while. Now that educational program I put on—"

"It was very good," interrupted the Exec. "And I have no doubt it had something to do with the improvement."

"I saved a lot of water in the galley too," said the Paymaster smugly.

"And I started a new system in the laundry saving thousands of gallons," said the First Lieutenant, climbing on the bandwagon.

"How about your department, Chief?" asked the Captain, eyeing the Chief Engineer narrowly. "No doubt the Black Gang had a lot to do with this phenomenal improvement, too . . . didn't you stop a lot of leaks—tighten up on loose gaskets—and maybe find more economical ways of running the engines?"

"Well, sir," said the Chief warily, "I would prefer to let results speak for themselves. I'm sure you know at least as much as the rest of us about what . . . er . . . actually transpired . . . so I don't think it's necessary to hash over the details."

"You're absolutely right, Chief," said the Captain. "There's no use borrowing trouble by trying to decide who had most to do with this improvement. The main thing is to continue our efforts and hold the gains we have made. However, we can cancel water-rationing tomorrow for the time being. Thank you, gentlemen and good night."

Down in the incinerator, Fatso Gioninni was saying, "Pass the salt, butter, and onions, please."

"Just give me three eggs with my steak, Bellyache," said Beer Bottle Bates. "I ain't very hungry tonight."

Controversialist: Admiral Firecracker

BEYOND AUTOBIOGRAPHY and fiction, the other genre Gallery engaged in repeatedly was argument. While his storytelling (both his nonfiction and his fiction) clearly indicates much about the man, controversy defines perhaps an even more essential part of his character.

Gallery's first published disputation was a brief rebuttal of some pro–Air Force articles in the April and May 1948 issues of *Aero Digest*. There air force proponent Cy Caldwell had argued that certain circumstances of modern war required the "utter destruction of the enemy nation," even a "war of extinction."[1] In his essay Caldwell threw barbs at fictionalized senior naval authorities (Admirals "Brassbound," "Tinney," "Porpoise," and "Blowhard"), and especially attacked an Admiral "Firecracker" who had recently proposed in a secret memo to have the navy take over strategic bombing from the air force.[2] Obviously he was referring to the "Gallery Memorandum," and "Admiral Firecracker" was Dan Gallery.

Gallery responded in the July issue of the magazine, likening himself to the paper-mâché figure at whom Caldwell had scoffed:

> After reading Cy Caldwell's stories in the April and May issues about "salt encrusted admirals," I went over to Patuxent the other day and took a *Phantom* out to see if I could . . . blow some of the salt out of my whiskers. After tucking my beard inside my flying

suit, to make sure it wouldn't foul up the controls, I went roaring
off into the wild blue yonder and, while up there, thought about
several things that Cy ought to be told about. . . .

I thought that one of the major lessons we learned last time was
that the formula of "unconditional surrender" didn't pay off. Now
Cy goes a lot further than that and calls for utter extinction. He will
not be satisfied to overthrow a political system or uproot an
ideology. He wants to obliterate a whole continent of people. . . .

. . . This method is simply a *reductio ad absurdum* of the so-called
strategic bombing of Germany which turned out to be so utterly
futile.

In a follow-up letter to the editor of the magazine (also signed "Admiral
Firecracker") Gallery distinguished between World War II bombing that
was quite effective—like the destruction of the German rail system—and
the mass bombing that in Gallery's view had had little strategic effect. As
the admiral commented, "To many of our Pentagon strategists any bomb
that fell off an Air Force plane, was ipso facto a strategic bomb, no matter
where it hit." [3]

After Gallery's articles in *Aero Digest,* there followed the very controversial (but heartfelt) articles Gallery published while serving in the Pentagon. Then, in 1949, after some direct warnings from the CNO that he
was on a very dangerous track, Gallery abandoned polemics for a time.
As he wrote Rear Adm. Ralph Ofstie from the Mediterranean,

I am confining my literary efforts to fiction these days—you don't
get as many ulcers from fiction as you do from articles. But even in a
fiction story you can slip in a few derogatory and slanderous remarks
about our sister services. [4]

Although he stopped writing essays in favor of fiction for a year or two,
Gallery really hadn't abandoned polemics; he was simply delivering his
speeches backstage.

For instance, Arleigh Burke was head of the navy's Strategic Plans
Division in 1952, and a question apparently arose at one point in a conversation between him and Gallery as to how to reply to future Communist aggression. Gallery suggested an idea about possible action in
the Black Sea, and followed up with a letter. The context and details are

less important than Gallery's willingness to take losses for a worthwhile objective, a recurrent Gallery theme:

> I would [proceed] with a 3 ship Task Group, 2BB, 1 CVB, because in this way you have three tough ships that can shake off a few bomb hits or even torpedo hits, all high speed, all with very powerful AA batteries.
>
> . . . suppose the thing ends in disaster and we lose the entire Task Group. This possibility seems extremely remote to me, but if it happened would we lose control of the seas? We would not. We would still have dozens of big carriers and battle wagons left.
>
> What's the use of having all this fleet of ships if we are afraid to risk it especially when we are playing for keeps?[5]

Burke responded by praising Gallery for proposing "an aggressive attack instead of sitting on the ditty box awaiting orders," and went on to lament the lack of original thinking in much of the rest of the navy. In Burke's opinion, the observable tendency in the navy of the time was "to restrict thought processes within the limit of pieces of paper that come down from on high," something he found deplorable.[6] Gallery seldom restricted *his* thought processes within the given assumptions, and Burke always admired Gallery for his creative imagination and out-spokenness.

Incidentally, one should not get the impression from the letter cited above that Gallery was a loose cannon operationally, likely to get the United States into a shooting war by accident. In 1957 Gallery again wrote Burke (who had meantime become CNO) on how to deal with Soviet submarines detected near the East Coast. He inveighed against the "drastic measures" that a recent high-level position paper had implied should be used by American ships against the submarines. As usual, Gallery's thought and phrasing were lively:

> I feel we should treat these possible sub contacts more calmly than we do. My approach to the thing would be to show great interest in them, and curiosity about them, more or less in the way that a group of scientists interested in ichth[y]ology would observe the habits and behavior of a new type of whale. Let's track him, sniff around at him, and bounce sonar echoes off his hide,

but under no circumstances hurt the son of a bitch—unless he actually tries to bite us. . . .

. . . if we get too jittery about this, we may find ourselves in the position of taking flagrantly illegal hostile action against a Soviet sub that was on a "legitimate" mission on the high seas where he had just as much right to be under international law as we have.[7]

What Burke thought of this particular suggestion is not recorded. But his opinion of the Gallery of 1952 is worth quoting: "At that time, one of the most energetic and independent and aggressive lads in the navy was Dan Gallery. . . ."[8]

Not everybody appreciated Gallery's ideas. This was particularly true of Judge Advocate General Ira Nunn and others who, in 1953, were trying to work with Congress to improve the newly adopted Uniform Code of Military Justice (UCMJ). Many officers of Gallery's era were most upset with the UCMJ—not without some justification. Gallery wrote Nunn proposing to write an article attacking the new code. Nunn replied to Gallery's proposal with the comment, "The news causes me some concern—[partly] because I've had some peripheral contact with your writings in the past. . . ." Nunn went on to say, "I'm afraid that the emphasis you're almost certain to give will be harmful in securing much needed changes. . . ." Nunn asked that instead of writing for publication, Gallery lay out his views to the UCMJ advisory committee.[9] Gallery did correspond with the chair of that committee, but despite Nunn's request, he also went ahead and wrote the article, and then sent it in for official clearance.

Gallery argued (in part) that by cutting commanding officers' powers at captains' mast the new code undermined discipline; that it made junior legal officers responsible for the discipline that senior line officers ought to enforce; and that it created a new bureaucracy that tied things down in paperwork. In reaction to such arguments Gallery received comments of various sorts and in sometimes voluminous detail. The Advisory Committee's head, Rear Adm. Robert J. White, CHC (retired), responded in three closely typed pages that publication would do a great disservice to the navy. Although he agreed with Gallery's central criticisms, he argued that the piece would outrage Congress (which had created the Code), militate against the chance of improving the situation, and generally muddle the issue with its many inaccuracies.[10] Somewhat later, at another admiral's request, Comdr. Joe Taussig, Jr. (writing from the Naval Institute) wrote a nine-page critique of what he saw as the article's unfair criticisms and many factual errors.[11]

Admiral Nunn himself wrote the navy's chief of Security Review, strongly recommending Gallery's article not be cleared for publication:

> It contains some inaccuracies, but, more importantly, it is
> unnecessarily inflammatory and critical of the Congress in enacting
> the Uniform Code of Military Justice. It impugns the motives of
> some of those who urged enactment of the Code.[12]

So Gallery didn't get clearance.

But then he wrote another letter, asking whether publication of the article *even without clearance* would violate any rule. Again, Nunn took it upon himself to respond, agreeing that publication of Gallery's article would not violate any present regulation, but continuing to request that Gallery not publish anything.[13] Still one additional exchange of letters took place between Gallery and Nunn (on May twenty-fifth and twenty-eighth)—evidence of the trouble Gallery's correspondents took to keep Admiral Firecracker out of print.

However, a reading of the files suggests that despite all his letters threatening to, *Gallery had never intended to publish such a piece in the first place!* He made this clear early on in a letter to his friend Ralph Ofstie (now a vice admiral); Ofstie, incidentally, agreed wholeheartedly with the article, based on his recent experience with naval justice in Tokyo.

> P.S.   I'm sending the enclosed piece to CHINFO and requesting
> clearance with a perfectly straight face—because at present I have
> no intention of publishing it. But can't you imagine how many
> Pentagon characters will piss in their pants when they read it?[14]

No doubt Gallery believed what he said about the code, and apparently by threatening publication he was simply using a rather novel and audacious method to get important people to pay attention to his criticisms. It was not a method calculated to win him admirers, however.

The episode had an interesting sequel in early 1954. Gallery explained in a letter to his agent, Harold Matson:

On Tuesday, I attended a conference in the Pentagon in which Admiral Nunn teed-off on the UCMJ and ripped it to pieces even more thoroughly than I do in this [my] piece. He said, incidentally, that the JAGs of the Army, Navy, and Air Force all feel the same way and that they are recommending extensive revisions to the next Congress.

When I finished his talk, I asked him, "What do you think of my blast now?" Reply, "It ought to be published." [15]

Although after this latter incident Gallery did submit the article for consideration, he apparently never published it.

This whole UCMJ controversy possibly sheds some light on the reason Gallery didn't get selected to vice admiral by the selection boards that considered him about this time. Gallery's part in the "Revolt of the Admirals" controversy did not necessarily preclude his selection. Admiral Radford and others (including many senior naval authorities) had applauded at least some of those articles, after all, and while Gallery was (over time) at odds with several prestigious civilian officials, selection boards are comprised of naval officers, not civilians. In the arguments outlined above, however, we not only see that Gallery has earned a reputation within the service for uncontrollable outspokenness, but we also sense that now (if he had not already) he has also developed an appetite for flamboyance. It would be pretty natural, after all, that someone who had gained national notoriety as early in his senior naval career as Gallery had would begin to feel his oats and come to believe in his own perceptions a bit too much. If selection board members concluded this was true, nonselection would have been a natural consequence. Gallery's fiery temper (and occasional lack of tact) perhaps also factored into the equation.

On the other hand, maybe Dan's outspokenness alone was the main issue against him. If so, it is possible to argue that while no one as absolutely irrepressible and forthright as Gallery had become was likely to be promoted to the highest governmental positions, these latter habits on his part were not therefore *vices*: the military needs some who are absolutely fearless—and damn the selection boards. It is true that Gallery was disappointed that he did not go higher up the navy ladder, but one doubts he would have piped down substantially had he foreseen his failure to select. A friend wrote Gallery, musing on his own attempts to reach high rank and on the suffocating "careerism" that those attempts generated, "I liked the way *you* played it." Others may feel the same way.

All of this controversy over the UCMJ remained buried in private and inter-navy correspondence. But on other matters, Gallery soon abandoned his moratorium on public controversy. For instance, in the May 1953 *Reader's Digest* he had published a piece entitled, "Sea Power— Keystone of Air Power." [16] There his argument was what is now the long-familiar one that the United States imports so much of its raw materials that it desperately needs a navy (and a strong naval air arm). Arleigh Burke reviewed the piece ahead of time, and as he was particularly concerned with the growing Russian submarine fleet, he wrote back that he agreed wholeheartedly with Gallery's argument. In this piece Gallery was again taking on the Air Force Association, as he had while in the Pentagon; specifically, he was defying its attempt to stop the completion of the carriers *Forrestal* and *Saratoga*. Nevertheless, this particular article seems not to have caused any big stir, possibly because of its relatively quiet tone. Much of the essay seems purely expository.

One might point out that Gallery also wrote several other essays that seem on the surface to be primarily informative pieces. Yet, just as the admiral would take swipes at the sister services when he wrote his humorous stories and use his autobiographical books as platforms for political or social commentary, so even his mainly expository articles often had a rhetorical edge. For example, his 1953 article, "Don't Get Hysterical About Guided Missiles," is mainly a straightforward explanation of how guided missiles work, how they can be destroyed, and what dangers they do and do not pose to air, sea, and ground targets. However, in this essay Gallery also incidentally attacks "experts" who predict the end of navies, others who argued against the *Forrestal*-class carriers, and past authorities who formulated the misguided strategic bombing policies in World War II. [17]

Indeed, any superficially expository piece of the admiral's was likely to have a hidden agenda. Let us offer one especially flagrant example. In 1953 Gallery published an article entitled, "The 13 Wild Weeks of the USS *Princeton*" in the *Saturday Evening Post*. This article traced the reactivation of the carrier *Princeton* from mothballs in a record thirteen weeks, in time to help embark the marines at Hungnam, and also in time to participate fully in high-tempo flight attack operations for eight months. The article explained the many achievements of the carrier (including its fabled destruction of the Hwachon Dam with navy torpedoes, when regular bombs had no effect), and it stressed the fact that the carrier performed as well or better than the five veteran navy carriers it served with.[18]

Besides giving credit to every member of the crew and the embarked air group, the article attributed the ship's success especially to its captain at the time—who happened to be named W. O. (Bill) Gallery. One might think that in writing this essay (which Gallery signed with the pseudonym Patrick Curtis Shane III), besides praising the navy generally, Dan was simply patting his brother on the back. This was not the case. In fact, the article was the key piece of an audacious (actually, outrageous) scheme on Gallery's part to get his brother promoted.

Gallery had been bitterly disappointed to learn in July 1952 that Bill had been passed over for admiral.[19] The selection rate for flag is always tiny, and many superb captains do not make it. Still, Dan's knowledge of his brother's considerable abilities combined with his extremely powerful family loyalty and affection to convince him that Bill had gotten a raw deal. He swung immediately into action. Knowing Bill could still be promoted by the following year's flag selection board, and also knowing regulations did not permit any direct approach, he decided to use his own writing abilities and magazine connections to ensure the next board was thoroughly aware of Bill's virtues as a naval officer. Within a week he had written a preliminary draft of an article on Bill and the *Princeton*. Then he queried knowledgeable people, gathered information from official and unofficial sources, followed his regular policy to include salty words for greater impact and realism, and produced an impressive narrative. Within five weeks he had sold it as an 8,500 word article to the *Post*.[20] Calling it "the best thing I've ever written," he remarked, "Actually, I aimed it at the 9 guys who will be on the next selection board whoever they are. I guess you could say that's really using a blunderbuss when you blast away at several million readers hoping to hit 9!"[21]

Gallery also undertook a "whispering campaign," including writing on Bill's behalf to at least one person he was pretty sure was going to be a board member, attempting to get some of Bill's former bosses to upgrade fitness reports already on file, and generally doing whatever he could get away with to sway the decision.[22] Although the *Post's* editors had been in on the scheme from the start, they balked at his request to send an offprint of his article to every admiral in the navy. However, they did promote it thoroughly in Washington, and also arranged to have a newsreel on the demothballing of the *Princeton* aired on CBS News.[23] Gallery no doubt spread some offprints around himself.

Overall, Bill could hardly have had a more tenacious advocate. In the event, however, despite the efforts of brother Dan and Patrick Curtis Shane III, he was not selected the second time around either; upon retirement he received a "tombstone" promotion to rear admiral, as had brother Phil.

Although no doubt Dan thought he was justified in this scheme and that Bill's failure to promote was an injustice requiring extraordinary action, clearly he was skating on awfully thin ice. Gallery's readiness to ignore the rules may have been yet another factor working against his own promotion to vice admiral. Overall, though, while it may seem that Dan Gallery sometimes behaved just as irregularly as some of his wayward fictional characters, comparatively few of Gallery's arguments were primarily self-serving. Usually Gallery wrote to support a national cause in which he deeply believed. Whatever he wrote, he typically employed an innovative imagination. Both of these qualities—deep principle and an active imagination—were evident in one of his most famous controversial endeavors—his arguments in 1954–55 as to how to respond to Communist treatment of American prisoners of war.

Like many Americans, during the Korean War Gallery had become enraged over Communist "brainwashing" techniques that involved the torture and isolation of many prisoners, techniques which not only resulted in some prisoners attempting suicide but caused many American prisoners to make public "confessions" to the use of germ warfare or other fancied atrocities. To defeat such tactics, Gallery proposed a characteristically innovative solution—that all Americans who might possibly become POWs should be ordered ahead of time to "confess" to obvious lies. In a 1954 letter to the CNO, Adm. Robert B. "Mick" Carney, Gallery used as precedent Cardinal Mindszenty, the Hungarian prelate who, just before his 1948 arrest by the Communist government, wrote a statement specifically disavowing in advance any confessions he might later make:

> In the case of Mindzenti the propaganda value of his confession was vitiated because he foresaw and disavowed his confession ahead of time in a manner that was widely publicized. Why can't we do the same thing for all of our military personnel who are subject to capture and brain washing? . . .
>
> I think this would forestall whatever propaganda value such confessions might have. In addition, the issuance of such a directive, if skillfully done, could have great anti-communist propaganda value. . . . We would be publicly recognizing the fact that their barbarous treatment of prisoners required drastic revision of laws by which all other nations have been bound up to now.[24]

Carney replied that these thoughts came very close to his own feelings, but that he was not entirely convinced of the propaganda tactic.[25]

Having submitted his idea up the chain with no apparent result, Gallery decided to go public. He did get clearance of a sort—he sent a draft of a proposed article on the subject to his old chaplain on the *Guadalcanal,* Chris Weldon, now a Catholic bishop, to see if, theologically speaking, men who told fairy stories to the Communists would be guilty of lying. When the bishop said no,[26] Gallery drafted an article and sent it to his old friends at the *Saturday Evening Post.* The editors objected mildly about the harm the article's publication might do to "Dan the fire-eater"'s career, but of course readily published the piece anyway.[27]

Though the article is well written and cogent, we have no space to study it in depth here. We can only suggest his basic argument by quoting a passage reprinted in *Time* magazine a week later:

> Suppose the President of the United States were to issue an Executive Order to the armed forces right now, telling our men that, if captured by the Reds, they may sign any document the Communists want them to or appear on radio or TV programs and deliver any script the Reds hand them. Tell them they can confess that the United States poisoned Lenin and Stalin; they can call the President a capitalist, warmongering dog of Wall Street. . . . Give

the Reds anything they want for propaganda purposes and defy them to use it![28]

Gallery's general complaint about this whole issue was about the *clumsiness with which the United States handled enemy propaganda.* "We follow the book; our actions are unimaginative and perfectly predictable. The Reds know it, and use us as if they owned us. They sold the Big Lie on United States germ warfare to the whole Orient."[29]

Gallery would later claim that President Eisenhower's appointment of a commission to study the brainwashing problem—a commission that eventually wrote the military "Code of Conduct"—came about partly as a result of this article.[30] Others said the article contributed to the Defense Department's tightening restrictions on statements by military men, announced on March 30, 1955, by the secretary of defense![31] Anyway there are good reasons that the Code of Conduct did not reflect Gallery's suggestions—primarily, the damage such "confessions" might do to the prisoners' own morale. However, we note again that, as usual, Gallery was not only taking a hard line (and once again risking his career)—he was also using his imagination.

Gallery was also speaking from the heart and with considerable plausibility when, many years later, he published his last major work, which again dealt with American encounters with North Korean communists.

In January 1968, Comdr. Lloyd Bucher achieved a kind of historical symmetry with Gallery. The first capture of an enemy vessel in combat since the War of 1812 had taken place under Gallery's command; the first surrender of a U.S. naval vessel since the War of 1812 occurred under Bucher's. Bucher's vessel USS *Pueblo* was a slow and slightly-armed navy intelligence-gathering ship working off the coast of North Korea. When fired upon by North Korean gunboats that he could neither outrun nor outfight, Bucher surrendered to save the lives of his crew. Having spent eleven months in captivity they returned home after making false confessions, and after the U.S. government had provided (while disowning) a groveling "confession" on their behalf. (One notes—and Gallery was to note with irony—that the government itself here did what Gallery had suggested it order American soldiers to do in such circumstances: "confess" to what the Communists demanded, while publicly disowning the obvious lie!) Anyway, partly because of the crew's ill treatment, Bucher was viewed sympathetically—even as a hero—in many quarters, and appeared on the covers of *Life, Newsweek,* and the *New York Times Magazine* in early 1969. At the time of the *Pueblo's* capture, though, the case of another notorious U.S. Navy commanding officer, already nearly two years old, was making renewed headlines.

Lt. Comdr. Marcus Aurelius Arnheiter, of the destroyer escort *Vance (DER-387),* had been summarily relieved after ninety-nine days in command, on March 31, 1966. The case was amazingly reminiscent of Herman Wouk's best-selling novel, *The Caine Mutiny.* Arnheiter's officers, some of whom had been keeping a log of his allegedly improper activities, uniformly testified against him. Was Arnheiter another Queeg or a victim of mutinous conspiracy by his officers? All of Arnheiter's efforts to restore himself failed. The following May, congressional hearings opened on the *Pueblo* affair.[32]

Now in retirement, Gallery was not directly involved with either the Arnheiter case or the *Pueblo* affair. However, his own feeling about their significance to the navy and the country compelled him to speak out. He aired his views on the Arnheiter case in a letter to the *Chicago Tribune* in December 1967. He later wrote the secretary of the navy, Paul Ignatius. His position was that the navy did not look good in the public eye, and Arnheiter should get the court of inquiry or court-martial he wanted. His concern was partly the credibility of the navy as an institution, but most importantly "the right of a commanding officer to run his ship without taking a Gallup poll among his junior officers to see if they like the way he is doing it."[33] Examining the official records and corresponding with Arnheiter and others, Gallery drafted a nonfiction book and also a novel, largely based on the Arnheiter affair, both of which embodied his position. (Neither was published.) Throughout, his interest was clearly not in Arnheiter personally (actually, when Arnheiter wrote him, Gallery counselled him that he had no legal case[34]), but in what he saw as an erosion of the authority of commanding officers.

Gallery did publish *The* Pueblo *Incident,*[35] his first and only published book-length argument, and one of only a few books on the subject (Bucher's own narrative, *My Story,* came out a few months after Gallery's). While, in blaming Bucher, Gallery's argument ran rather against the general tide, his sentiments were shared by many in and out of uniform. The strength of his book is in the comprehensiveness and plausibility of his many criticisms—criticisms not only of Bucher, but of various figures in the navy, the Department of Defense, and to some extent of the social order itself.

Gallery was not entirely unsympathetic to Bucher; he thought the commander had been placed in an impossible situation, and had performed rather well once imprisoned. But Bucher had committed the capital naval sin of surrendering his ship without fighting back. In a letter to Gallery Bucher complained that in the modern navy there were lots of gray areas, no black and white.[36] To this Gallery responded, "Certain things were black and white in my time, and one of them was you don't surrender without a fight."[37] Gallery pointed out that Bucher had made no attempt when under siege to man the ship's .50-caliber machine guns forward—and also blamed him for obeying orders and keeping the guns covered in the first place: "There comes a time when it is an officer's duty to disobey a stupid order."[38] Gallery was dumbfounded by the fact that Bucher's men had not used their ten Thompson submachine guns and seven .45-caliber pistols to repel the Communist boarding party. Hence the "incredible picture" of eight or ten North Koreans meeting no resistance when they scrambled aboard to take possession of eighty-two submissive American prisoners and an American ship. Gallery deftly portrayed the basic absurdity involved:

> That small boarding party had every reason to expect they would be greeted by a blast of gunfire and killed. If they had reasoned the way [the *Pueblo* crew] did, they would have said, "No. It's too dangerous. We won't go aboard." But they don't reason that way.[39]

Above all, then, Bucher was highly blameworthy for failing to fight the Communists. In one of his nicer ironies, Gallery pointed out that whatever else one thought of Marcus Arnheiter's character as a commanding officer (and Gallery admitted that Arnheiter was "strong medicine"[40]), given Arnheiter's forethought about attempted boardings and his general combativeness (which Bucher so greatly lacked) this man certainly would never have surrendered the *Pueblo* so listlessly had he been in command.

Gallery also blamed Bucher for failing to disable his ship. With proper planning it would have been possible in fifteen minutes—but of course no one had given previous thought to the subject. Failing that, Bucher could have (and should have) had the ship itself put on fire—but that would have required some risk to the men, and no one on the *Pueblo* showed any interest in taking risks. Gallery reached further back, to his own blackshoe training, and argued that Bucher could have disabled his main engine; he could have lowered an anchor and disabled his anchor engine; he might have jammed his rudder hard over and disabled the rudder engine. All of these maneuvers could have bought time—and how was Bucher to know what might have happened with a couple more hours? Gallery painted the laughable spectacle that, in contrast, actually occurred. Once the North Koreans took over, a pilot "rang up full speed, and Bucher's men in the engine room obediently revved the engines up to $12\frac{1}{2}$ knots."[41] The ship steamed full ahead into Wonsan harbor on her own engines.

Again, had anybody thought ahead about such a contingency, the whole disaster might have been avoided. One of Gallery's most invincible criticisms was that despite previous recent problems when the American military went spying—harrassment of other snooper ships on the high seas, Russia's shooting down of our U-2s, and the debacle of the spy ship USS *Liberty,* which had been attacked by the Israelis several years before (the *Liberty* lost dozens of men but had still managed to put up a fight)—no one in the navy from Bucher to those at the highest levels of responsibility seemed to have believed an attack on a ship like the *Pueblo* was remotely possible. On the one hand, Bucher had never practiced destroying his classified material—indeed, the inquiry established that after giving the destruction order he was astonished to know how much such material his own ship carried. On the other hand, no plan at all had been drawn up by naval or other planners to help the ship if she got in trouble.[42] Poor foresight had thus been a woeful and comprehensive deficiency.

Gallery admitted he was speaking from hindsight, here, but his own habits and reputation suggest he would have been more farseeing. As we have seen, Arleigh Burke had praised him once for not restricting his assumptions to those issued from on high—a habit of Bucher and his superiors. Also, as we have seen, while in Iceland Gallery had gone to great lengths (and great trouble) to prepare for the possible emergence of the *Tirpitz* into the Denmark Strait. His own crew's imitating him by manning the gun emplacements long before sunrise on Easter Sunday of 1942 in Iceland—just in case—is another indication of Gallery's personal habit of preparedness.

Gallery went on to criticize higher-ups for a myriad of problems, too numerous to catalogue fully here. He was especially hard on the "Whiz Kids" or civilian managers who worked for Secretary of Defense McNamara. In his autobiography Gallery had made this incisive criticism of the so-called leadership of the Department of Defense:

> The Pentagon Whiz Kids are, I think, conscientious, patriotic people who are experts at calculating odds, figuring cost effectiveness, and squeezing the last cent out of contract negotiations. But they are heavy-handed butchers in dealing with that delicate, vital thing called "morale." . . .[43]

In *The* Pueblo *Incident,* one of the sharpest attacks by this master of morale upon DOD leadership concentrated on its policy of usurping military command and exercising it directly from the Pentagon. This (Gallery believed) tended to stifle initiative and paralyze military judgment. Gallery found evidence of such inertia at virtually every level of naval command involved. This included the flag officer in charge of the carrier *Enterprise* itself, which, though just a couple of hours' flying time away from the *Pueblo,* inconceivably had never launched planes. (Ironically, Gallery gave full credit to the air force general on Okinawa who, on his own, ordered planes to aid the beleaguered ship. Unfortunately they were too far away and could not reach the *Pueblo* in time).

Finally, Gallery reserved a choice comeback for the argument about the danger of escalation put forth by Adm. U.S. Grant Sharp, commander in chief, Pacific, at the time of the incident. Sharp had testified:

> Once the *Pueblo* entered Wonsan Harbor, any major U.S. countermoves would then be of a retaliatory nature. I therefore viewed the situation from this point on as one involving major U.S. forces in a confrontation that could result in a second Korean War.

To this Gallery responded,

> Come, come now, Admiral! This is like saying that if someone punches you in the nose you won't punch him back because it might start a fight.[44]

With contempt Gallery suggested that the Whiz Kids' style of thinking had infected the highest levels of naval leadership.

Perhaps inevitably, Gallery raised his fire at last to social issues, specifically, to the state of the national character. According to Gallery, "The real cause of the fiasco is our present way of life, the false values we are adopting and our cynical attitude toward the old-fashioned virtues that made this country great."[45] Gallery attacked the Great Society, welfare programs that overturned traditional values of thrift and self-reliance, gangster-ridden labor unions, the decline in law and order, pornography masquerading as literature, and so on. Gallery also lamented the Vietnam-era tendency to "run Marine recruiters off the campus, and make heroes of deserters who find refuge in Sweden."[46]

In the late 1990s the nation has had second thoughts about some of the social issues Gallery raised, what with new programs of workfare, "the end of welfare as we know it," and so on. In the 1960s, though, Gallery's assessment of social and moral values, was (as in his other books) not entirely successful with reviewers or with readers in general; his arguments were not fresh and incisive enough fully to support his conservative social criticism. There were also some other faults in Gallery's presentation, faults for which editors who struggled with this especially stubborn author cannot really be blamed. The book is somewhat repetitive, for one thing; for another, his allusions toward the book's end to "flower-children," "hippies," and other social nonconformists were neither flattering nor calculated to win readers. Especially problematic was Gallery's tone, which, while it came to be regarded as "punchy" by some readers, seemed "testy" or even "hysterical" to others.[47] Finally, Gallery shared the inability of many at the time to see the degree to which the Vietnam conflict increasingly (though by no means exclusively) was at the root of the social evils he perceived.

On the other hand, most of his social arguments did relate to the *Pueblo* incident itself in one way or another; they were not as gratuitous as in that last chapter of his autobiography. Gallery believed the increasing disorder in society (which was partly a result of antiwar feeling) had direct relevance to the *Pueblo* occurrences. Seeing deserters applauded, protestors coddled, and police accused of brutality, Gallery considered that the crew members of Bucher's ship were "the product of the times we are living in. They are all young men, who have grown up in a permissive and submissive society. . . . They saw nothing very wrong in submitting to piracy on the high seas."[48] In a letter to Gallery complaining about his criticisms, Bucher argued that the navy of 1969 was not the navy Gallery knew.[49] Although somewhat self-serving (for Gallery or another excellent leader might have transformed even Bucher's crew into a genuine fighting team), Bucher's comment tends to buttress Gallery's case.

To summarize, then, though somewhat flawed, overall *The* Pueblo *Incident* was Gallery's most sustained and solid argument. We have dwelt at some length on this brief and admittedly uneven book partly because in its strongest points it is so characteristic of its author. A great deal about Gallery from his childhood on is epitomized in the operational criticism found here: his pride in the navy, his fighting character, his understanding of command, his concern for good leadership and morale, his great patriotism, even his insistence that commanders overlook stupid orders (which of course he had done himself many times). Every instinct in his character told him the *Pueblo* capture was an unmitigated disaster, and that had the captain, crewmembers, and authorities been doing their job, it would never have happened. On the other hand, the fact that the capture *had* happened he saw as symptomatic of great problems in the nation he so loved and admired. (And there was some truth even here.) The fact that Gallery's method of stating this problem was not entirely successful is less important than the character and understanding he again displayed in evaluating that problem and going to bat against it. His was the single major voice to trumpet forth to the public the classic naval perspective surrounding the *Pueblo* calamity. At least in operational terms, his assessment was pretty even-handed—and he pulled no punches. As he had not flattered Arnheiter when the *Vance*'s former commander wrote to him, so in the *Pueblo* case Gallery was willing to blame commanders at all levels—and he did. In his writing as in his naval leadership, Dan Gallery first and last remained a fighting man.

TOWARD THE END of *The* Pueblo *Incident,* Gallery turned to a discussion of American character as manifested in naval history—essentially a discussion of principle. There is no doubt that the argument in the chapter excerpted below embodies some of his deepest convictions as a naval professional.

Some readers may find parts of this essay outdated. Not only does Gallery quote the MacCauley poem that was required reading in his schooldays throughout the country, but the "Cold War" mentality that conditions some parts of his thinking is often parodied in our time. For example, Gallery here finds (in 1970) the possibility of pulling out of Vietnam unthinkable. If that view seems foolish to some people now, one should balance it against Gallery's absolute scorn for Robert McNamara and the kind of thinking that got us into the moral catastrophe of the Vietnam War in the first place.

One other thing. In our era, whoever reads this segment might be jarred by Gallery's use of a derogatory, crass term for the North Koreans. Early in his professional career, with the rest of the nation Gallery had grown out of the kind of ethnic slurs—"wop," "spic," "kike"—to which his childhood had accustomed him (and which dot his adolescent letters and diaries). However, in this book Gallery both rhetorically and willfully chose an "inimical" pejorative. As he explained in a prefatory note: "By 'gook' I mean precisely an uncivilized Asiatic Communist. I see no reason for anyone who doesn't fit this definition to object to it."[50] Gallery's language choice here was formed not only by the Cold War, but also by his revulsion at the extreme barbarity of the North Koreans' treatment of American prisoners of war—which, of course, was later to be repeated by the North Vietnamese. Given the nature of those actions (which, by any civilized standard, were unconscionable in the extreme) one doubts that he would change his mind and use a different term, even today.

From "What Price Human Life?"

Since public sympathy in this affair was clearly on the side of Commander Bucher, it is well to take a close look at some of the basic principles involved.

A Navy court of inquiry, consisting of five admirals, spent over a month looking into this thing, and did a good job, as far as it went, which was only up to the first level of command above the *Pueblo*. Of course, blunders were made clear up the chain of command all the way to the White House, so the court merely exposed the tip of the iceberg. But that's all this court was supposed to do.

You certainly can't expect a court of Navy admirals to point an accusing finger at anyone senior to them in the chain of command.

Gallery stands by his convictions. *U.S. Navy*

Had it done so, it would have shown lack of common sense, raising grave doubt as to the fitness of its members for promotion to high command themselves.

The big question that this court had to answer was a very simple one—"When a U.S. Navy ship, engaged in its country's business, is confronted with superior force, should it surrender?"

The court's answer was, "No. The skipper who does surrender should be court-martialed." I fully approve of this verdict.

The Secretary of the Navy, exercising his civilian control, decided that because of the many high-level blunders that put Commander Bucher on the spot, there would be no court-martial. This was all right too.

The professional Navy had to take a hard-nosed view of this matter. If it had officially condoned surrender without a fight, it would be time for the Navy to go out of business and turn its job over to the Coast Guard.

At 0352 Z on January 23, 1968, Commander Bucher was on the horns of a grim dilemma. He had a perfect right to be where he was and doing what he was. Navy tradition and regulations said, "Fight, no matter what the odds." But Bucher was convinced that fighting would not save his ship and would result in the slaughter of his crew. He thought the only way to save his crew was to surrender. Surrender would violate three of the great guiding laws in a naval officer's code: (1) The Navy Regulations (2) Executive Order 10631 (Code of Conduct for the Military Forces), and (3) long-standing hallowed Navy traditions.

Article 0730, Navy Regulations, reads: "The commanding officer shall not permit his command to be searched by any person representing a foreign state nor permit any of the personnel under his command to be removed from the command by such persons so long as he has the power to resist." Navy regulations are federal law, so far as the Navy is concerned.

The Code of Conduct says:

"1. I am an American fighting man. I serve in the Forces which guard my country and our way of life. I am prepared to give my life in their defense.

"2. I will never surrender of my own free will. If in command I will never surrender my men while they still have the means to resist."

Naval tradition also says that U.S. men-o'-war do not surrender. They go down with guns blazing and colors nailed to the mast. Navy regulations cover practically every problem that can ever come up aboard ship—except how to surrender. Until the *Pueblo* case, all Navy men accepted it as one of the facts of life that you never surrender.

Commander Bucher chose to do so. The Navy is now officially on record condemning his action.

Bucher's defenders justify what he did by saying that to fight meant certain death for all hands and would serve no useful purpose. But we will never *know* what would have happened if he had chosen to fight. Perhaps he and his whole crew would have been slaughtered. But *maybe* the gooks would have put their tails between their legs and run. "Hopeless" causes have often been saved by putting up a fight against the odds. The *Pueblo* gave up without taking her gun covers off.

Besides, surrender to a gang of ruthless savages gave Bucher no assurance that the lives of his crew would be spared. In fact, later his captors threatened to beat his men to death one by one in front of him unless he signed a false confession. Bucher says under oath he believes they would have done it.

Suppose he had chosen to fight, and his crew had been slaughtered. Would their deaths have been useless? That depends on how you value certain things.

One of the big differences between our way of life and the Communists' is the value we place on human life. It has become popular these days to say that preserving human life takes precedence over everything else.

This sweeping generality just doesn't hold water. If we really meant that and intended to live by it, the Communists would soon rule the world, and we would have their low valuation of life rammed down our throats.

And obviously we don't believe our own valuation. Otherwise, how do you justify our fleet of Polaris submarines with their nuclear missiles constantly zeroed in on the big cities of Russia, aimed, cocked, and ready? If we ever turn these missiles loose, one hundred million human lives will be snuffed out. The countdown for this holocaust right now, at this very moment, is "one minute and *holding*."

How does this jibe with the idea that preservation of human life takes precedence over everything else? Obviously there are other things to which we give higher precedence—one of them being preservation of freedom. Perhaps honor, patriotism, and duty to God and country should have a higher place too.

If the *Pueblo* had fought, her men would not have died uselessly. The biggest thing the Koreans got out of the *Pueblo*'s capture was a smashing propaganda victory. A ship of the supposedly invincible U.S. Navy was boarded and captured by the tiny navy of the Republic of North Korea. The Reds broadcast to the world, "Confronted by the brave sailors of the People's Democratic Republic, the cowardly imperialist warmongers surrendered without even a fight."

In the Orient, "face" is one of the most important facts of life. The United States can never regain the face it lost in the *Pueblo* fiasco. Propaganda is what the Koreans were after, and they reaped a bonanza of it. They also got a windfall of top-secret intelligence papers and our most hush-hush electronic black boxes. But this stuff was of no interest to them. They gave it all to the Chinese. What they wanted was to humble the United States and gain face for themselves in the Orient. This they did, beyond their wildest dreams.

If they had taken the *Pueblo* after a bloody fight, the propaganda value would have been small. But taking it as they did was the greatest Oriental victory over the West since Pearl Harbor. We will not live it down in our lifetime. Even among our friends and allies, we lost face.

This matter of face requires a word of explanation. Most Occidentals have no real idea of what it stands for in the Orient. They think it is more or less the same as status, dignity, a social standing. But these things are merely the trimmings of face. It means far more than that. It means honor, integrity, trustworthiness, and everything of moral value. When an Oriental loses face, he is utterly degraded and becomes a nobody. It's almost as bad as having all your credit cards revoked in our Great Society. And usually, you can only lose it once. Once you have lost it, a lifetime is too short to regain it.

This is what happened to the United States throughout the Orient when the *Pueblo* surrendered without a fight. We are powerful enough so that we are still feared. But we are no longer respected.

At Pearl Harbor, we were humiliated; but whether we lost face or not remained to be seen. It depended on what came after. What came after eventually turned the tables, and the Japanese were the ones who lost face. The Koreans expected a violent reaction to the capture of the *Pueblo*. It never came. A year later, to get the crew back, we meekly signed a "confession" that we had violated their territorial waters. We will never gain back the face we lost by this.

The last time a U.S. Navy ship was boarded on the high seas without a fight was in 1807. Then, H.M.S. *Leopard* boarded and searched the U.S.S. *Chesapeake* off our Atlantic Coast and removed four of our sailors from her. This, and similar cases of shanghaiing our sailors off merchant ships, led to the War of 1812, fought primarily over the issue of freedom of the seas.

The captain of *Chesapeake* in 1807 was James Barron. He is remembered in history now as the man who killed Stephen Decatur in a duel over derogatory comments Decatur made about the boarding.

Later, the *Chesapeake* won herself a place in history. During the War of 1812, off Boston Harbor, she was boarded, captured, and taken to a British port by H.M.S. *Shannon*. Her captain, David Lawrence, and many of her crew were killed in this battle. Lawrence's dying words on his quarter-deck have become a watchword in the U.S. Navy. Ironically, they were, "Don't give up the ship."

Neither of these episodes in which the *Chesapeake* figured shed any glory on the U.S. Navy. But the second makes better reading in the history books than the first, even though no lives were lost when Barron submitted to search and seizure.

Incidentally, Article 0730 of Navy Regulations was written as a result of Barron's craven action.

Ever since "civilization" began, soldiers and sailors have been expected as a matter of course to be ready to die for their country. This has been one of the basic facts of life in the Christian era—and before. I know of no military man who has won an honored place in history by surrendering without a fight. Certainly Barron didn't! But we seem bent on giving Bucher one now.

This idea of valuing human life above all else is a high-sounding booby trap. It can lead to national suicide. If we really believe it, we can live in peace with the Communists and save a great many lives by simply doing what Bucher did—submitting. But, of course, what we will get for doing it will be the same as what Bucher and his men got during their year of imprisonment. Those who would "rather be Red than dead" can have their "druthers" any time they want them, at the price of slavery, as Hungary and Czechoslovakia are finding out.

We honor the early Christian martyrs now who chose death in the Colosseum rather than deny their faith. But *if* preservation of human life takes precedence over everything else, then these men and women were misguided zealots and fools!

The *reductio ad absurdum* of this preservation-of-life idea is the current wave of hijacking airliners. Airliner crews are supposed to be intrepid birdmen—adventurous, daredevil types. But whenever some greasy young punk pulls a knife on a stewardess . . . off we go to Havana. Nobody has the guts to find out that the hijacker really hasn't got any guts. This is just a miniature preview of how the Communists will take over the country someday if we keep on as we are going.

I had first-hand experience with this fallacy of preserving lives at all costs during my last tour of active duty when I was Commander,

Caribbean sea frontier, in San Juan, Puerto Rico. We had an incident with Castro that turned out to be a miniature preview of the *Pueblo* affair.

In 1958 Castro was still a guerrilla; and he and his gang of bandits were hiding up in the hills of Oriente province at the east end of Cuba, near our naval base of Guantanamo. At that time, we allowed sailors from the base to make weekend liberties to nearby Guantanamo City. In the early hours of a Sunday morning, a bus bringing back thirty sailors to the naval base was hijacked by four of Castro's bandits and taken up to his hide-out in the hills about thirty miles from the naval base. Our sailors were held captive for several weeks and newspapers friendly to Castro, like The New York *Times,* had themselves quite a story.

Guantanamo was part of my bailiwick, and these were my men. I wanted to send the Marines from the naval base up into the hills and rescue these men. But in these days of instant communication, you can't do a thing like that on your own. You must get an O.K. from the Pentagon. Admiral Arleigh Burke, the CNO at that time, was in favor of sending the Marines too. But when he, in turn, asked permission to do this the answer was, "No! The bandits might kill all our men." So the State Department, who were covertly backing Castro at this time, opened negotiations with him and about three weeks later, our men were returned. Meantime, Castro reaped a windfall of favorable publicity in our far-left press.

Incidentally, I met this group of sailors when they returned to the naval base and there wasn't a bullet wound, broken bone, or even a black eye among them. Talk about submissiveness! Here was a group of thirty American sailors who were captured and kidnaped by four crummy Cuban bandits. They came back without a mark on them.

This affair, disgraceful and humiliating as it was, was not as bad as the *Pueblo* affair. But our country's reaction to this flagrant crime against our sovereignty was exactly the same as in the *Pueblo* case. It was to get the boys back safely, no matter what the cost to our standing in the community of nations.

I wanted to get the men back—safely if possible—but to get them back as fast as the Marines could get to them. I am still convinced that Castro at that time was not crazy enough to murder our men. But if he had, you can depend on it, the Marines would have wiped out him and his whole gang. If this had happened, it would have changed the recent history of Latin America. There would have been no Bay of Pigs and no Cuban missile crisis, in which the world teetered on the brink of an atomic holocaust for several days. This world would be a better world to live in today, and our men would not have died in vain.

I wonder what those thirty men are doing now to make this a better world. I wonder if they will brag to their grandchildren that they were one of that submissive band who came back that morning without even a black eye?

By far the most important thing about this affair was the effect it had on Castro and on our standing in the eyes of all the other American countries. Here were thirty of our sailors, kidnaped in uniform, without even any pretense that they had done anything wrong. Our reaction was simply to say, "Tut, tut. You shouldn't have done that. Please, Mr. Castro, let us have our men back."

How could you expect Castro to have any respect whatever for this country after we let him get away with that? How could you expect other Latin American countries to respect us? Or Asiatic countries either, for that matter—where The New York *Times* circulates. If there were any lingering doubts after this happened about whether we were a paper tiger or not, the Bay of Pigs removed them.

The fatal error in this, as well as the *Pueblo* case, is the starry-eyed proposition that preservation of human life takes precedence over everything else in this world. This is one of those high-sounding ideas that we piously proclaim, but don't live by. Taking issue with it is like attacking home, mother, and the American flag. But to try to live by it is out of the question.

Automobiles kill over fifty thousand human beings in the United States *each year*. If we abolished automobiles, we could save all those lives. But obviously, getting where we want to go in a hurry is more important than fifty thousand lives. The fact that many of us, when we get where we are going in such a hurry, will just sit down, scratch ourselves, and have a drink, has no bearing on this subject.

In eight years of war in Vietnam, we have lost thirty-five thousand men killed. We could save thousands of American lives next year by simply pulling out of Vietnam tomorrow. But this is just as impossible as abolishing automobiles—which take many more lives each year. Maybe this sort of double-think, saying one thing but living by something else, is what drives the hippies and flower children up the wall.

It's time to sweep out a lot of this peace-at-any-price and rather-Red-than-dead rubbish, and to reaffirm some of the old "corny" ideas that helped to make the country great. One of them was that we must be ready to die in defense of the country.

Unless this country has got something that is worth dying for, and unless we are willing to die for it, it won't remain great much longer. And it won't deserve to!

One rather shocking way to explain the *Pueblo*'s surrender without a fight is to say that they just didn't think that this country was worth fighting for. I doubt that anyone on the *Pueblo* felt that way on the afternoon of the surrender. But maybe a week later, they did.

At any rate, when the *Pueblo* sent her SOS, we didn't think *they* were worth fighting for. Several of the *Pueblo* crew have testified that they fully expected this country to react fast and forcibly to save them and that they were perfectly willing to accept whatever happened to them in a fight to get them back. They were amazed, and ashamed, when we made no move to help them.

True, their own skipper had surrendered them without firing a shot—to save them from "certain" slaughter. No good military commander leads his men to certain death in a hopeless cause, and Bucher says he thought this was hopeless.

But few things are certain on this earth, and lost causes sometimes have been turned into glorious victories, although if you surrender without firing a shot, you will never know what might have happened if you had fought.

Back in 1779, when the captain of H.M.S. *Serapis* hailed John Paul Jones and asked, "Have you struck your colors, sir?" the U.S.S. *Bonne Homme Richard* was a battered, water-logged hulk, dismasted and burning. Jones had plenty of reason to answer, "I surrender." But he answered otherwise—and fought on to board and capture the *Serapis*.

If George Washington had valued human life above everything else, he would have run up a white flag at Valley Forge, and there would be no U.S.A. today.

In World War II, in the Battle of the Bulge, the Germans had General McAuliffe's outfit surrounded and apparently all set up for the kill. When they asked McAuliffe, "Are you ready to surrender?" his reply might well have been, "Affirmative." Instead, it was, "Nuts."

In each of these cases bright pages were written into our history books. Each had its price in human lives. Was it worth the price? I think so.

There is a verse in Macaulay's poem, *Horatius at the Bridge,* that answers this question about the value of life better than anything else I know. The Etruscan army is bearing down on Rome and the Romans are trying frantically to destroy the last bridge over the Tiber before they get there. The vanguard of the invaders is in sight, and it looks like the Romans won't get the bridge down in time. They call for volunteers to fight at the far end of the bridge and hold the invaders up long enough for them to finish the job. It looks like a suicide mission for anyone who volunteers—and for a moment, no one does. Then Horatius steps forward.

> Then out spake brave Horatius,
>   The Captain of the Gate:
> "To every man upon this earth
>   Death cometh soon or late;
> And how can man die better
>   Than facing fearful odds
> For the ashes of his fathers
>   And the temples of his gods?"

Admiral Arleigh Burke tells of an incident during the Okinawa invasion when he was Admiral Mitscher's Chief of Staff on the *Bunker Hill.* The kamikazes were giving us a bad time then, and our destroyers far out on the radar picket line were catching hell.

Sometimes freak atmospheric conditions carried voice radio transmissions way beyond their normal range to the horizon. One morning on the *Bunker Hill's* flag bridge, the TBS (talk between ships) loudspeaker picked up a destroyer on the picket line over a hundred miles away.

"Songbird to Eagle—Songbird to Eagle—URGENT. Ensign Jones talking—we just took a kamikaze on the bridge—it's real bad—others coming—captain and exec dead—I think I'm the only officer left—. . . I've only been in this Navy a little while, so if I do anything wrong, that's why—but I'm going to fight this ship as long as she stays afloat—Songbird out."

There was a dead silence on the bridge of the *Bunker Hill*. Everyone was too choked up to say anything. Mitscher, Burke, and the others just glared at each other defiantly—and proudly—and went on about their business.

That's how it used to be—only twenty-five years ago.

Epilogue

In the early 1970s, having begun to donate his papers to Special Collections in the Nimitz Library in the Naval Academy, Gallery decided to offer some of his early, unpublished stories to navy-related publications. In March of 1971 the Naval Academy alumni magazine *Shipmate* published "St. Brendan's Day Eve." Gallery had written this story years earlier, maybe not long after his Sixth Fleet task group had visited the Italian naval port of Taranto (which is the story's setting) in the early 1950s.

This story has a religious theme. As we have seen, from his Chicago childhood on Dan Gallery believed firmly in God, and throughout his life he regularly participated in the rites of his church. The Catholic faith, of course, has some deeply mystical aspects, somewhat like those found in this story, which—in that respect—is unique among Gallery's writings. Presenting this story will thus provide an appropriate conclusion to this biography of a career naval officer who, whether sailing on the sea of Galilee as a young ensign, ordering daily prayer for his ship's sailors in wartime, or having an audience with the Pope as an admiral commanding a carrier group, always regarded God as superintending and comprehending his life.

"St. Brendan's Day Eve"

Half an hour before midnight, in Taranto, Italy, in a night back in 1950 that will always seem like last night as long as I live, I was leaning on

Officers of the *Pittsburgh* (including Dan, second from left) set sail on the Sea of Galilee at Tiberius. The ship visited the Holy Land in March 1923. *Courtesy of Mrs. Daniel V. Gallery*

the railing in a little park on top of a hill that overlooks the waterfront and the Mare Piccolo. "Mare" means sea, "piccolo" means "little."

I was alone and the park was deserted. I came ashore for a walk that evening and told my barge crew I would be back at the dock around midnight. My walk had taken me to this park with a wonderful view of Mare Piccolo, and I paused here to admire it and the brilliant star-lighted sky.

Looking up at the clear night sky out into the depths of space, I allowed my mind to browse around among the stars. There were millions of them that night, all in the duly appointed places assigned to them by proper authority, swinging across the sky in the paths ordained for them by the great code of laws that governs all things. Perfect order, peace, and harmony prevailed among the giant orbs out there thousands of light years away. . . .

Gazing out into the infinity of the universe like that, it is hard to see how anyone can doubt that this is all run by a much greater Intellect than man's. It is obviously an all powerful Intellect, which can do things so wondrous that man cannot understand them. And, not understanding, man often arrogantly refuses to believe them.

Coming back to earth I gazed out over the Mare Piccolo and began thinking of ships, the sea, and of men like myself who spent their lives going down to the sea in ships. This harbor had seen every type of ship from the Greek Triremes to my flagship, an atomic carrier, now anchored in the Mare Grande. The triremes had made Greece great in the days when men fought with swords. Ships, both of war and commerce, were still the key to national greatness even now, when one atomic bomb can obliterate whole cities. . . .

Just below the park where I was standing lay the naval base, with its long row of decommissioned ships in the Italian mothball fleet. Moored with its sterns to the sea wall was the fleet which had waged such spectacular reviews for Mussolini—but which wouldn't fight for him.

On the left end of the line were the battleships *Andrea Doria* and *Italia,* still ponderous and powerful looking giants, though now obsolete. The *Doria,* flagship of what was left of the Italian navy, was in reduced commission. *Italia* was in mothballs. Extending to the right was the line of a dozen heavy cruisers and scores of destroyers, all out of commission. At the far end of the line was the *Amerigo Vespuccio,* a majestic full-rigged sailing ship, relic of a past era, still used for training midshipmen. . . .

[These ships] probably never would go to sea again, unless dragged out ignominiously at the end of a towline, bound for a wrecker's yard. To a sea-faring man there is something sad about a dead ship, and I felt sorry to intrude on their privacy and witness their humiliation.

Then I heard seven bells struck by the *Andrea Doria,* indicating a half hour until midnight, and I became aware of a man leaning on the rail alongside me. I hadn't noticed his approach, and he must have been there some time before I saw him. As I glanced his way he touched his cap in an easy, informal sort of a salute and said, "Good evening, Admiral; a blessed evening, sir."

His deduction was an easy one to make. There were no tourists in Taranto. American naval officers in civilian clothes are usually unmistakable, and everybody in Taranto knew that the *Iwo Jima,* flagship of the U.S. Mediterranean Fleet, had anchored in the Mare Grande that afternoon. My gray hairs and wrinkled face meant I had to be either a Warrant Officer or the Admiral, and my picture had been in the afternoon paper.

"Yes," I answered, not too sure that I wanted to get into a conversation with a stranger in this secluded spot. But he was a harmless-looking old codger and his appearance aroused my curiosity.

He was a stocky, square-shouldered man of indefinite age, somewhere between 50 and 80, I thought. His gnarled hands had anchors tattooed on the backs. He had a silver chain around his neck, with a medal and cross on it, wore a sailor's jacket of a kind I didn't recognize, and had large gold earrings in both ears. He looked as salty as the sea itself, and his weather-beaten face was like a rocky headland which had been hammered by the surf of a thousand storms. I sized him up as a retired fisherman and wondered where he picked up his good English. He seemed to be quite at ease, as if chatting informally with Admirals was nothing unusual for him.

After a few moments he said, "You Americans haven't got a bad navy . . . in some ways it's pretty good . . . but we used to be good sailors too, you know."

I was a bit taken aback by his patronizing reference to the greatest navy in the world, and by his somewhat belligerent pride in the past of the Italian navy. I turned my head to get a better look at him, and at the same time he cocked his head toward me. His eyes had obviously squinted into the teeth of many a howling gale and seemed to look right into me and see what was inside me. "Glittering" is the only way I can describe them, and I couldn't help thinking of the Ancient Mariner. I had a strange feeling there was much more to this old man than met *my* eyes.

Being unable to remember, offhand, just when the Italian navy had been so great, I replied to his challenge with a non-committal, ". . . So?"

The old man seemed to read my thoughts. He said, "Perhaps you have forgotten that we have been sailing this Mediterranean Sea for over 3000 years. Don't you remember Syracuse?"

That was reaching pretty far back, and as I remembered it, the Syracusians were Greeks; but I conceded, "Of course I do. They were great sailors in *those* days."

He picked me right up on the implication that this was all very ancient history. "And it wasn't only in those old-time days, either. Rome, Genoa, Naples and Venice produced great sailors. It was an

Italian fleet that beat the Turks at Lepanto and saved the Christian world."

"So it was, my friend," I admitted; and then I rashly added, "but it was an Austrian admiral in command."

"Hah!" snorted the seafarer. "A youth 24 years old, hardly out of his swaddling clothes! He didn't yet know a clove hitch from a bowline on a bight. He was a mere figurehead. The real commander in that battle was an Italian bosun who told him what to do. If you're going to argue that way, it makes it easy for me."

Actually, I didn't want to argue at all. But there was something about this old man that drew me out, and without intending to get involved, I was pretty well committed. . . . I couldn't resist the temptation to say, "[Actually,] we Americans have done more in a couple of hundred years at sea than you have in the past 3000." I knew as soon as I said it that I was too close to the wind on that tack.

"Yes," said the old man with dignity, "from some points of view you have. In the recent war our navy did not do well. At Cape Matapan, and here in the Mare Grande, we were disgraced. There were reasons . . . our hearts were not with Mussolini . . . we had no radar . . . we had no naval air arm. . . . But what's the use of making excuses? We are doing our penance now. . . . And what you say is quite true. You Americans command the sea now. First it was the Phoenicians, then the Greeks, the Romans, the Spaniards, the British, and now you. Your country has a great responsibility on its shoulders. Those who command the sea can rule the world. I hope you are worthy of the honor, and equal to the responsibility."

I wondered if we were. I thought of the mad scramble in the USA to get something for nothing. I thought of how the pioneer virtues of hard work and thrift had fallen into disrepute, and how nearly everyone felt that their American birthright now entitled them to security from the cradle to the grave. I thought of gangsters and punk racketeers openly defying the Congress of the United States.

I wasn't too sure we were equal to the responsibility or worthy of the honor.

"I didn't mean to say your sailors weren't brave," I said hastily.

"Individually they were brave," he said proudly. "Our frogmen did great deeds at Suda Bay, Alexandria, and Gibraltar. Ask the British what happened to the *York, Barham* and *Rodney*. Ask them about Lieutenant Cabrini."

"I don't have to ask them; I know," I said, glad to be able to soothe his wounded feelings. "My country has its naval heroes, too. Did you ever hear of John Paul Jones?"

"Yes, I know him well," he replied. "Good seaman. Handled a full-rigged ship as well as anybody I know."

I was amused and a little puzzled to hear him speak of John Paul Jones as if he were a contemporary of ours. I said, "He died several hundred years ago. I didn't realize you Italians would know about him. Is he in your history books?"

"Oh, no," said the old man. "But I know them all—your Jones, Farragut, Dewey, the Frenchman Villeneuve, Tromp the Dutchman, and the Britishers, too, Nelson, Rodney, Jellicoe and Beatty."

I was impressed by his knowledge of the great naval captains of the past, but noting that the ones he had named were all long dead, I said, "How about the great admirals of the last war? King, Halsey, Nimitz, Cunningham—don't you know them?"

"Not yet," said the old timer, cryptically, "except King, slightly. But we will. They all die eventually. I do know some of your contemporaries—Mitscher, McCain, Scott-Phillips—"

Mitscher and McCain died right after the war. I remembered that Scott-Phillips was the British admiral who went down in the *Hood* when the *Bismarck* sank her up in Denmark Straits.

I was getting a very queer feeling about this old man. "Why do you only know the dead?" I asked.

He ignored my question. "Nelson is the greatest of them all. He's an example that proves what I was saying about seamen. Nelson's crews were a rabble swept up from the European waterfronts. They were the riff-raff of all nations—but they were good seamen."

"Don't you give Nelson himself any credit?" I asked. "Didn't his leadership have a lot to do with winning the battles?"

"Of course it did," he replied scornfully. "But Lord Nelson was a real sailor and seaman himself. That's why he was great. There have been plenty of admirals who were no more seamen than Balaam's ass."

There was no profit in arguing that point. Looking out over the Mare Piccolo I saw in the moonlight that the *Doria* had cast off her moorings and was moving out from the mole. This was a surprising thing in the middle of the night. I said, "Look. *Doria* is getting underway."

My companion glanced toward the naval base and said, "Yes, *Doria* leads out tonight." Then, resuming his discussion of admirals where he had left off. "Lots of officers spend so much time on social and political affairs trying to get themselves made admirals that they don't have time to learn about being seamen on the way up. When they finally become admirals, they are a menace to navigation if they ever go to sea again. Many admirals who are now dead would lead different lives if they ever had another chance."

"I guess that applies to almost everyone who ever lived, doesn't it?" I asked. "Except the saints."

"Maybe to some of them, too," replied my friend. "But I don't know many saints very well. We seafaring men don't produce many of them. The only ones I can think of offhand are St. Nicholas of Bari, just up the coast a ways, St. Elmo, and the Irishman, St. Brendan, the patron saint of sailors. This is the eve of his feast day, do you know."

I hadn't known it, but I thought it politic to say, "Yes, of course."

"He is a very powerful saint," said the old man. "We old sailors would have a hard time without him."

I noticed two more big ships leaving their berths. One was the battleship *Italia,* which I knew was out of commission. I said, "Hey, what's going on here? The *Italia* is standing out! She is out of commission!"

The old man glanced at the waterfront and said, "Yes, that's the *Italia.* But don't get excited about it. It's only for a short cruise. She will be back at her berth in mothballs before sunrise."

Sunrise was only five hours away. Something extraordinary was going on here. You can't recommission a battleship in the middle of the night and take her out on a cruise lasting for only one watch. I had been aboard the thoroughly mothballed *Italia* that very afternoon. Yet there she was, standing out. It was unbelievable, uncanny. A fantastic idea was trying to shove its way to the front of my mind. I pushed it back, grasped the railing with both hands and said, as calmly as I could:

"Old man, what's this all about? What is happening here?"

"Don't be alarmed, Admiral," said the seafarer. "It's just a routine operation. It happens every year at this time."

That statement was absurd. "How can that be?" I demanded. "Where do the crews come from to man those ships?"

"From everwhere Italian seamen have sailed," said the old man. "They come from Italy, America, and from all the seven seas of the world."

"Just for a four-hour cruise?" I asked, unwilling to grasp the full implications of his words.

"Yes, sir."

"Who are they, anyway—naval reserves?" I asked, grasping for a straw.

"You might call them that," he said. "Most of them saw service in the navy at one time or another. A lot of them out there tonight served in the *Roma,* the *Victor Emmanuel,* and the *Caesar.*"

"But those three ships got sunk, and there were few survivors from them," I protested, still unwilling to admit what I was beginning to know.

"Very few survivors," the old man agreed.

I looked back at the Mare Piccolo, and now over a dozen of the mothballed ships had cast off their lines and were forging ahead into open water. All this was done silently, without any of the usual shouting to line handling parties on the dock and adjacent ships; no testing of whistles and sirens: it was as quiet as a graveyard. Getting a large fleet like this underway at night would be a difficult and noisy operation even for the U.S. Navy.

My scalp began to tingle. Certain things the old man had said, and the way he had said them, were beginning to add up.

Once more the Ancient Mariner read my thoughts. "You see, they *are* good seamen," quoth he.

A cruiser and destroyer turning in opposite directions seemed to be on the point of swinging into each other. I reached for my companion's elbow and said, "Look, they are going to collide."

The old man showed no concern. "Don't worry," he said. "They won't hurt each other."

My hand found no elbow, and groped in the empty air, although the old man was still there. I watched, spellbound, while the destroyer backed full speed and got clear.

"Admiral Donatelli is taking that cruiser out," the old man explained. "He was a political admiral and couldn't even handle a rowboat in a lily pond. He's lucky to be here at all. But the destroyer captain is my grandson. He's a real seaman."

By this time the battleship *Doria* was approaching the narrow canal connecting Mare Piccolo and Mare Grande. Any prudent skipper would slow to bare steerage way before taking a big ship through that bottleneck, but *Doria* was barging ahead at about 20 knots. I thought, "Well, you *can* go through at high sped if everything breaks exactly right, and if you don't mind smashing up the fishermen's boats with your bow wave and wash."

Doria was just entering the canal now, only a hundred yards from the bridge, still making 20 knots when I saw that the bridge was closed!

"The bridge!" I gasped. "It isn't open yet. They'll hit it."

"Steady as you go," said my ancient friend. "It's all right. Nothing bad is going to happen."

I stood rooted to the spot. As *Doria*'s bow reached the closed span I braced myself for the rending crash of steel tearing through steel—but it never came. *Doria* steamed right through the bridge as if it wasn't there—or was it the battleship that wasn't there? My mind tugged at its moorings and was on the point of dragging its anchor when the salty voice beside me said,

"You see. She got through all right. There's nothing to be afraid of. This is not an evil thing you are watching here tonight. The Devil would stop it if he could, but St. Brendan, our sailor's saint, won't let him."

Things began falling into place in my reeling mind, places which had been empty up to this moment. The explanation of all this was simple if you disregard some of the superstitions of modern science, which accepts the miracle of the universe without batting an eye, but scoffs at the miracles of Lourdes. All I had to do to see a greater miracle than the one I was watching in the Mare Piccolo was to look up into the starry sky.

The normal physical laws of this world did not apply to the sortie now in progress, because the ships and their crews were not of this world. I began to understand why the people manning those ships tonight came from ships like the *Roma,* which had been sunk, and why my friend did not yet know Admirals Halsey and Nimitz.

I suppose I should have been frightened out of my wits to be talking casually to an inhabitant of the other world. But strangely enough I was not afraid. I knew that this old sailor beside me could do me no harm as long as I was in this world, and he might be a good shipmate to know in the next. The only feelings I had were those of wonder and awe, and of salty comradeship with this old man who spoke the language of the sea.

"Watch that destroyer go through the canal," the old man said proudly. "My grandson is at her helm tonight. He was Don Juan's bosun at the battle of Lepanto . . . knows more about steering sailing ships than he does about these modern craft."

"Old Timer," I said, "why do they do this?"

"It's an old seagoing custom. It happens every year on the eve of St. Brendan's feast day. Those sailors who have finished their cruise on this earth but are not resting easy come back and take a deserted ship out for a cruise on the mid-watch of their patron saint's day."

"Do they all come here to Taranto?" I asked.

"No, they are doing this all over the world tonight—wherever men go down to the sea in ships and wherever there are boneyards of old ships like this. We are more open about it in Italy because our people are accustomed to wondrous things, to miracles, and to matters of the other world. This will happen in your country, too, tonight. Bayonne, New Jersey, is the place, I think; but nobody will see it because in your country you have no faith."

"But why must they come back like this?" I asked with simple faith.

"Because the way they died wasn't according to the regulations. Their duty hadn't been properly done. Some went down in battle on ships that should have been afloat at the end of the battle accepting the enemy's surrender. Some died in shipwrecks that shouldn't have happened. Some saw shipmates drown because of their lubberly carelessness. They all have to come back and stand watch until they have worked off the extra duty the Captain gives them when they report aboard in the other world without proper discharge papers from this one."

"But there are so many of them, Old Timer. There must be thousands of them out there tonight."

"Aye—many thousands. Everybody who got sunk here in the Mare Grande and at Cape Matapan is out there now, atoning for their failures."

"Do they have very long to serve?" I asked.

"Not too long. The Captain is soft-hearted with old sailors. Kings, archbishops, generals, bankers—they have a bad time when they come up before the Mast. Admirals and captains . . . nearly always catch Hell. But any simple sailor who can spin Him a good yarn gets off with a couple of hundred years of this business you're seeing tonight. In a way, the Old Man is a seafaring Man Himself, you know. After all, He created the oceans. And He must have liked them better than He did the land, because He made three times as much of them."

I took no issue with him on that, so my friend went on. "Few of these men here tonight go back any further than Columbus, so you can see He's not very hard on sailors. You can't fool Him, of course, but He'll always listen to a sailor's story and pretend He believes it."

"Are there many admirals out there tonight?" I asked.

"A few," he said.

I was taking some comfort from the reply when he added, "Most of the admirals are down below. Way down below, in the bottom bilges of Hell, with the archbishops, kings, and others who were very important people on earth."

He cocked a quizzical eye at me as he made this statement, and seeing my obvious concern he went on, "But not all of them, sir. Your John Paul Jones, Nelson, the Spaniard Cervera, and some others have navigated through the Pearly Gates. That admiral on the cruiser that I was telling you about, he got in by the skin of his teeth. He saved himself by giving his life jacket to his orderly and going down with his ship at Matapan. He only got 500 years extra duty . . . so you see, not all admirals go below. Even you might still get in, sir, if you're careful. . . ."

By this time the only ship left at the mole was the old full-rigged *Amerigo Vespuccio*. The old man nodded his head toward her and said, "Well, sir, I must be going. We get underway in 20 minutes. This may be my last cruise tonight, because one more watch settles up my account."

He hitched up his trousers, squared his shoulders, and said, "In a way I'm sorry this is the last time. I'm going to miss these cruises. To tell the truth, it gets monotonous for sailormen, up in heaven. There's no waterfront there, and I get pretty well fed up with those angels whanging away on their harps all day long, singing nothing but hymns. They're a sanctimonious bunch, too, and you've got to watch your language all the time. And most of the saints are lubberly swabs who never saw salt water. Except for Jonah and Noah and, of course, St. Nicholas and St. Brendan, there isn't a one of them that would even know how to get a rat out of the lee scuppers. It's a treat to get away

Daniel V. Gallery, Jr., at sea. *U.S. Navy*

from them for a while, and get back on the deck of a seagoing ship even for only four hours. . . .

"Maybe I can work out a deal with St. Brendan to let me come back each year and teach some of these rubber swab handles your atomic age is producing how to reef a topsail. . . . I know about something St. Brendan did one night when he was ashore in Dublin, that he might not want to get noised about in heaven . . . but I must shove off now."

I still had many things I wanted to ask him—so many I hardly knew where to begin. I didn't even know his name, so I said, "Before you go, Old Timer, at least tell me . . . who are you?"

"I was Columbus' bosun in the *Santa Maria,*" he said proudly. "She was a good ship. Just a little spit kit, you would call her; you could hoist her aboard that aircraft carrier of yours. But we really showed the world something with her. I must hurry now, they are singling up the lines and I'm sailing *Amerigo Vespuccio* out tonight."

He touched his cap and said, "Goodbye, Admiral. I wish you fair winds, smooth passage, and God bless you," and he strode off, rolling down toward the waterfront.

As he vanished into the night I called after him.

"Good luck to you too, Old Timer. . . . and may you rest in peace. I'll be seeing you later—I hope!"

On January 16, 1977, Daniel V. Gallery, Junior, died of emphysema, after a long illness. His nephew Phil recounted in a May 28, 1998, interview that Dan seemed pensive in his last few months, but that he had confidence he was going to a better place. He had done his duty and was ready to go; he figured God would have room even for someone like him. Dan was buried in Arlington National Cemetery, where he now rests alongside his two navy brothers, William Onahan and Phil.

On December 20, 1980, the United States Navy launched the frigate USS *Gallery* (FFG-26), named for the Gallery brothers Dan and Phil "and as a living memorial for members of the Gallery family as they serve the Navy." It has since been decommissioned.

Notes

An Irish Childhood in Chicago

1. Daniel V. Gallery, *Eight Bells and All's Well* (New York: Norton, 1965), 11.
2. Dan's grandmother on his mother's side (Margaret Duffy Onahan) was born in Boston. See "Reminiscences of Rear Admiral Daniel V. Gallery, U.S. Navy (Retired)," U.S. Naval Institute, June 1976, Annapolis, Md. (hereafter cited as Gallery, oral history), 1–2.
3. Frank C. Clare, "A Gallery of Fighting Gallerys," *Extension: The National Catholic Monthly* (October 1944) 14.
4. Daniel V. Gallery, *Eight Bells,* 18–99.
5. Ibid., 32.
6. Ibid., 25.
7. Ibid., 19–20.
8. Mary Onahan Gallery, *Life of William J. Onahan: Stories of Men Who Made Chicago* (Chicago: Loyola University Press, 1929), 45–46.
9. Ibid., 50.
10. Ibid., 50–51.
11. Ibid.
12. Clare, "A Gallery of Fighting Gallerys," 14.
13. Daniel V. Gallery, *Eight Bells,* 26.
14. Ibid., 27.
15. Ibid., 23. See also photos in the scrapbooks Dan's father kept for him, in Box 67 of the Gallery papers.
16. Daniel V. Gallery, *Eight Bells,* 23–24.
17. See photos of these "watches" in scrapbooks, Box 67.
18. Gallery, 2–3.
19. Daniel V. Gallery, *Eight Bells,* 28–29.

20. Gallagher wrote Gallery a second time on April 14, 1917.
21. Entry for July 14, 1917 from "Daniel V. Gallery, Jr., His Log," kept by Daniel V. Gallery, Sr. (hereafter cited as the Gallery log).
22. Gallery log, August 1, 1917.
23. See Daniel V. Gallery, *Eight Bells,* 30; scrapbook entries; and Gallery log, March 13, 1917.
24. This letter can be found in Box 73 of the Gallery papers.

Three Years at Annapolis

1. Daniel V. Gallery, *Eight Bells,* 31.
2. See Gallery's letter to his father, November 1, 1936, and Halsey's letter to the selection board, November 30, 1931.
3. See Gallery's letter to King (commanding USS *Lexington*), October 7, 1931, and King's reply, October 29, 1931.
4. Daniel V. Gallery, *Eight Bells,* 32.
5. Gallery log, June 3, 1920.
6. See Washburn's letters of January 12 and February 2.
7. Daniel V. Gallery, *Eight Bells,* 30.
8. Gallery, letter to father, January 25, 1920.
9. Ibid.
10. Ira H. Nunn, letter to Gallery, May 21, 1953.
11. Gallery, letter to father, October 20, 1918.
12. Daniel V. Gallery, *Eight Bells,* 22–23.
13. Ibid., 39.

14. See Gallery, log, February 22, 1919.
15. Daniel V. Gallery, *Eight Bells,* 41.
16. Gallery, telegrams to parents, February 21, March 6, and March 13, 1920.
17. Scrapbook, clipping dated March 26, 1920.
18. Gallery log, July 14 and July 27, 1920.
19. Gallery log, August 16, 1920.
20. Daniel V. Gallery, *Eight Bells,* 47.
21. Gallery log, August 16, 1920.
22. Daniel V. Gallery, *Eight Bells,* 48–49.
23. Ibid., 48.
24. Gallery, letter to father, December 15, 1936.
25. See 1921 edition of the Naval Academy yearbook *Lucky Bag,* 84.
26. Gallery, oral history, 5.
27. Gallery log, August 10, 1926.

Gallery as a Blackshoe

1. Gallery, letter to father, August 16, 1918.
2. Daniel V. Gallery, *Eight Bells,* 51.
3. Gallery, letter to father, February 27, 1921 (incorrectly dated 1920).
4. Gallery, letter to father, March 14, 1921.
5. Gallery, letter to father, May 23, 1921.
6. Gallery, letter to father, February 27, 1921.
7. Daniel V. Gallery, *Eight Bells,* 53.
8. Gallery, letter to father, July 6, 1921.

9. Gallery, letter to father, August 31, 1921.
10. Gallery, letter to father, April 11, 1922.
11. Gallery, letter to father, January 20, 1922.
12. Gallery, letter to father, November 20, 1921.
13. Gallery, letter to father, February 25, 1922.
14. Gallery, letter to father, September 11, 1921.
15. Gallery, telegram to father, October 13, 1921.
16. Gallery, letter to father, October 14, 1921.
17. Gallery, letters to father, March 15 and April 2, 1922.
18. Gallery, letter to father, April 25, 1922.
19. Lt. P. V. H. Weems, "Decommissioning Destroyers at Philadelphia," U.S. Naval Institute March 1923 *Proceedings*, 449–52. Retiring in 1933, Weems became a prolific author and expert on navigation (see Oliver Jensen, "Ensign Weems," *Life,* December 29, 1941, 54–60, especially page 58).
20. Gallery log, June 10–25, 1922.
21. Gallery, letter to father, September 11, 1922.
22. Gallery log, "November to December 31," 1923.
23. Ibid., October 22, 1922 to January 1924; Gallery, oral history, 18.
24. Gallery, letter to father, October 25, 1921.

25. Daniel V. Gallery, *Eight Bells,* 55–63.
26. Ibid., 57.
27. Ibid., 60.
28. Gallery, oral history, 18.
29. Gallery log, June 11, 1924.
30. Record of proceedings of the board of inquest into the deaths of Lt. Comdr Rhodes and Seaman First Class George Everett Clark, November 3, 1924.
31. Gallery log, November 3, 1924.
32. Gallery, letter to Capt. P. D. Butler of the SS *Illinois,* September 8, 1952.
33. Daniel V. Gallery, *Eight Bells,* 70–71.

From Pensacola to "The Gun Club"

1. Daniel V. Gallery, *Eight Bells,* 15–16.
2. Gallery, oral history, 15.
3. Gallery log, June 23 and July 5, 1924, and September 1924.
4. Gallery, oral history, 20–21.
5. Gallery log, September and December 1926.
6. Gallery heard from his mother on May 28, 1927 (see Gallery log).
7. Gallery, oral history, 21.
8. Ibid., 22.
9. Gallery, letters to father, February 27, March 6, April 4, and April 15, 1927.
10. Gallery, letter to father, June 5, 1927.
11. Gallery log, February 21 and 25, 1927.

12. Ibid. September 9, 1927.
13. Daniel V. Gallery, *Eight Bells,* 95.
14. Gallery, oral history, 23.
15. Ibid., 24.
16. See penned comments near scrapbook photos of Dan's Pensacola class.
17. Gallery, oral history, 23.
18. Daniel V. Gallery, *Eight Bells,* 79–81.
19. Gallery log, September–October and October–November (1927), respectively.
20. Gallery, oral history, 25.
21. Gallery, letter to father, March 24, 1929.
22. "The Reminiscences of Vice Admiral Paul D. Stroop, USN (Retired)," 1970, U.S. Naval Institute, Annapolis, Md., 24–25.
23. Gallery log, May 19 and August 1928; see also scrapbook entries.
24. "The Reminiscences of Rear Admiral Samuel B. Frankel, U.S. Navy (Retired)," 1972, U.S. Naval Institute, Annapolis, Md., 40–41.
25. Gallery, letter to father, May 7, 1931.
26. Gallery, letter to father, February 27, 1931.
27. Court-martial proceedings at U.S. Naval Air Station, Pensacola, in the case of John A. Smith, seaman second class (V-5), USNR, January 22, 1931.
28. Gallery's note on the court-martial folder.
29. Gallery, letter to father, April 4, 1931.
30. Gallery, letter to father, May 7, 1931.
31. Daniel V. Gallery, *Eight Bells,* 91.
32. Chief of Bureau of Aeronautics, letter to commandant, Naval Air Station, Pensacola, October 24, 1931.
33. Chief of Bureau of Ordnance, letter to Gallery, April 9, 1935.
34. Chief of Bureau of Aeronautics, letter to Gallery, April 14, 1936.
35. Untitled and undated manuscript beginning "My subject tonight is Naval Aviation," found in folder "Memorabilia," Box 69.
36. Gallery, letter to father, February 11, 1934.
37. "Engine Stops with Ship 1,000 Feet in Air Over Stamford," page 2 of the April 26, 1934 issue of a Stamford, Connecticut newspaper. Clipping is in scrapbook, vol. 3. See also Gallery's letter to Trouble Board, Naval Reserve Aviation Base, Brooklyn, New York. April 30, 1934.
38. "Pilot Averts Crack Up on Greendale Farm," *The Hudson Register,* Wednesday, August 10, 1938, 1, in scrapbook, vol. 3.
39. "Postage Stamp Was No Word For It!" *Naval Aviation News,* March 1972, 33.
40. "Postage Stamp," 34.
41. Gallery, letter to father, May 8, 1936.
42. "Postage Stamp," 33.
43. "Postage Stamp," 34, and Daniel V. Gallery, *Eight Bells,* 92–93.

44. Daniel V. Gallery, *Eight Bells,* 94.
45. Gallery, letter to father, March 18, 1937.
46. Gallery, letter to father, March 14, 1938.
47. Gallery, letter to father, October 12, 1937.
48. Gallery, letter to father, August 9, 1937.
49. Gallery, letter to father, March 14, 1938.
50. Gallery, oral history, 31–33; Daniel V. Gallery, *Eight Bells,* 98.
51. Gallery, oral history, 36–37.
52. Gallery, letter to Malcolm "Red" Schoeffel, May 20, 1939.
53. Gallery, memo for the Chief of Bureau of Ordnance, March 17, 1939.
54. Gallery, letter to Schoeffel, May 20, 1939, 3.
55. Ibid., 5.
56. "The Reminiscences of Rear Admiral Malcolm F. Schoeffel, U.S. Navy (Retired), 1979," U.S. Naval Institute, Annapolis, Md., 350.

Private Life

1. Gallery log, December 25, 1924.
2. Gallery log, November 11, 18, and 21, 1927.
3. Mary Onahan Gallery, *The Life of William J. Onahan* 16.
4. Daniel V. Gallery, *Eight Bells,* 34.
5. *Lucky Bag,* 1921 edition, 84.
6. Diary, February 3, 1920.
7. Gallery, letter to father, November 2, 1921.

8. General photo album number 2; photo taken March 1923.
9. Daniel V. Gallery, *Eight Bells,* 71.
10. Mrs. Vee Gallery, interview, February 11, 1997.
11. Gallery, letter to father, July 12, 1935.
12. Mrs. Vee Gallery, interview.

Camp Kwitcherbelliakin

1. Assigned to the American Embassy in London, Gallery's formal titles were assistant naval attaché and assistant naval attaché for air. See "Chronological Transcript of Service," Container List, Gallery collection (hereafter cited as chronological file).
2. Daniel V. Gallery, *Eight Bells,* 105.
3. Ibid., 102–3.
4. Ibid., 99–100, 105–6.
5. *Eight Bells,* 106, says March; the chronological file says May.
6. Daniel V. Gallery, *Eight Bells,* 107.
7. Gallery, letter to Rear Adm. A. L. Bristol, c/o the Navy Department. November 20, 1941.
8. Ibid.
9. Daniel V. Gallery, *Eight Bells,* 109.
10. Diary, December 6, 1941.
11. Ibid., December 8, 1941.
12. Ibid., January 15, 1942.
13. Daniel V. Gallery, *Eight Bells,* 114.
14. Gallery, letter to Comdr. Jim Carney, NAS Norfolk, [April] 4, 1942.
15. Diary, March 4, 1942.

16. Gallery, letter to Capt. Henry Mullinix, USS *Albemarle,* April 4, 1942.
17. Daniel V. Gallery, *Eight Bells,* 117.
18. Gallery, letter to Carney, [April] 4, 1942.
19. Diary, March 29, 1942.
20. Interview with Manuel Luke, November 18, 1998. Luke was one of the four chiefs mentioned. Recently Luke learned that an attack he piloted while flying out of Iceland did in fact bag a German U-boat; Gallery had only given him credit for "damage" at the time. See "Never Too Late for Ex-Pilot to Get His Flying Cross," *Navy Times,* November 16, 1998, 17.
21. Daniel V. Gallery, *Eight Bells,* 122, and "Talk to the Crew," November 16, 1942.
22. Daniel V. Gallery, *Eight Bells,* 118.
23. Ibid., 109.
24. Gallery, letter to Rear Admiral Bristol.
25. Undated "Talk by Commander Gallery to Officers of Iceland Air Detachment," 2.
26. Daniel V. Gallery, *Eight Bells,* 126.
27. In a July 29, 1942, letter, E. J. King congratulates Gallery on his "fine work" in getting NAS into a going concern, and says he looks forward to placing the "duly autographed photograph of the palm trees" in his headquarters.
28. Daniel V. Gallery, *Eight Bells,* 137.
29. William J. Lederer, letter to Marty Somers, December 1, 1948.

Command of the USS *Guadalcanal*

1. Text of Gallery's speech to ship's officers, September 22, 1943.
2. Daniel V. Gallery, *Clear the Decks!* (New York: Morrow, 1951), 48.
3. Gallery, letter to J. A. Jennings, Jr., July 30, 1943.
4. News release, Chaplains Division, Bureau of Personnel, n.d. (September 1943).
5. Ibid.
6. Gallery, letter to Chaplain C. J. Weldon, September 3, 1943.
7. Gallery's memo of July 14, 1943, in ship's paper *Scuttlebutt,* September 1943.
8. Gallery, letter to Rear Adm. A. C. Davis, August 10, 1943.
9. Daniel V. Gallery, *Clear the Decks!* 69.
10. Ibid. 75.
11. Gallery, letter to D. P. Potter, May 1, 1959.
12. "U-505: The Secret Around Felix," *Kristall,* 3d qtr. 1956 (in German: English translation), Gallery files, Box 37.
13. Daniel V. Gallery, *Eight Bells,* 150–53.
14. Ibid., 147.
15. Gallery, letter to Air Commodore K. B. Lloyd, RAF, May 29, 1944.
16. Daniel V. Gallery, *Eight Bells,* 147–48.

"Away Boarders!"

1. Gallery, oral history, 68–69.
2. Ladislas Farago, *The Tenth Fleet*

(New York: Ivan Obolensky, 1962); see especially pp. 154–56 and 170 on Gallery and the *U-505.* Perhaps for security reasons, Gallery does not name or give full credit to the Tenth Fleet in his published work, though he did privately (Farago, *The Tenth Fleet,* 170).

3. Daniel V. Gallery, *Eight Bells,* 168.
4. Ibid., 169.
5. Ibid., 171.
6. Timothy P. Mulligan, *Lone Wolf: The Life and Death of U-Boat Ace Werner Henke* (Westport, Conn.: Praeger, 1963), 208. For Gallery's remark, Daniel V. Gallery, *Eight Bells,* 176.
7. A. Denis Clift, editor of U.S. Naval Institute *Proceedings,* letter to Gallery, November 19, 1965.
8. Gallery, letter to Draper Kaufman, December 3, 1965.
9. Dan Gallery, ". . . Nor Dark of Night," U.S. Naval Institute *Proceedings,* April 1969, 85–90.
10. Daniel V. Gallery, *Eight Bells,* 177–78; Gallery, oral history, 90–91.
11. Gallery, oral history, 95.
12. Ibid., 268.
13. Memorandum for OP-20 from Comdr. J. N. Wenger, July 13, 1944, cited in Clay Blair, *Hitler's U-boat War: The Hunted, 1942–1945* (New York: Random House, 1998), 555.
14. Blair, *Hitler's U-boat War,* 553.
15. "*U-505:* The Secret Around Felix."

16. Daniel V. Gallery, *Twenty Million Tons,* 297–98. Gallery tells of an American fishing the German from the sea to ask the question, then throwing him right back. According to Zenon Lukosius and Wayne Pickles, members of the *Pillsbury* boarding party, this is a misapprehension—the German had been rescued by, and was put back into, a boat from the *Jenks.* Zenon Lukosius and Wayne Pickles, interview by Gilliland, June 2, 1998.
17. Rear Adm. Earl Trosino, USN (Ret.), interview by Gilliland, July 7, 1998.
18. "*U-505:* The Secret Around Felix." Gilliland's interview of July 7, 1998, with Trosino confirmed this account as accurate.
19. Gallery memo to Admiral McCann, March 6, 1945. Bednarczyk received a Commendation Ribbon and a Navy and Marine Corps Medal.
20. When asked during an interview with Gilliland, Trosino did not remember seeing Ewald in the regular interrogations of the crew. Gallery apparently had already decided to give Ewald special treatment.
21. Gallery, "Memo to Whom it May Concern," March 4, 1948.
22. "*U-505:* The Secret Around Felix."
23. Ibid.

24. Gallery, "Memo to Whom it May Concern."

25. Trosino, interview July; Blair, *Hitler's U-boat War,* 554. Gallery's write-ups consistently and repeatedly emphasize Trosino's courage and resourcefulness but never mention Rucker.

26. Trosino, interview.

27. Ibid.

28. Axel Loewe, letter to Gallery, September 29, 1955.

29. Gallery, letter to Bednarczyk, December 20, 1944.

30. Trosino, interview.

31. See various letters to and from Gallery in Box 37.

32. Lohr, letter to Gallery, March 18, 1957.

Gallery and "The Revolt of the Admirals"

1. "Recollections of Rear Admiral Henry J. Miller, USN (Ret.)" 1970, U.S. Naval Institute, Annapolis, Md., vol. 1, pp. 101–2.

2. "Letter of young Watts to his Dad," October 5, 1945, in chronological file.

3. Daniel V. Gallery, *Eight Bells,* 215.

4. Danny Gallery (Dan III), interview by Shenk, June 12, 1998.

5. "Reminiscences of Vice Admiral Lawson P. Ramage, U.S.N. (Ret.)," June 1975, U.S. Naval Institute, Annapolis, Md., 206–9 (hereafter cited as Ramage, oral history).

6. Jeffrey G. Barlow, *Revolt of the Admirals: The Fight for Naval Aviation, 1945–1950* (Washington, D.C.: Naval Historical Center, 1994), 58; Mr. Stephen F. Leo, interview by Dr. George M. Watson, Jr., August 18, 1982, United States Air Force Oral History Program, 30, 54 (hereafter cited as Leo, oral history).

7. Barlow, *Revolt of the Admirals,* 53.

8. Gallery, letter to Clark, January 12, 1968.

9. "The Rear Admiral Daniel V. Gallery Memorandum," *Army-Navy–Air Force Register,* December 11, 1954, 22.

10. Barlow, *Revolt of the Admirals,* 120.

11. Ibid., n. 55, ch. 4, cites Denfeld, memo to SECNAV, April 8, 1948.

12. "Sullivan Censures Top Navy Official," *New York Times,* April 10, 1948, 7.

13. Gallery, letter to Rear Adm. J. W. Reaves, April 21, 1948.

14. Gallery, letter to Cy Caldwell, August 26, 1948.

15. Gallery, letter to Deputy CNO (Air), November 9, 1948.

16. Grosse Isle Address, Approximate Text, 1, Box 84.

17. Ibid., 7.

18. Ibid., 6.

19. Ibid., 10; *Science Illustrated* (February 1949).

20. Denfeld, memo to Gallery, February 21, 1949.

21. Daniel V. Gallery, *Eight Bells,* 223.

22. Barlow, *Revolt of the Admirals,* 198–99.
23. The "Gambling" article became "An Admiral Talks Back to the Airmen," *Saturday Evening Post,* June 25, 1949.
24. Gallery, letter to Marty Somers, March 29, 1954.
25. Leo, oral history, 80.
26. Ibid., 67.
27. Daniel V. Gallery, *Eight Bells,* 230–31.
28. Byrd, letter to Gallery, April 27, 1949.
29. Memo of uncertain date, probably late April 1949, Box 57.
30. Mrs. Vee Gallery, interview.
31. Gallery, letter to Ben Hibbs, June 9, 1949.
32. Gallery to Somers, May 5, 1949.
33. Gallery, letter to Hibbs, May 16, 1949.
34. Hibbs, letter to Gallery, May 17, 1949.
35. Ramage, oral history, 220–21. (Ramage mistakenly recalls the article in question as "If This Be Treason.")
36. Daniel V. Gallery, *Eight Bells,* 228.
37. "The Armed Services Battle it Out," *Life,* June 6, 1949, 42.
38. *Life,* June 27, 13.
39. C. T. Durgin, letter to Gallery, September 23, 1949.
40. Arthur W. Radford, *From Pearl Harbor to Vietnam: The Memoirs of Admiral Arthur W. Radford,* ed. Stephen Jurika, Jr. (Stanford, Calif.: Hoover Institution Press, ca. 1980), 195.
41. Daniel V. Gallery, "Don't Let Them Cripple the Navy!" *Saturday Evening Post,* October 27, 1949, 46.
42. Gallery, letter to Cole, November 12, 1949.
43. Daniel V. Gallery, "If This Be Treason," *Collier's,* January 21, 1950.
44. Daniel V. Gallery, *Eight Bells,* 225.
45. Gallery, letter to Louis Ruppel, January 30, 1950.
46. Gallery, letter to Jocko Clark, January 21, 1968.
47. Gallery, letter to Crommelin, January 23, 1950.
48. Gallery, letter to Clark, January 21, 1968.
49. Barlow, *Revolt of the Admirals,* 56.
50. Holloway, letter to Gallery, July 8, 1949; King, letter to Gallery, January 18, 1950; Hart, letter to Gallery, July 13, 1949.
51. Mary Dockstader, letters to Gallery, August 23, September 4, and October 5, 1949.
52. Barlow, *Revolt of the Admirals,* "Conclusions," 291–94.
53. Opening words of lead for Dan Gallery, "Don't Damn the Carriers," *Science Illustrated* (February 1949).
54. Barlow, *Revolt of the Admirals,* 244.

Admiral at Sea

1. Gallery, letter to Phil Gallery, early November 1949.
2. Gallery, letter to Capt. W. W.

Smith, USN (Ret.), November 18, 1949.

3. Gallery, letter to Capt. Malen Durski, USN, July 27, 1950.

4. Daniel V. Gallery, *Eight Bells,* 236.

5. "Dan Gallery was writing for the *Saturday Evening Post* and *Collier's* at the time, so it was a great treat to be with him, because he was always out for a story. . . ." "Reminiscences of Admiral James S. Russell, USN, 1984–85, U.S. Naval Institute, Annapolis, Md. 292–93 (hereafter cited as Russell, oral history).

6. Daniel V. Gallery, letter to Adm. A. W. Radford, August 28, 1952.

7. Capt. Edward L. Beach, interview, February 11, 1997.

8. From Wouk's speech to the Naval Institute, reprinted as "Herman Wouk's Navy," U.S. Naval Institute *Proceedings,* June 1995, 28.

9. Mrs. Vee Gallery, interview.

10. See especially Gallery's letters to Wouk of May 9 and June 2, 1971.

11. Mrs. Vee Gallery, interview.

12. Russell, oral history, 307.

13. Gallery, letter to Lt. Comdr. Frank Metzner, September 22, 1952.

14. Russell, oral history, 298.

15. Daniel V. Gallery, *Eight Bells,* 243.

16. Russell, oral history, 298.

17. Ibid., 298–99.

18. See Gallery's note to editor, *Naval Aviation News,* October 3, 1951.

19. Russell, oral history, 300.

20. This story constitutes the concluding episode of Gallery's collection, *Now, Hear This!* (New York: Norton, 1965), 236–54.

21. Beach, interview.

22. Daniel V. Gallery, *Eight Bells,* 240.

23. Russell, oral history, 293.

24. Ibid., 292.

25. Daniel V. Gallery, "Could We Stop a Red U-Boat Attack?" January 31, 1953, 29.

26. Ibid., 88.

Admiral Ashore

1. Daniel V. Gallery, *Eight Bells,* 245–46. Gallery had additional duty as commandant of the Ninth Naval District, Great Lakes, the last two years he was there.

2. At San Juan he had additional duty as commandant, Tenth Naval District, and commander, Antilles Defense Command (from October 1957).

3. Daniel V. Gallery, *Eight Bells,* 263–64.

4. Ibid., 265–67.

5. Dan Gallery III, interview.

6. Daniel V. Gallery, "The Secret of the Great Upset," *Saturday Evening Post,* December 1, 1951.

7. Beach, interview.

8. Daniel V. Gallery, *Eight Bells,* 256–58; Shirley Povich, "This Morning," *Washington Post,* August 15, 1962, sec. D, p. 1; and Jack McDonald, "Short Wave Can Make Coach a Mere Flunkie," *San Francisco Call-Bulletin,* October 17, 1956.

9. Dan Gallery, III, interview.

10. Daniel V. Gallery, *Twenty Million Tons,* 312–13.

11. Memorandum For Under Secretary Charles Thomas, March 19, 1953.

12. Daniel V. Gallery, *Twenty Million Tons,* 314.

13. "Adm. Roy S. Benson, Oral History," 1984, U.S. Naval Institute, Annapolis, Md., 347.

14. Daniel V. Gallery, memorandum to Capt. Walter Karig, November 29, 1948.

15. Daniel V. Gallery, letter to Rear Adm. R. F. Hickey, USN, October 10, 1950.

16. Beach interview.

17. Gallery, letter to Hickey.

18. Daniel V. Gallery, *Twenty Million Tons,* 316; R. A. Ofstie, letter to Gallery, April 1, 1953.

19. Daniel V. Gallery, *Twenty Million Tons,* 319.

20. Daniel V. Gallery, *Eight Bells,* 248.

21. Keith Gill, collections coordinator, Museum of Science and Industry, conversation with editors, June 3, 1998.

22. Keith Gill, conversations with editors, July 1, 1998.

23. Daniel V. Gallery, *Eight Bells,* 272.

24. Daniel V. Gallery, "My Steel Band," *Shipmate,* January–February, 1974, 31.

25. Ibid., 31.

26. Gallery, oral history, 196–97.

27. Daniel V. Gallery, "My Steel Band," 31, and Daniel V. Gallery, *Eight Bells,* 274–75.

28. "Dan Gallery Band Charms President," *Chicago Daily News,* February 23, 1960.

29. Gallery, letter to Rudy F. Onsrud, president, Onsrud Machine Works, May 4, 1957.

30. Pete Seeger letter to Gallery, signed by TAS [Toshi-Aline Seeger], July 8, 1957.

31. Gallery, letter to Sommers, May 24, 1957.

32. Itinerary, U.S. Navy Steel Band, October 25–November 7, 1971.

33. Senior Chief Dennis Allard, band leader of the Navy Steel Band, telephone conversation with Shenk, October 24, 1997.

34. Daniel V. Gallery, *Eight Bells,* 252.

35. Gallery, letter to father, February 25, 1922.

36. Gallery log, May 5, 1922.

37. Gallery log various entries, March–November, 1923.

38. *Idaho Yarn,* Saturday, July 17, 1926.

39. Gallery, letters to father, April 11 and 15, 1927.

40. Gallery, letter to father, March 21, 1937.

41. Daniel V. Gallery, *Clear the Decks!* 36.

42. Dan Gallery III, interview.

43. USS *Hancock* (CV19) Release No. J-1, December 1, 1945, 1–2.

44. Ibid., 3.

45. Statistics for Gallery's OpDevFor baseball performance can be found on stat sheet in file labelled "Memorabilia" (Box 69).

46. Daniel V. Gallery, *Eight Bells,* 252–54.

47. The article, "Play by the Rules? Nuts!", *Sports Illustrated,* February 4, 1957, 46–47, appeared after Gallery had been transferred to Puerto Rico.

48. Gallery, letter to Commissioner Landis, June 12, 1942. Gallery was answered by Thomas Connolly, umpire-in-chief of the American League.

49. *Sports Illustrated* summarizes the controversy in "The Admiral Laughs Last," May 6, 1957, 31; see also Gallery's letter to the magazine on page 81.

50. Daniel V. Gallery, "Pitcher in a Jam? Call the Weatherman!", *Sports Illustrated,* April 15, 1957.

51. Daniel V. Gallery, *Eight Bells,* 255–56.

52. Daniel V. Gallery, letter to Rear Adm. J. P. Womble, Jr., May 25, 1956.

53. Gallery, letter to Vice Adm. A. K. Doyle, July 13, 1956.

Autobiographer

1. See Gallery's letter to Arleigh Burke, December 16, 1957, and Burke's reply, January 14, 1958.

2. Daniel V. Gallery, *Eight Bells,* 251, 281.

3. Burke, letter to Gallery, January 21, 1960.

4. Daniel V. Gallery, *Eight Bells,* 281–82.

5. See Gallery's diary of European cruise on USS *Pittsburgh,* 1922–24.

6. Mrs. Vee Gallery, interview.

7. Gallery, letter to "dear Phil," July 22, [no year], Box 34.

8. Daniel V. Gallery, letter to Bill Gallery, May 15, 1967.

9. Gallery, letter to "Dave" at Kollmann Instruments, January 29, 1964.

10. Daniel V. Gallery, letter to Bill Gallery, May 15, 1967.

11. Daniel V. Gallery, *Clear the Decks!,* 58–59.

12. Ibid., 158.

13. Ibid., 63.

14. Published in 1956; printed in 1957 in England in revised form as *We Captured a U-Boat;* later republished in America as *U-505.*

15. Copies of this film are held at the Museum of Science and Industry at Chicago, at the United States Naval Academy, and by The Department of Defense Joint Combat Camera Center.

16. Capt. Herbert Lange, letter to Gallery, September 1, 1949. (Box 39).

17. Daniel V. Gallery, *Twenty Million Tons,* 168–69.

18. Blair, *Hitler's U-Boat War,* 554.

19. Ibid., 244, 294.

20. Ibid., 309, 310, and 311, respectively.

21. Samuel Eliot Morison, letter to Gallery, January 6, 1957.

22. Adm. Friedrich Ruge, letter to Gallery, January 6, 1957.

23. Lotte Meyer, letter to Gallery, December 14, 1956.
24. Grossadmiral Dönitz, letter to Gallery (trans.), Dec. 14, 1956.
25. Eric Swenson, letter to Gallery, December 15, 1964, Box 7.
26. Gallery, letter to Herman Wouk, April 25, [1965].
27. *Virginia Kirkus Bulletin,* August 1, 1965.
28. See Gallery, Daniel V. [Patrick Custis Shane III, pseud.], "The 13 Wild Weeks of the USS *Princeton*," *Saturday Evening Post,* March 14, 1953.
29. Gallery, letter to Metzner, August 31, 1952.
30. Gallery, letter to Metzner, September 22, 1952.
31. Gallery, letter to Metzner, August 31, 1952.
32. Pages 225–26.
33. Gallery, letter to Marty Somers, August 4, 1953.
34. Gallery, letter to J. M. Macheskey, February 3, 1959.
35. Daniel V. Gallery, *Twenty Million Tons,* 9.
36. Gallery, letter to Henry Regnery, April 22, 1959.

Fiction Writer

1. He published others in such journals as *Collier's* and *Nation's Business.*
2. Retitled "Fatso's Bomb-Disposal Job," in *Now, Hear This!;* see 169.
3. Herman Wouk, "Herman Wouk's Navy," U.S. Naval Institute *Proceedings,* June 1995, 28.
4. H. C. Rand, letter to Gallery, November 29, 1966.
5. Daniel V. Gallery, *Now, Hear This!,* 42.
6. Ibid., c. 2. However, it was titled "Phantom of the Fleet" in the September 11, 1954, issue of *Collier's.*
7. Lt. D. C. Lory, Canadian Armed Forces Special, April 1966.
8. "Monkey Business at Mers el Kebir," *Collier's,* September 22, 1951.
9. Anonymous note to *Collier's,* September 23, 1951.
10. Merrill Pollack, letter to Gallery, August 2, 1963.
11. C. S. Forester, letter to Gallery, September 27, 1963.
12. "Books of the Times: End Papers," Harry Gilroy, *New York Times,* uncertain date.
13. Robert Poos, EPS, "Fatso's Skullduggery Below," review of *Now, Hear This!,* by Daniel V. Gallery, uncertain date.
14. David L. McDonald, letter to gallery, March 19, 1965.
15. Arleigh Burke, letter to Gallery, December 29, 1964.
16. George Kenney, letter to Gallery, July 11, 1966.
17. "The Reminiscences of Vice Admiral Paul D. Stroop, USN (Ret.)," 1970, U.S. Naval Institute, Annapolis, Md., 29.
18. S.H., "Admiral Unloads His

Opinions," *San Antonio Express,*
October 6, 1988.

19. Burke, letter to Gallery with critiques, February 12, 1968.

20. Win Pendleton, copy for WKIS (Orlando 740), review of *Now, Hear This!* by Daniel V. Gallery, May 14, 1970.

21. Shirley K. Sullivan, *Macon (Georgia) Telegraph and News,* review of *Now, Hear This!* by Daniel V. Gallery, December 7, 1969.

22. Clark Kinnaird, *Parade of Books,* King Features Syndicate, January 23, 1965.

Controversialist: Admiral Firecracker

1. "The Elephant, the Whale and the Eagle," *Aero Digest,* April 1948, 110.

2. "The Defense of the Navy," *Aero Digest,* May 1948.

3. Gallery's short article, "Take It Easy, Cy" was published in the July issue of *Aero Digest* (p. 39) under the pseudonym "Admiral Firecracker"; his letter to Frank Tichenor, *Aero Digest,* was dated July 14, 1948.

4. Gallery, letter to Rear Adm. Ralph Ofstie, August 17, 1951.

5. Gallery, letter to Burke, August 6, 1952.

6. Burke, letter to Gallery, August 12, 1952.

7. Gallery, letter to Burke from San Juan in the late 1950s (date uncertain).

8. "Reminiscences of Admiral Arleigh Burke, USN, Retired," 1973, Annapolis, Md.: U.S. Naval Institute, vol. 2, p. 209.

9. Ira Nunn, letter to Gallery, January 2, 1953.

10. Rear Adm. Robert J. White, letter to Gallery, January 31, 1953.

11. Comdr. Joe Taussig, Jr., letter (with critique) to Adm. F. S. Withington, May 21, 1953.

12. Ira Nunn, letter to Gallery, March 23, 1953.

13. Nunn, letter to Gallery, May 21, 1953.

14. Ofstie, letter to Gallery, February 18, 1953.

15. Gallery, letter to Harold Matson, December 2, 1954.

16. Daniel V. Gallery, "Sea Power—Keystone of Air Power," *Reader's Digest,* May 1953, 29–35.

17. In the June 13, 1953, issue of *Saturday Evening Post.*

18. March 14, 1953, issue of the *Post,* 28.

19. Daniel V. Gallery, letter to Mrs. W. O. Gallery, July 28, 1952.

20. Daniel V. Gallery, letter to Capt. W. O. Gallery, August 31, 1952.

21. Daniel V. Gallery, letter to Capt. P. D. Gallery, September 8, 1952.

22. Daniel V. Gallery, letters to Capt. W. O. Gallery, August 5, 1952; Rear Adm. Wendell G. Switzer, June 26, 1953; and Vice Adm.

Ralph A. Ofstie, February 19, 1953.

23. Martin Somers, letter to Gallery, March 12, 1953.

24. Gallery, letter to Adm. Robert B. "Mick" Carney, March 24, 1954.

25. Carney, letter to Gallery, March 29, 1954.

26. "Chris" Weldon, letter to Gallery, October 13, 1954.

27. See Sommers, letter to Gallery, November 10, 1954.

28. "We Can Baffle the Brainwashers!" *Washington Post,* January 22, 1955, 94. *Time* presented its summary in its January 31 issue, p. 18.

29. "We Can Baffle," 94.

30. Daniel V. Gallery, *The* Pueblo *Incident* (New York: Doubleday, 1970), 70.

31. Daniel V(incent), Gallery Jr., *Current Biography*, April 1966, 16.

32. See Neil Sheehan, *The Arnheiter Affair* (New York: Random House, 1971), for a full examination.

33. Gallery, letter to Paul Ignatius, May 16, 1968.

34. Gallery, letter to Arnheiter, February 3, year uncertain.

35. Daniel V. Gallery, *The* Pueblo *Incident.*

36. Comdr. Lloyd Bucher, letter to Gallery, April 10, 1970.

37. Gallery, letter to Bucher, April 22, 1970.

38. Daniel V. Gallery, *The* Pueblo *Incident,* 36.

39. Ibid., 40.

40. Ibid., 60.

41. Ibid., 41.

42. Ibid., 28.

43. Daniel V. Gallery, *Eight Bells,* 296.

44. Daniel V. Gallery, *The* Pueblo *Incident,* 64–65.

45. Ibid., 106.

46. Ibid., 108.

47. Compare Robert A. Liston, *The* Pueblo *Surrender* (New York: M. Evans & Co., 1980); *Life,* August 21, 1970; and Bernard Weinraub, *New York Times Book Review,* February 15, 1970, 40.

48. Daniel V. Gallery, *The* Pueblo *Incident,* 115.

49. Bucher, letter to Gallery, April 10, 1970.

50. Daniel V. Gallery, *The* Pueblo *Incident,* xi.

Acknowledgments

One of the true pleasures in making this book has been sharing it with those who have helped and supported us in the process. Above all, Mrs. Vee Gallery not only generously gave us access to her late husband's papers and permission to publish his writings, but also welcomed us into her home for a memorable interview. She, Danny Gallery, Phil Gallery, Jr., and Audrey Gallery gave us important family insights.

For help especially in connection with the *U-505*, we thank Keith Gill of the Chicago Museum of Science and Industry; Wayne Pickles and Zenon Lukosius, of the original boarding party; and especially Earl Trosino, who led the *U-505* salvage party and later was officer in charge of the submarine during her transit to Chicago.

Alice Creighton, director of Special Collections at the U.S. Naval Academy's Nimitz Library, where the Gallery Papers are held, had a lively, ongoing interest in this project, stemming in part from her prominent role in the original acquisition of the Gallery papers. She gave freely of her time and knowledge, as did her assistant Mary Catalfamo.

We thank Dan Doll and Paul Stillwell for reading the manuscript at various stages and for giving honest reactions and sound advice. Gordon Forbes, Keith Gill, Jeffrey G. Barlow, and Paul Stevens also helped by reading sections or offering their expertise. Edward L. Beach provided valuable naval perspective, particularly about the pitfalls of writing for publication while on active duty.

We most appreciate Herman Wouk's generosity in writing a foreword for this book, and in supporting the project from its inception. Thanks are due, too, to Jim Eisenhower and Dave Poyer for their encouragement.

Finally, Paula Shenk was not only ever-interested, but helped us search through parts of the large Gallery collection; Carol Gilliland patiently tolerated a neglect of many domestic projects in favor of this one.

Index

Barham, HMS, 296
Barlow, Jeffrey, 147, 149
Barron, James, 284–85
baseball, 32–33, 47, 63, 163, 196–204
BatDivThree, 54–55
Bates, George B. "Belly Tank," 178
battleships, 26–28, 37–39, 53–55
Bay of Pigs, 287
Bayonne, N.J., 300
Beach, Edward L., 160–61, 165, 187
Beatty, Sir David, 296
Bednarczyk, Leon, 127–29, 311 n.19
Benson, Roy, 186–87
Bermuda, 123, 129, 212
Bernhard, Alva, 43
Biscay, Bay of, 219–20, 224, 226
Bismarck, German battleship, 296
Blair, Clay, 125, 128, 214
Blandy, W. H. P., 79, 154, 157
Block Island, USS, 121
Bogan, Gerald, 150
"Bomb's Away," 234
Bon Homme Richard, USS, 288
boxing, 23–25
Brett, General, 109
The Brink, 162, 243–45
Britain. *See* England
British, 81, 89–92, 96
Brooklyn Dodgers, 200
Brown, Joe E., 193
Brussels, Belgium, 20–21, 193
Bryan, Joe, 143
Bucher, Lloyd, 273–88
Bunger, Willi, 230
Bunker Hill, USS, 289–90
Bureau of Ordnance, 55–58, 77, 79
Burke, Arleigh: advice to Gallery, 205; *Bunker Hill* experience, 289–90; and Castro, 286; critique of *The Brink,* 244–45; critique of *Now, Hear This!* 242; influence on Gallery, 163; praise of Gallery, 264–66, 276; promotion to rear admiral, 151; view of "sea bat," 242; view of sea power, 269

Busch Gardens, 195
Byrd, Richard, 143

Cabrini, Lieutenant, 296
Cadle, J. W., 116–17
Caesar, Italian warship, 298
The Caine Mutiny, ix–x, 161–62, 274
Caldwell, Cy, 263–64
Campbell, J. M., 169–70, 172
"can-do" motto, 99–101, 103, 122
Cannes, France, 165–66
Cape Finnestere, 220
Caribbean Sea Frontier, 181–82, 193, 205, 286–87
Carney, Robert B., 180, 271–72
Carrier Division 6, 159–60, 163–66, 168–80, 198, 238
Carrier Division 16, 134
carriers: arguments about use of, 137–57; Gallery's service aboard, 51–53, 97–109, 110–31, 132–34, 158–80; stories/novels set on, 233–43, 247–62
Casablanca, 121
Case, USS, 31
Casselman, G. C., 118
Castro, Fidel, 286–87
Catholicism: guardian angel, 40–41; lifetime participation in, 291; lies to communists, 272; and Lourdes, 299; mass attendance, 16–17; upbringing in, 1–5, 8; "Vee" Gallery and, 64–65; Wouk's and Gallery's religions, x. *See also* prayer, religion
CBS News, 271
Ceramic, S.S., 112, 213
Cervera, Pasquale, 301
Chatelain, USS, 115, 116–17
Chesapeake, USS, 284–85
Chicago: Gallery's childhood in, 1–13; experiences in, 181–85, 196, 199–201; movement of *U-505* to, 185–90
Chicago Bears, 185
Chicago Police, 200

About the Authors

C. HERBERT GILLILAND grew up in Gainesville, Florida, and earned both his bachelor's and master's degrees from the University of Florida. Commissioned in the U.S. Naval Reserve in 1966, he served as communications officer on a destroyer and destroyer staff before returning to the University of Florida, where he received his Ph.D. in English in 1976. Recalled to active duty, he was a member of the U.S. Naval Academy English Department from 1982 to 1985 before leaving to join the faculty of Virginia Military Institute. He later returned to the Naval Academy as a civilian professor, the position he currently holds. He is a retired captain in the U.S. Naval Reserve.

ROBERT SHENK saw his initial navy duty on a destroyer and on river patrol boats during the Vietnam War. Having earned his Ph.D. from the University of Kansas, he returned to active duty in 1979 to teach English, first at the Air Force Academy and then at the Naval Academy. He is currently professor of English at the University of New Orleans, where he has taught since 1985. Shenk is the author of *The Naval Institute Guide to Naval Writing,* editor of *The Left-Handed Monkey Wrench: Stories and Essays by Richard McKenna,* and editor of *Authors at Sea: Modern American Writers Remember Their Naval Service.* In 1993 Shenk retired from the reserves with a rank of captain.

THE NAVAL INSTITUTE PRESS is the book-publishing arm of the U.S. Naval Institute, a private, nonprofit, membership society for sea service professionals and others who share an interest in naval and maritime affairs. Established in 1873 at the U.S. Naval Academy in Annapolis, Maryland, where its offices remain today, the Naval Institute has members worldwide.

Members of the Naval Institute support the education programs of the society and receive the influential monthly magazine *Proceedings* and discounts on fine nautical prints and on ship and aircraft photos. They also have access to the transcripts of the Institute's Oral History Program and get discounted admission to any of the Institute-sponsored seminars offered around the country.

The Naval Institute also publishes *Naval History* magazine. This colorful bimonthly is filled with entertaining and thought-provoking articles, first-person reminiscences, and dramatic art and photography. Members receive a discount on *Naval History* subscriptions.

The Naval Institute's book-publishing program, begun in 1898 with basic guides to naval practices, has broadened its scope in recent years to include books of more general interest. Now the Naval Institute Press publishes about one hundred titles each year, ranging from how-to books on boating and navigation to battle histories, biographies, ship and aircraft guides, and novels. Institute members receive discounts of 20 to 50 percent on the Press's nearly eight hundred books in print.

Full-time students are eligible for special half-price membership rates. Life memberships are also available.

For a free catalog describing Naval Institute Press books currently available, and for further information about subscribing to *Naval History* magazine or about joining the U.S. Naval Institute, please write to:

Membership Department
U.S. Naval Institute
291 Wood Road
Annapolis, MD 21402-5034
Telephone: (800) 233-8764
Fax: (410) 269-7940
Web address: www. usni.org